D1049097

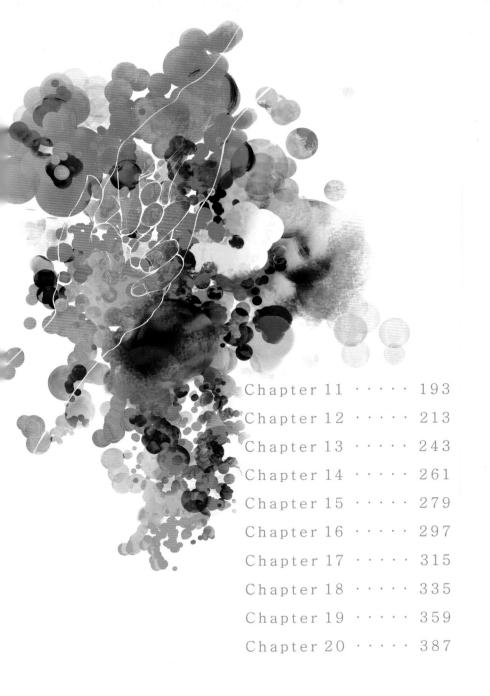

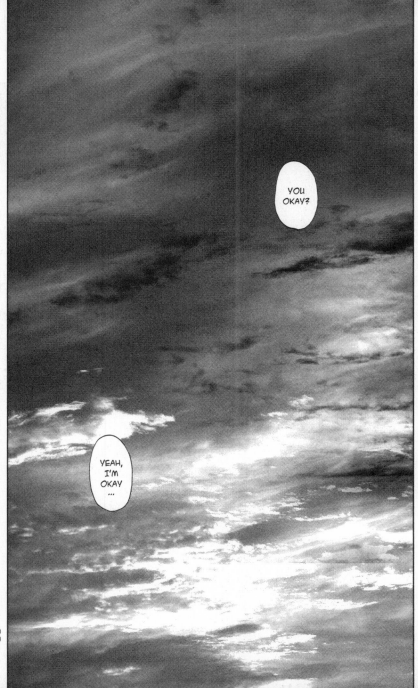

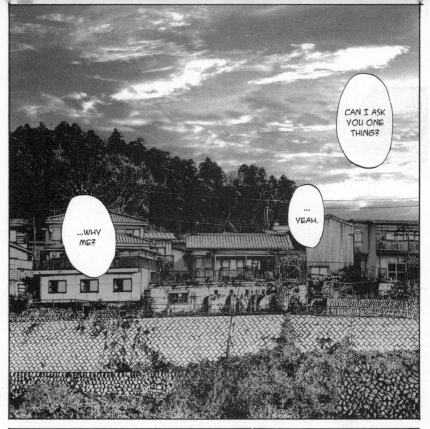

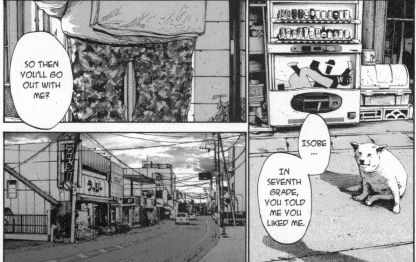

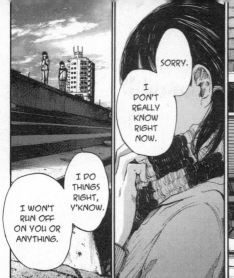
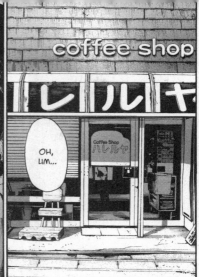
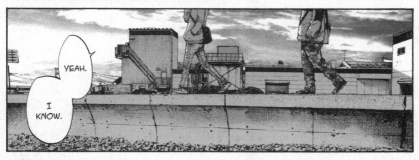
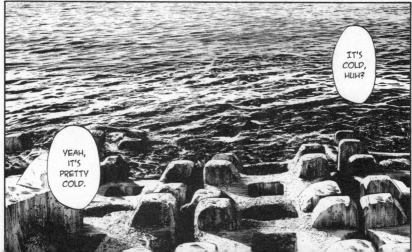

In town, there's a tiny beach that's never busy,
not even in the middle of summer.

I used to like walking there, looking for stuff.

Like old fireworks.

Or kelp.

A hat knocked off someone's head by the wind.

You basically never find what you were expecting to.

And maybe you weren't expecting to find
anything right from the start...

A

Girl

on the

Shore

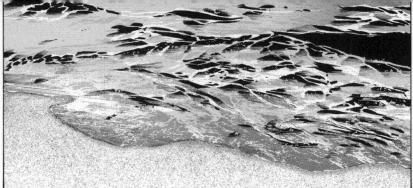

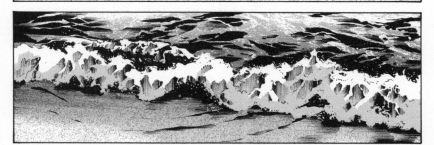

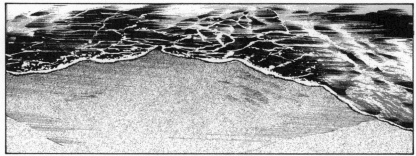

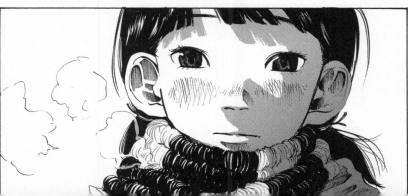

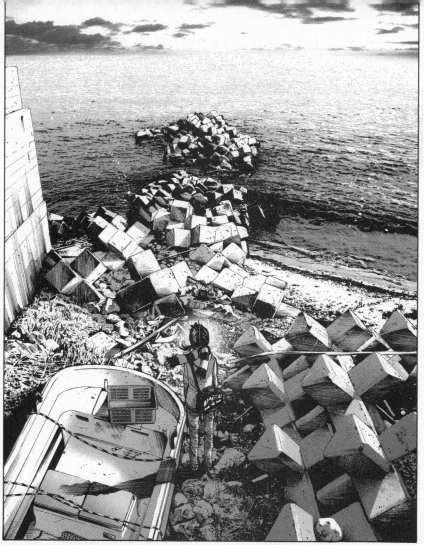

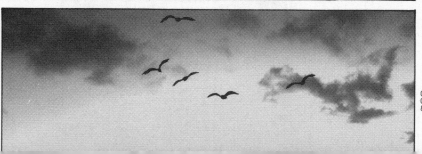

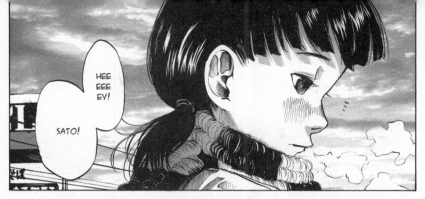

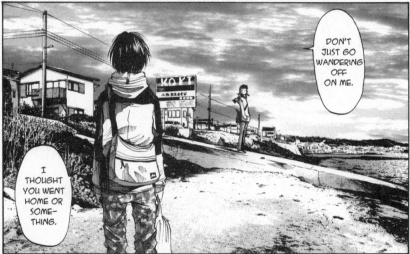

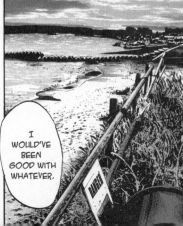

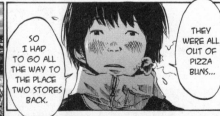

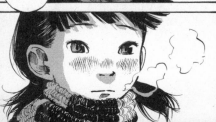

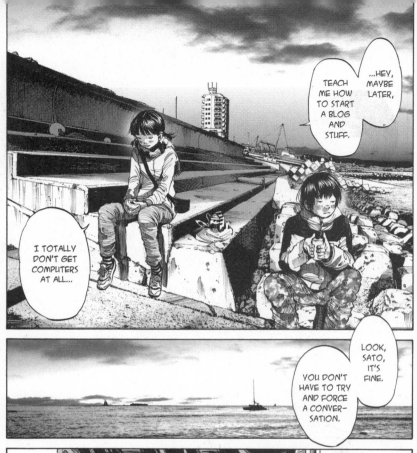

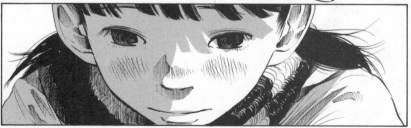

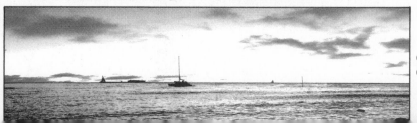

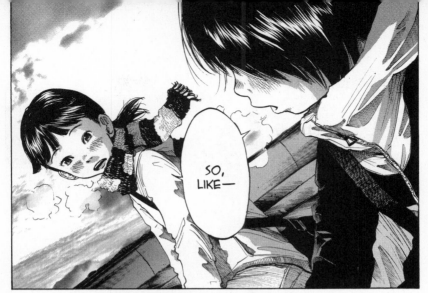

SO,
LIKE—

YOU CAN KEEP RANTING ABOUT HIM IF YOU WANT.

OH. SORRY.

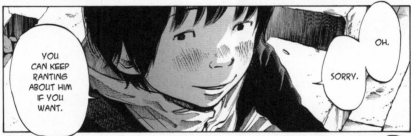

I WAS KINDA WONDERING IF YOU WERE OKAY. IT LOOKED LIKE IT HURT A LOT.

OH. I DUNNO.

I'M PRETTY MUCH DONE.

IT'S OKAY...

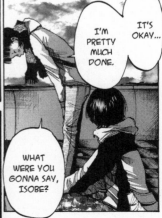

WHAT WERE YOU GONNA SAY, ISOBE?

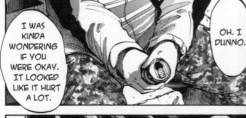

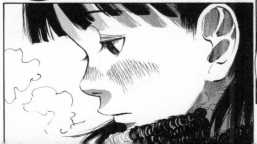

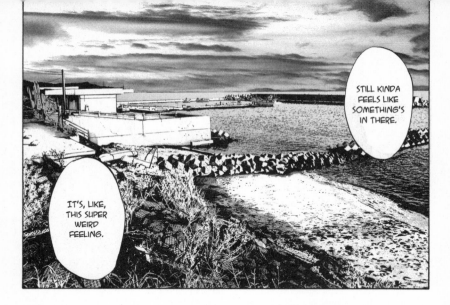

STILL KINDA FEELS LIKE SOMETHING'S IN THERE.

IT'S, LIKE, THIS SUPER WEIRD FEELING.

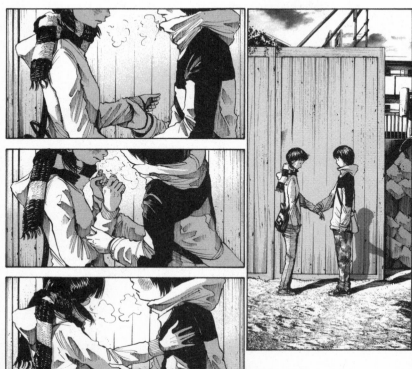

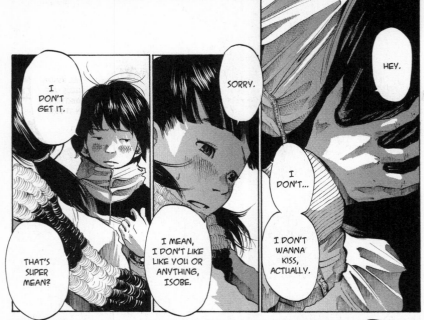

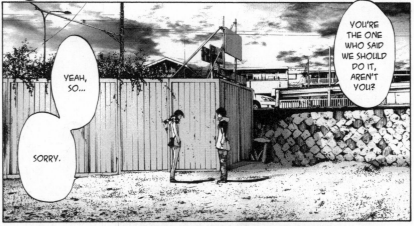

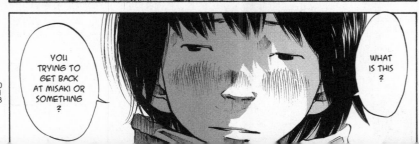

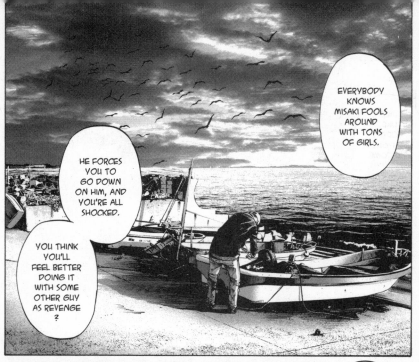

EVERYBODY KNOWS MISAKI FOOLS AROUND WITH TONS OF GIRLS.

HE FORCES YOU TO GO DOWN ON HIM, AND YOU'RE ALL SHOCKED.

YOU THINK YOU'LL FEEL BETTER DOING IT WITH SOME OTHER GUY AS REVENGE?

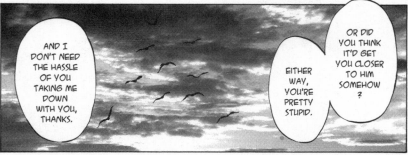

AND I DON'T NEED THE HASSLE OF YOU TAKING ME DOWN WITH YOU, THANKS.

EITHER WAY, YOU'RE PRETTY STUPID.

OR DID YOU THINK IT'D GET YOU CLOSER TO HIM SOMEHOW?

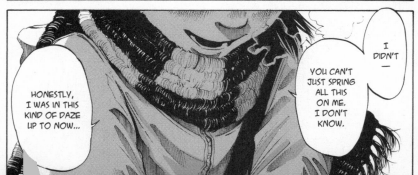

HONESTLY, I WAS IN THIS KIND OF DAZE UP TO NOW...

YOU CAN'T JUST SPRING ALL THIS ON ME. I DON'T KNOW.

I DIDN'T —

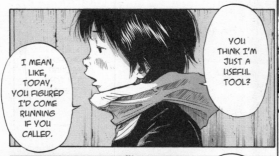

I MEAN, LIKE, TODAY, YOU FIGURED I'D COME RUNNING IF YOU CALLED.

YOU THINK I'M JUST A USEFUL TOOL?

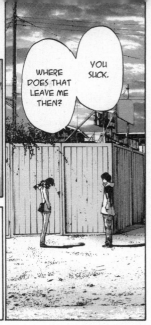

WHERE DOES THAT LEAVE ME THEN?

YOU SUCK.

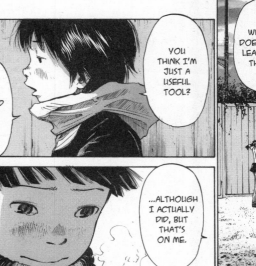

...ALTHOUGH I ACTUALLY DID, BUT THAT'S ON ME.

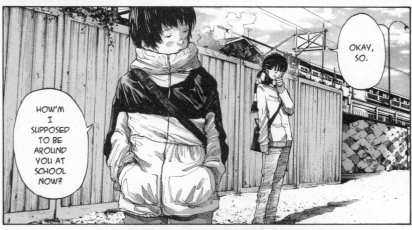

OKAY, SO.

HOW'M I SUPPOSED TO BE AROUND YOU AT SCHOOL NOW?

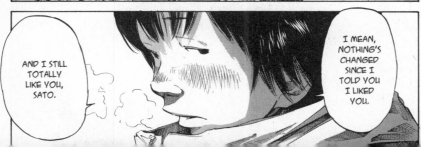

AND I STILL TOTALLY LIKE YOU, SATO.

I MEAN, NOTHING'S CHANGED SINCE I TOLD YOU I LIKED YOU.

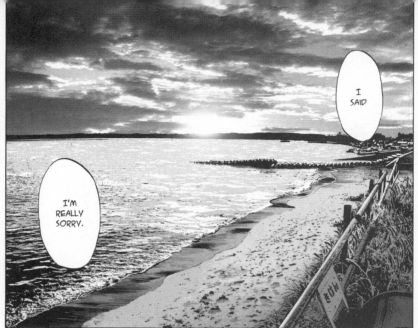

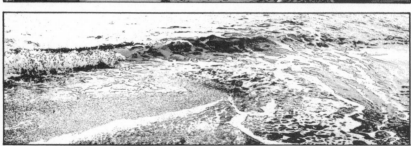

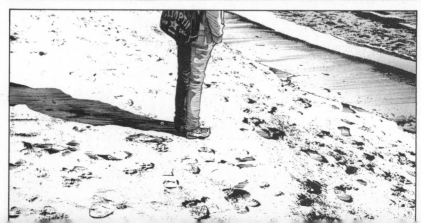

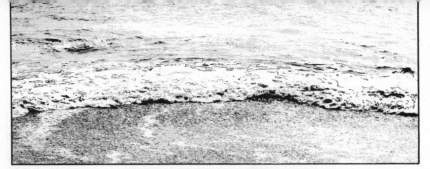

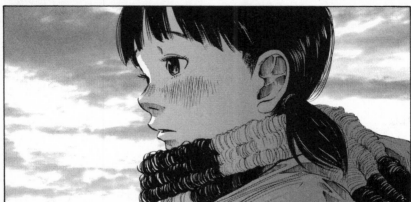

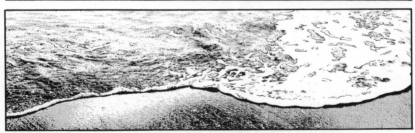

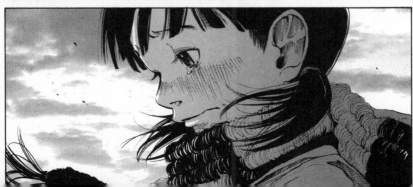

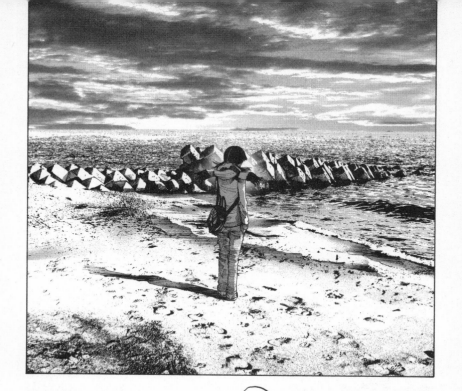

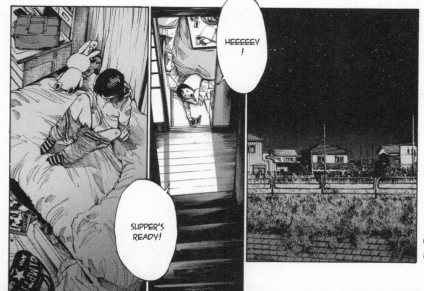

HEEEEEY
!

SUPPER'S
READY!

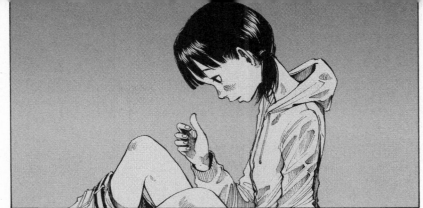

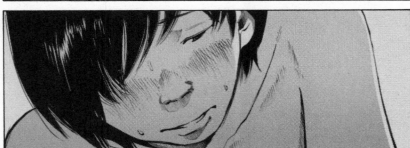

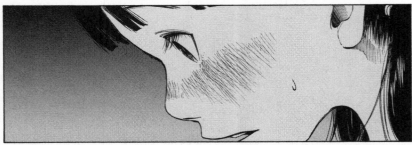

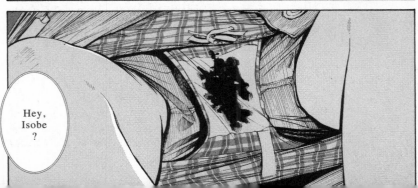

Hey,
Isobe
?

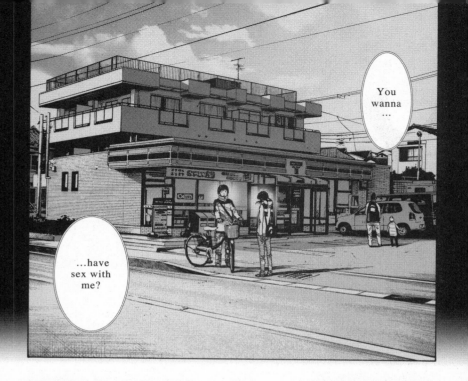

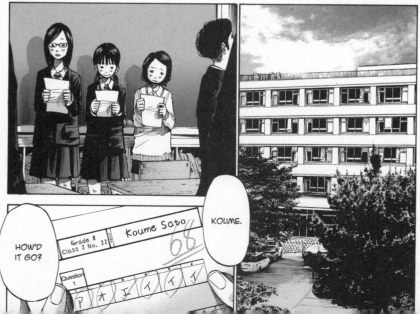

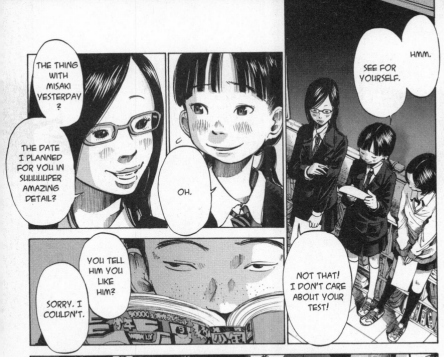

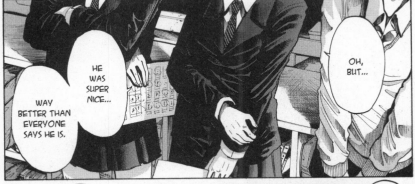

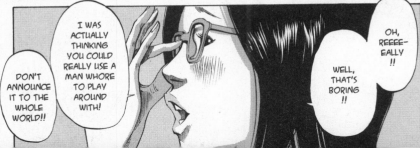

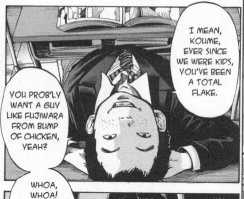

I MEAN, KOUME, EVER SINCE WE WERE KIDS, YOU'VE BEEN A TOTAL FLAKE.

SHUT UP, STUPID. GET LOST.

PFT! AS IF!!

WAIT, WHAT? KOUME'S GOT A BOYFRIEND NOW?

YOU PROB'LY WANT A GUY LIKE FUJIWARA FROM BUMP OF CHICKEN, YEAH?

WHOA, WHOA! DON'T GET CARRIED AWAY. YOU NEED TO TAKE A REAL LOOK AT REALITY!

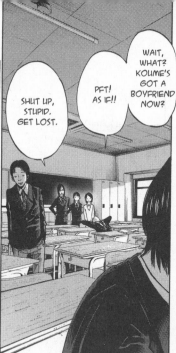

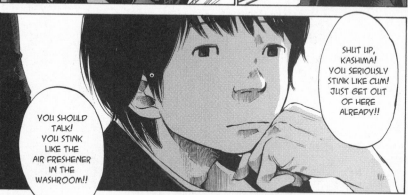

SHUT UP, KASHIMA! YOU SERIOUSLY STINK LIKE CUM! JUST GET OUT OF HERE ALREADY!!

YOU SHOULD TALK! YOU STINK LIKE THE AIR FRESHENER IN THE WASHROOM!!

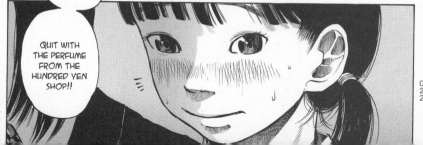

QUIT WITH THE PERFUME FROM THE HUNDRED YEN SHOP!!

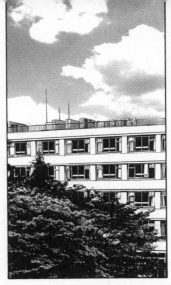

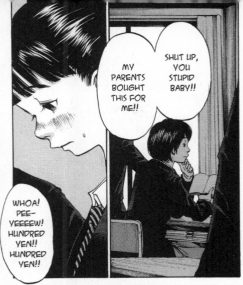

MY PARENTS BOUGHT THIS FOR ME!!

SHUT UP, YOU STUPID BABY!!

WHOA! PEE-YEEEEW! HUNDRED YEN!! HUNDRED YEN!!

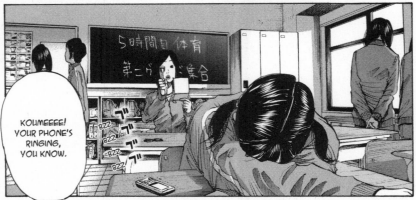

KOUMEEEE! YOUR PHONE'S RINGING, YOU KNOW.

BZZ BZZ BZZ BZZ

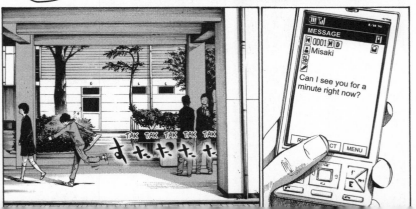

TAK TAK TAK TAK TAK TAK

MESSAGE

◄0001►

●Misaki

Can I see you for a minute right now?

REJECT   MENU

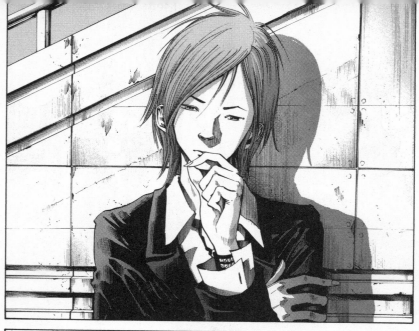

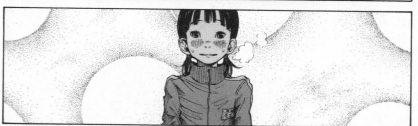

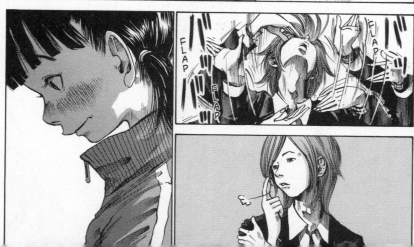

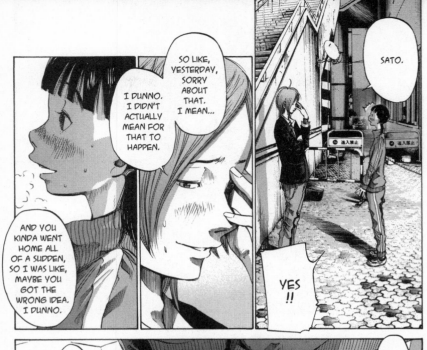

SO LIKE, YESTERDAY, SORRY ABOUT THAT. I MEAN...

I DUNNO. I DIDN'T ACTUALLY MEAN FOR THAT TO HAPPEN.

SATO.

AND YOU KINDA WENT HOME ALL OF A SUDDEN, SO I WAS LIKE, MAYBE YOU GOT THE WRONG IDEA. I DUNNO.

YES !!

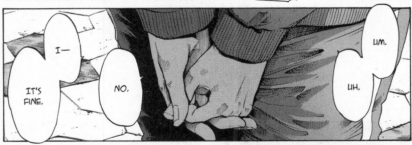

I—

IT'S FINE.

NO.

UM.

UH,

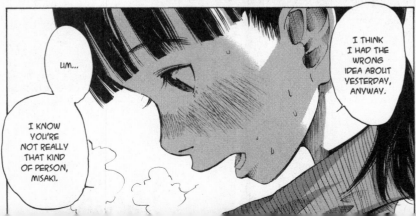

UM...

I KNOW YOU'RE NOT REALLY THAT KIND OF PERSON, MISAKI.

I THINK I HAD THE WRONG IDEA ABOUT YESTERDAY, ANYWAY.

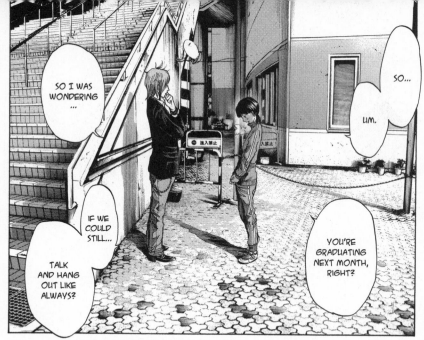

SO I WAS WONDERING...

SO...

UM.

IF WE COULD STILL...

TALK AND HANG OUT LIKE ALWAYS?

YOU'RE GRADUATING NEXT MONTH, RIGHT?

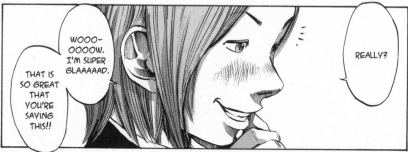

WOOO-OOOOW. I'M SUPER GLAAAAAD.

THAT IS SO GREAT THAT YOU'RE SAYING THIS!!

REALLY?

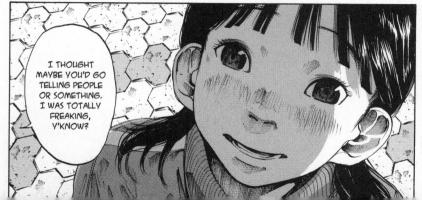

I THOUGHT MAYBE YOU'D GO TELLING PEOPLE OR SOMETHING. I WAS TOTALLY FREAKING, Y'KNOW?

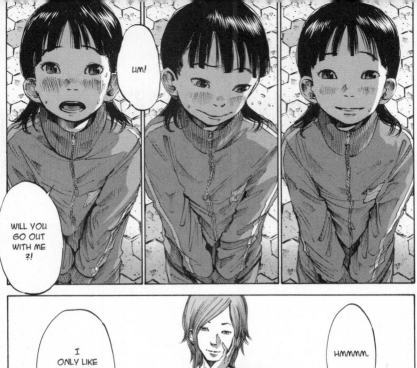

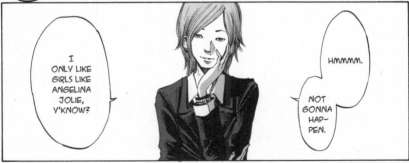

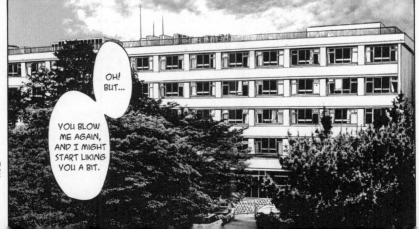

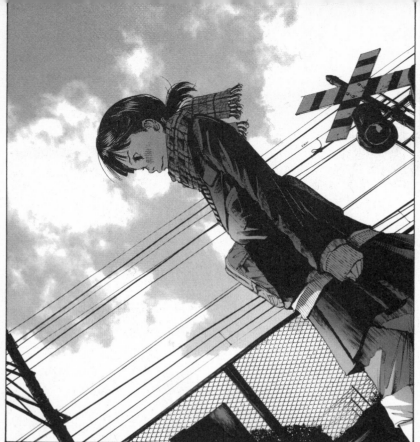

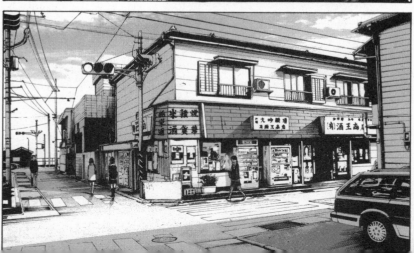

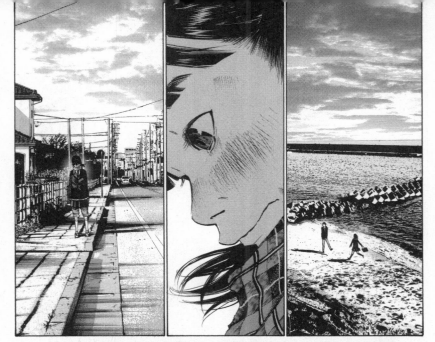

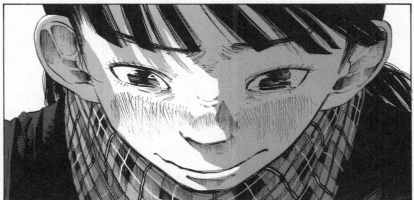

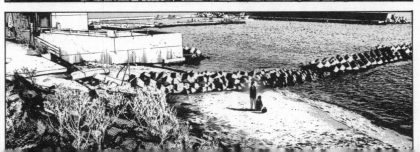

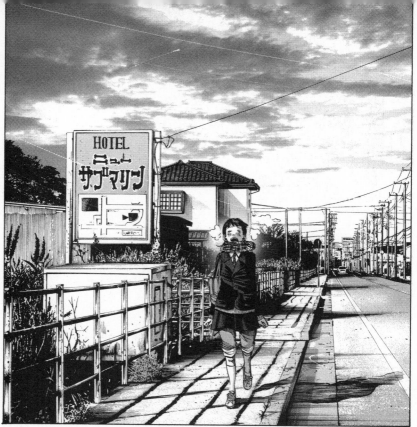

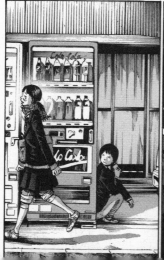
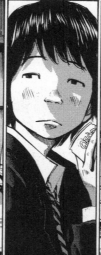
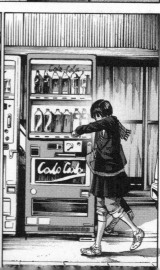

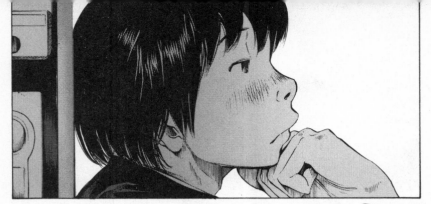

SATO!

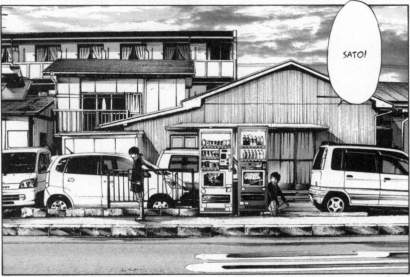

YOU HAD ANOTHER FIGHT WITH MISAKI?

THAT'S KINDA HILARIOUS.

FIRST, OKAY?

IT'S NOT LIKE I WAS SITTING HERE WAITING FOR YOU OR ANYTHING.

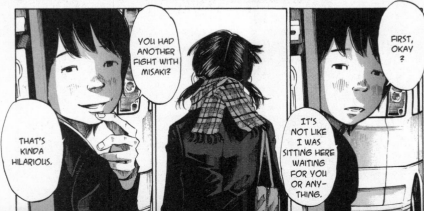

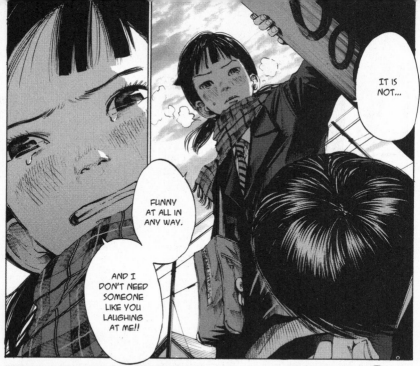

IT IS NOT...

FUNNY AT ALL IN ANY WAY.

AND I DON'T NEED SOMEONE LIKE YOU LAUGHING AT ME!!

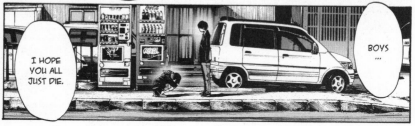

I HOPE YOU ALL JUST DIE.

BOYS...

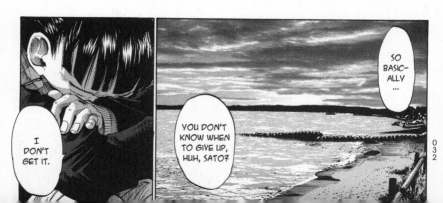

I DON'T GET IT.

YOU DON'T KNOW WHEN TO GIVE UP, HUH, SATO?

SO BASIC-ALLY...

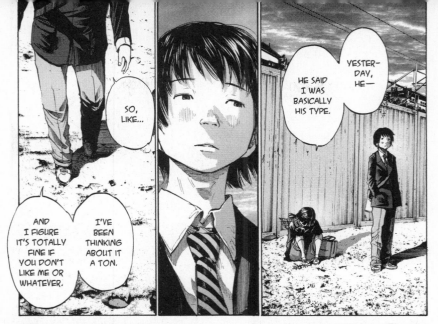

SO, LIKE...

HE SAID I WAS BASICALLY HIS TYPE.

YESTER-DAY, HE—

AND I FIGURE IT'S TOTALLY FINE IF YOU DON'T LIKE ME OR WHATEVER.

I'VE BEEN THINKING ABOUT IT A TON.

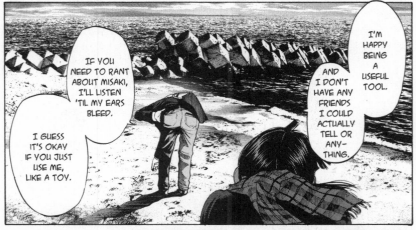

IF YOU NEED TO RANT ABOUT MISAKI, I'LL LISTEN 'TIL MY EARS BLEED.

I'M HAPPY BEING A USEFUL TOOL.

AND I DON'T HAVE ANY FRIENDS I COULD ACTUALLY TELL OR ANY-THING.

I GUESS IT'S OKAY IF YOU JUST USE ME, LIKE A TOY.

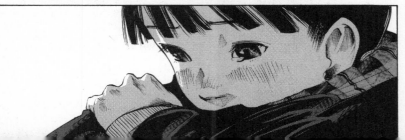

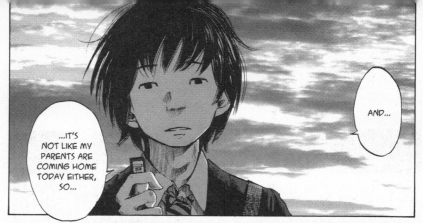

AND...

...IT'S NOT LIKE MY PARENTS ARE COMING HOME TODAY EITHER, SO...

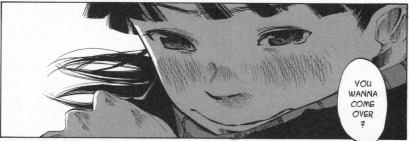

YOU WANNA COME OVER?

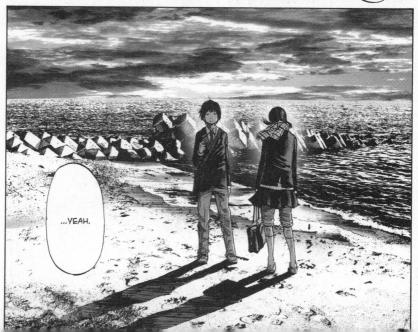

...YEAH.

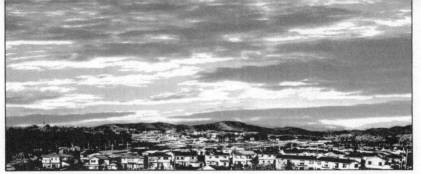

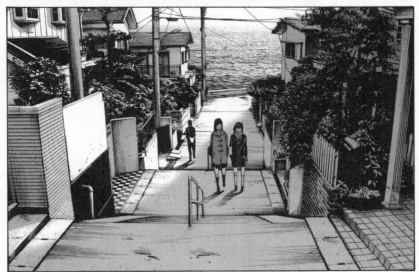

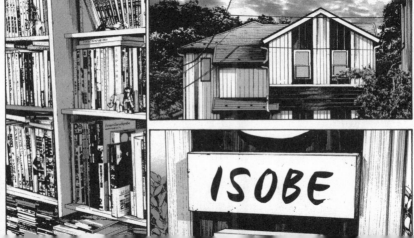

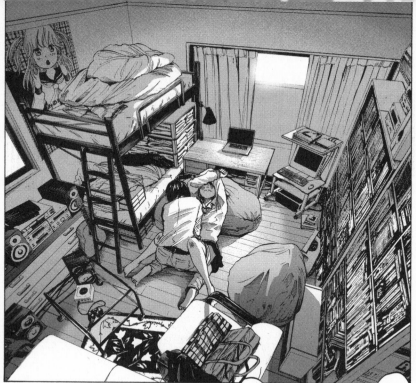

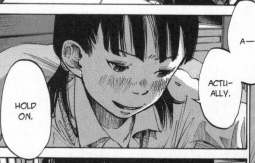

HEY...

A—

ACTU-
ALLY.

HOLD
ON.

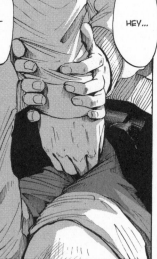

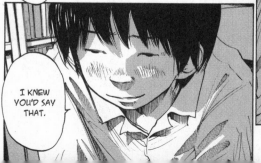

I KNEW
YOU'D SAY
THAT.

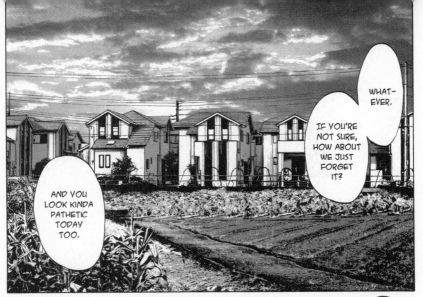

WHAT-EVER.

IF YOU'RE NOT SURE, HOW ABOUT WE JUST FORGET IT?

AND YOU LOOK KINDA PATHETIC TODAY TOO.

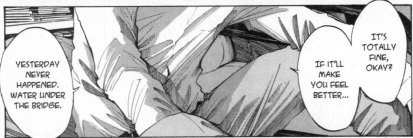

YESTERDAY NEVER HAPPENED. WATER UNDER THE BRIDGE.

IF IT'LL MAKE YOU FEEL BETTER...

IT'S TOTALLY FINE, OKAY?

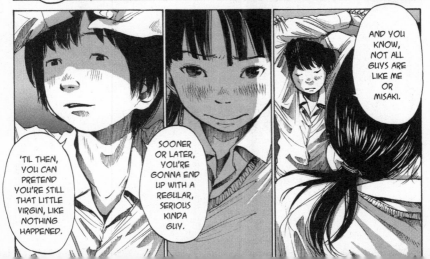

AND YOU KNOW, NOT ALL GUYS ARE LIKE ME OR MISAKI.

'TIL THEN, YOU CAN PRETEND YOU'RE STILL THAT LITTLE VIRGIN, LIKE NOTHING HAPPENED.

SOONER OR LATER, YOU'RE GONNA END UP WITH A REGULAR, SERIOUS KINDA GUY.

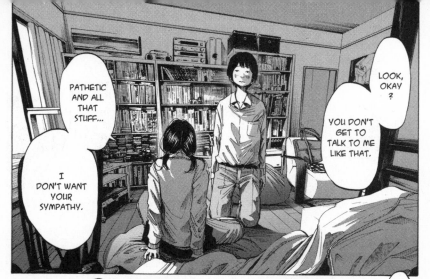

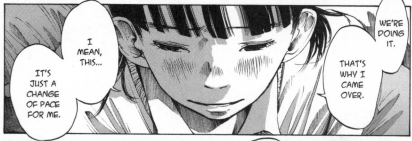

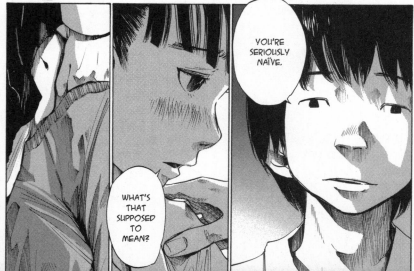

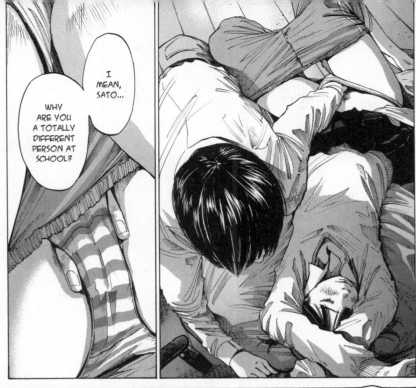

I MEAN, SATO...

WHY ARE YOU A TOTALLY DIFFERENT PERSON AT SCHOOL?

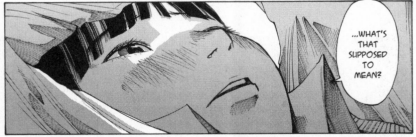

...WHAT'S THAT SUPPOSED TO MEAN?

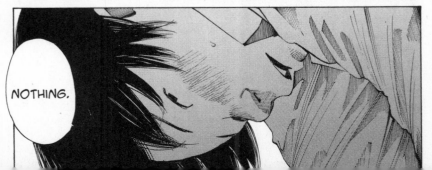

NOTHING.

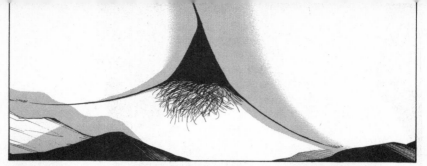

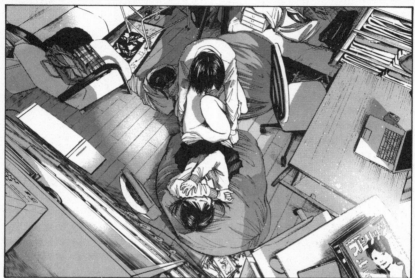

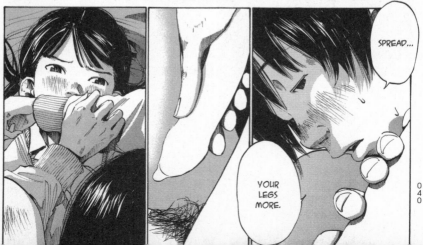

SPREAD...

YOUR
LEGS
MORE.

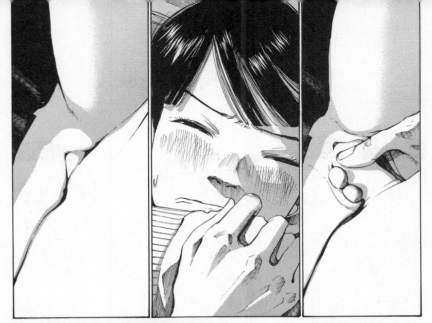

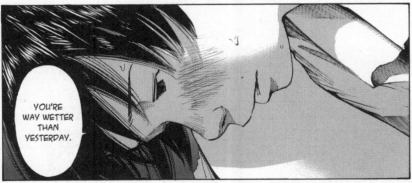

YOU'RE WAY WETTER THAN YESTERDAY.

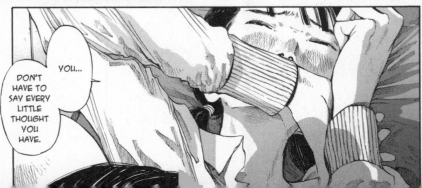

YOU...

DON'T HAVE TO SAY EVERY LITTLE THOUGHT YOU HAVE.

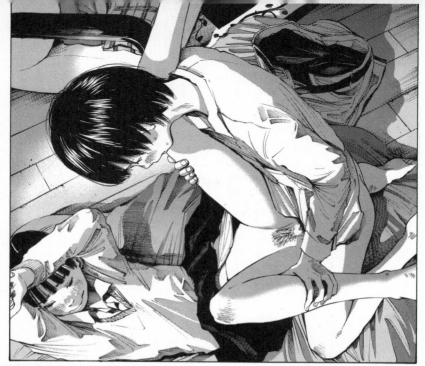

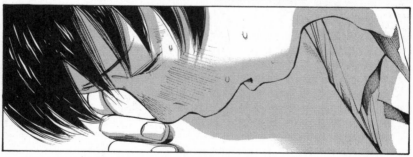

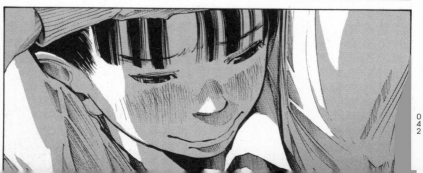

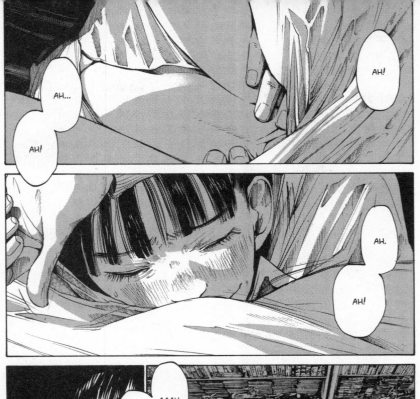

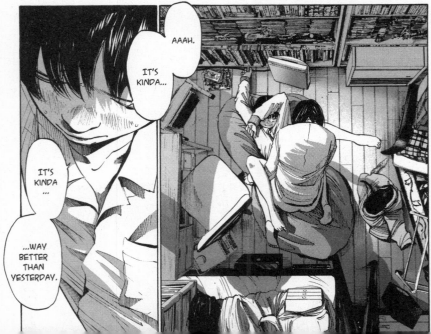

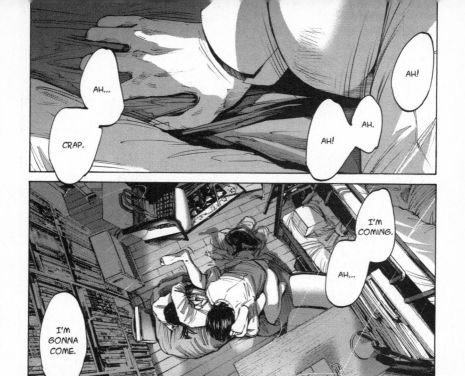

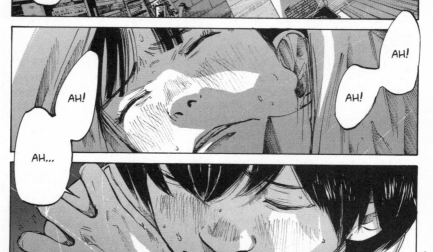

044

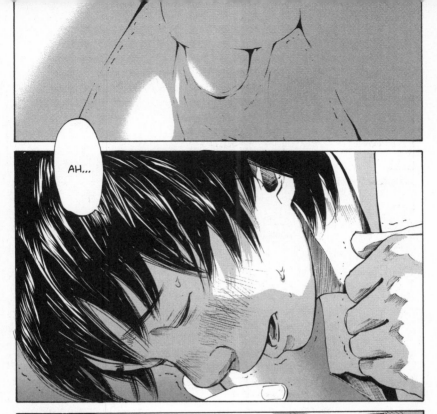

AH...

HAAH.

HAAH.

HAAH.

HAAH.

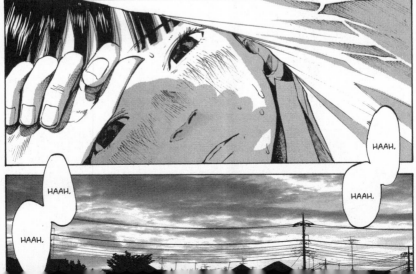

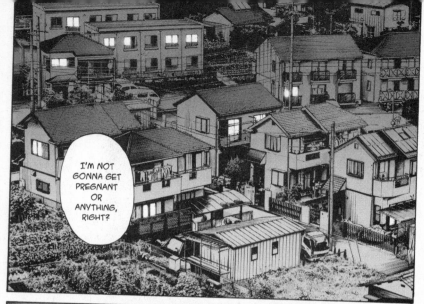

I'M NOT GONNA GET PREGNANT OR ANYTHING, RIGHT?

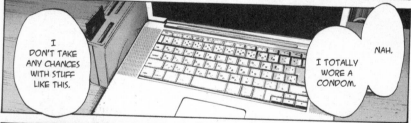

I DON'T TAKE ANY CHANCES WITH STUFF LIKE THIS.

NAH.

I TOTALLY WORE A CONDOM.

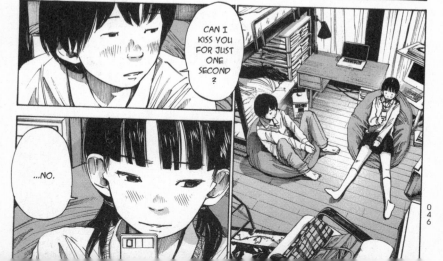

CAN I KISS YOU FOR JUST ONE SECOND?

...NO.

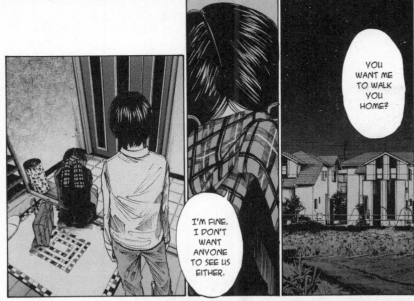

YOU WANT ME TO WALK YOU HOME?

I'M FINE. I DON'T WANT ANYONE TO SEE US EITHER.

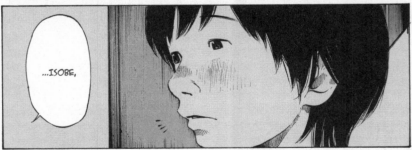

...ISOBE,

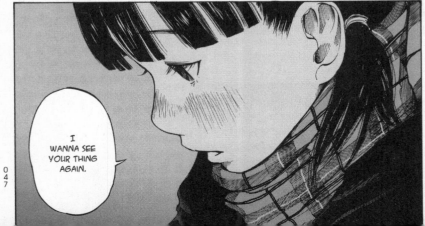

I WANNA SEE YOUR THING AGAIN.

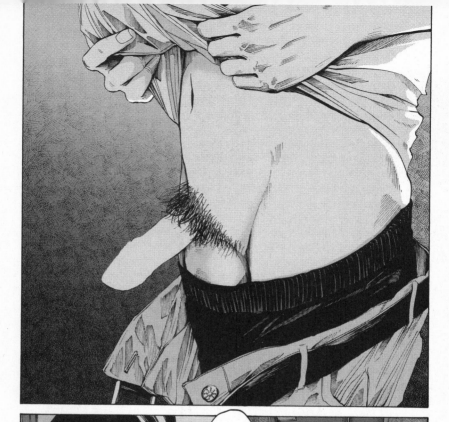

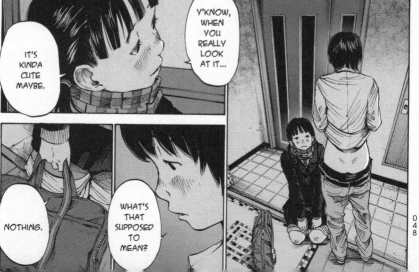

Y'KNOW, WHEN YOU REALLY LOOK AT IT...

IT'S KINDA CUTE MAYBE.

NOTHING.

WHAT'S THAT SUPPOSED TO MEAN?

048

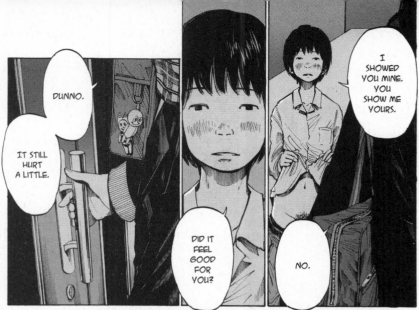

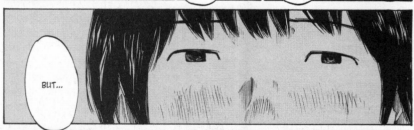

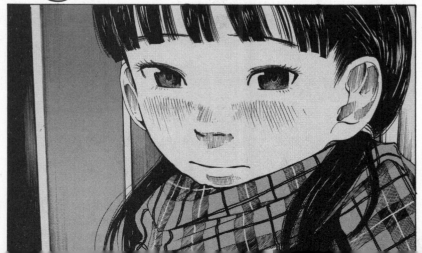

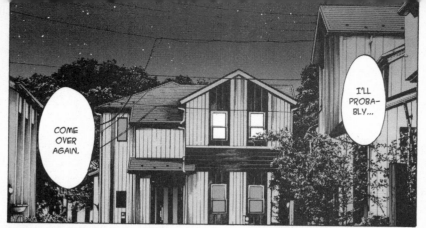

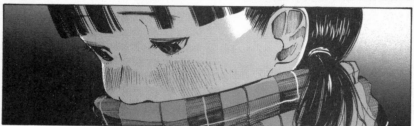

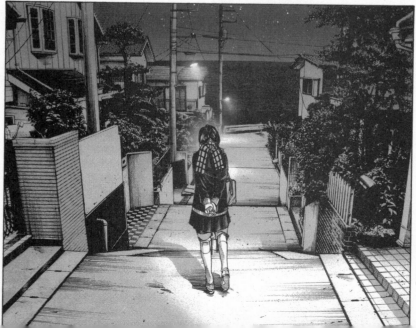

A

Girl

on the

Shore

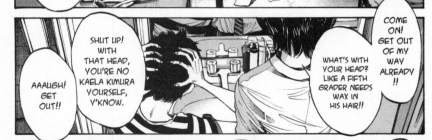
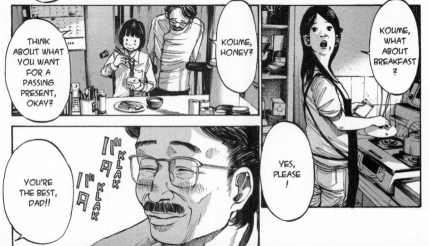

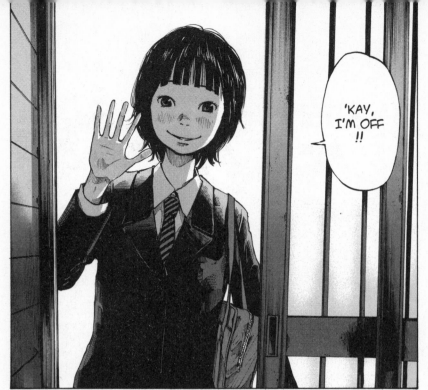

'KAY, I'M OFF !!

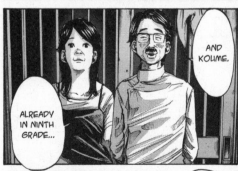

AND KOUME.

ALREADY IN NINTH GRADE...

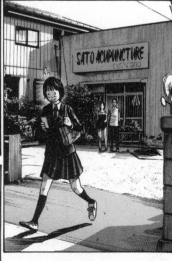

SATO ACUPUNCTURE

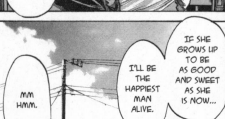

MM HMM.

I'LL BE THE HAPPIEST MAN ALIVE.

IF SHE GROWS UP TO BE AS GOOD AND SWEET AS SHE IS NOW...

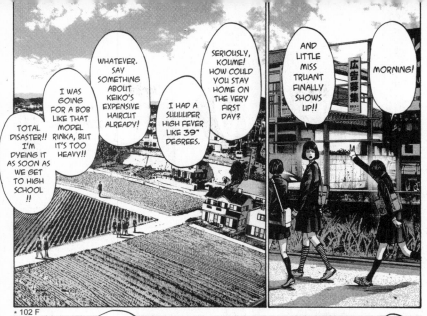

* 102 F

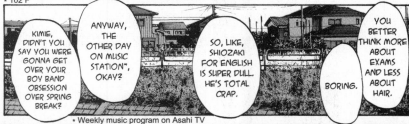

* Weekly music program on Asahi TV

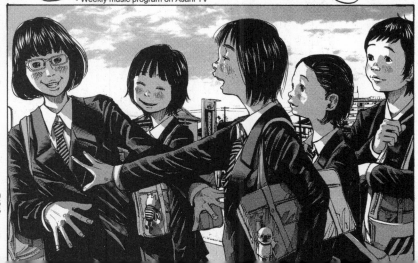

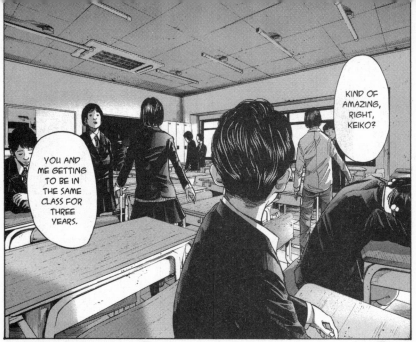

KIND OF AMAZING, RIGHT, KEIKO?

YOU AND ME GETTING TO BE IN THE SAME CLASS FOR THREE YEARS.

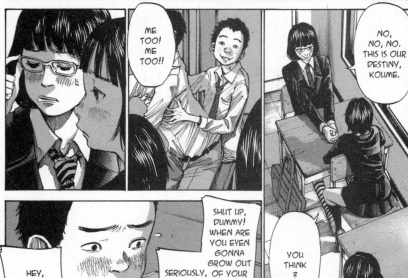

ME TOO! ME TOO!!

NO, NO, NO. THIS IS OUR DESTINY, KOUME.

SHUT UP, DUMMY! WHEN ARE YOU EVEN GONNA GROW OUT OF YOUR SHRIMPI-TUDE?!

SERIOUSLY, I'M SICK OF HOW SHORT YOU ARE!

HEY, THAT HURTS, YOU KNOW !!

YOU THINK ?

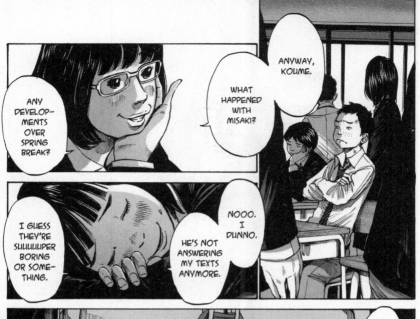

ANYWAY, KOUME.

WHAT HAPPENED WITH MISAKI?

ANY DEVELOPMENTS OVER SPRING BREAK?

I GUESS THEY'RE SUUUUUPER BORING OR SOMETHING.

HE'S NOT ANSWERING MY TEXTS ANYMORE.

NOOO. I DUNNO.

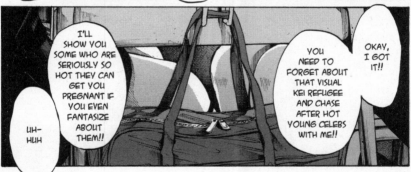

I'LL SHOW YOU SOME WHO ARE SERIOUSLY SO HOT THEY CAN GET YOU PREGNANT IF YOU EVEN FANTASIZE ABOUT THEM!!

UH-HUH

YOU NEED TO FORGET ABOUT THAT VISUAL KEI REFUGEE AND CHASE AFTER HOT YOUNG CELEBS WITH ME!!

OKAY, I GOT IT!!

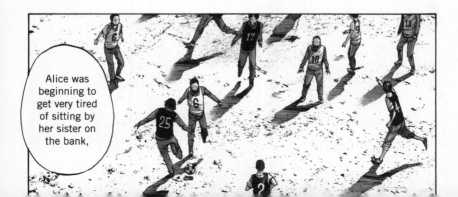

Alice was beginning to get very tired of sitting by her sister on the bank,

and of having nothing to do: once or twice she had peppered into

the book her sister was reading, but it had no pictures or conversations in it.

"and what is the use of a book," thought Alice,

"with out pictures or conversations?"

So she was considering, in her own

BZZ
BZZ
BZZ
BZZ

HEY! YOU!!

MESSAGES
Isobe
(no subject)
First floor south building
Girls · toilet first stall
Knock 5

REPLY
MENU

UM!

MR. BASEBALL! WAKE UP!!

HUH?

OH, YES SIR!!

AAAAH, WHERE DID WE READ UP TO THEN...

I KNOW THE TOURNEY IS COMING UP, BUT IF YOU'RE NOT CAREFUL, YOU'RE GOING TO GET LEFT BEHIND.

UH.

EXCUSE ME.

CAN I GO TO THE NURSE'S OFFICE?

I DON'T FEEL GOOD.

WHY
D'YOU
ALREADY
HAVE A
HARD-ON
?

YOU'RE
A
PERVERT.

C'MON
IN.

YOU'RE
ONE TO
TALK.

WE'RE IN DIFFERENT CLASSES NOW, HUH?

YOU SKIPPED OUT AT THE START OF GYM CLASS?

NOT MY FAULT IF THIS GOES ON YOUR RECORD.

WHAT- EVER.

I SAID I GET MIGRAINES AND STUFF.

AND I'M BAD AT THAT KIND OF GROUP COM- PETITION.

AH...

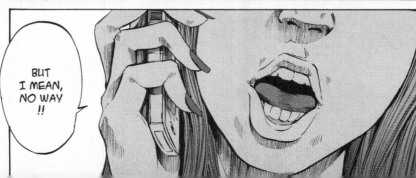

BUT
I MEAN,
NO WAY
!!

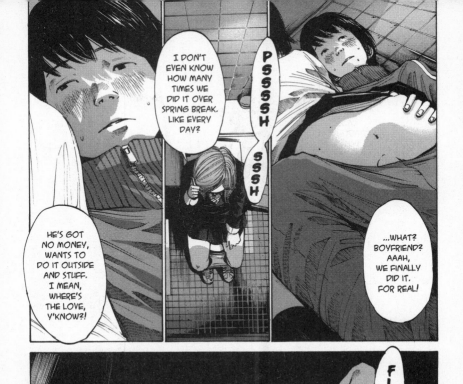

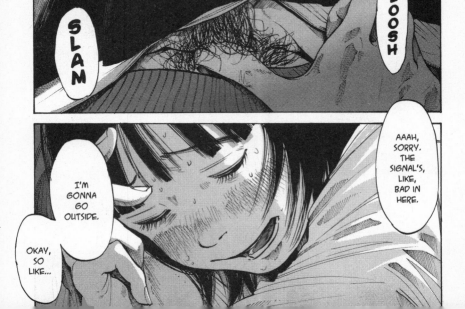

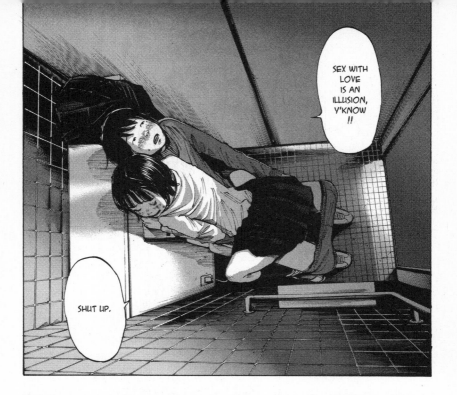

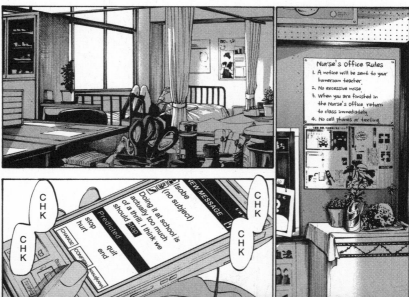

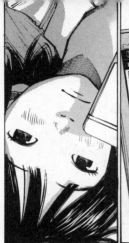

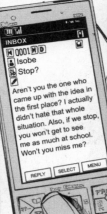

INBOX
☑ 0001 MD
👤 Isobe
🔖 Stop?
✏️ Aren't you the one who came up with the idea in the first place? I actually didn't hate that whole situation. Also, if we stop, you won't get to see me as much at school. Won't you miss me?

REPLY SELECT MENU

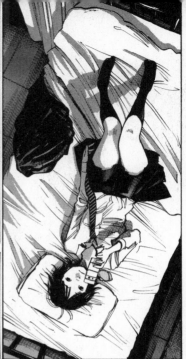

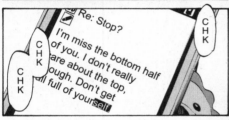

☑ Re: Stop?
I'm miss the bottom half of you. I don't really care about the top, though. Don't get full of yourself

CHK
CHK
CHK
CHK

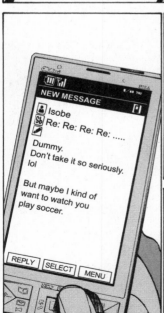

NEW MESSAGE
👤 Isobe
🔖 Re: Re: Re: Re: .....
✏️ Dummy.
Don't take it so seriously.
lol

But maybe I kind of want to watch you play soccer.

REPLY SELECT MENU

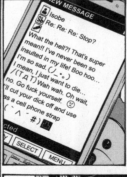

NEW MESSAGE
👤 Isobe
🔖 Re: Re: Re: Stop?
✏️ What the hell?! That's super mean!! I've never been so insulted in my life! Boo hoo. I'm so sad. (ﾉ´･ω･) I mean, I just want to die.... /(TДT) Wah wah. Oh wait, no. Go fuck yourself. I'll cut your dick off and use as a cell phone strap (´･ﾍ･ #)

SELECT MENU

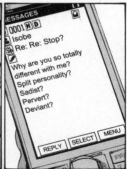

MESSAGES
☑ 0001 MD
👤 Isobe
🔖 Re: Re: Stop?
Why are you so totally different with me?
Split personality?
Sadist?
Pervert?
Deviant?

REPLY SELECT MENU

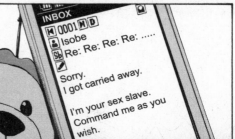

INBOX
☑ 0001 MD
👤 Isobe
🔖 Re: Re: Re: Re: .....
✏️ Sorry.
I got carried away.

I'm your sex slave.
Command me as you wish.

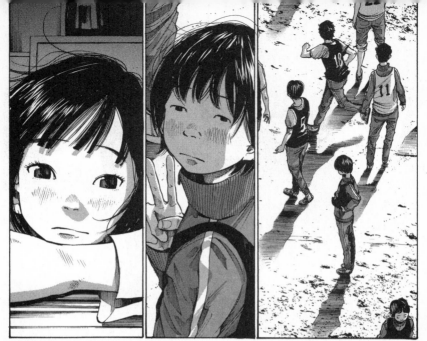

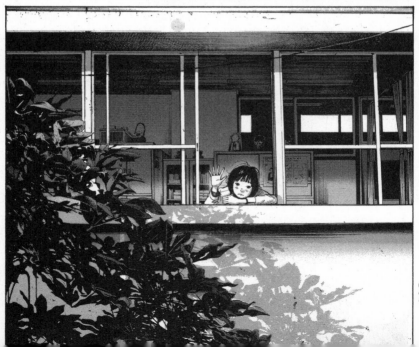

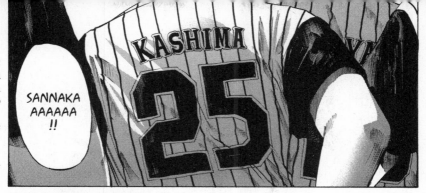

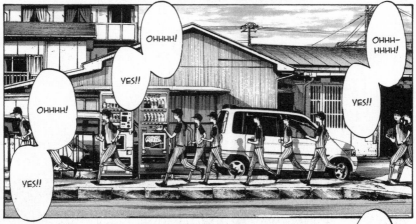

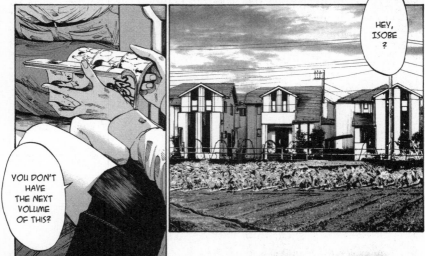

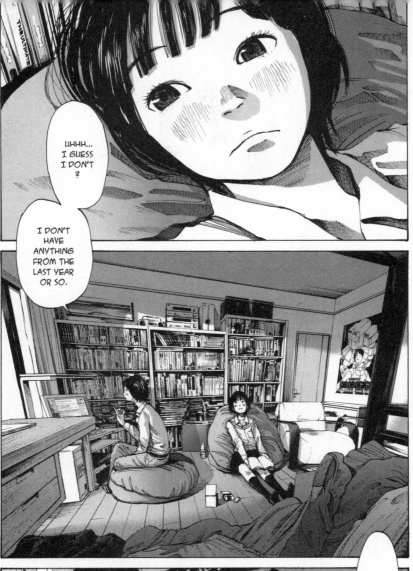

UHHH...
I GUESS
I DON'T
?

I DON'T
HAVE
ANYTHING
FROM THE
LAST YEAR
OR SO.

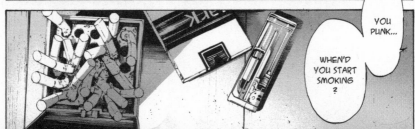

YOU
PUNK...

WHEN'D
YOU START
SMOKING
?

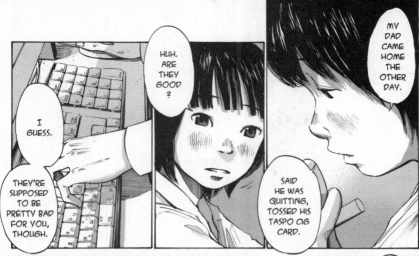

HUH, ARE THEY GOOD?

I GUESS.

THEY'RE SUPPOSED TO BE PRETTY BAD FOR YOU, THOUGH.

MY DAD CAME HOME THE OTHER DAY.

SAID HE WAS QUITTING, TOSSED HIS TASPO CIG CARD.

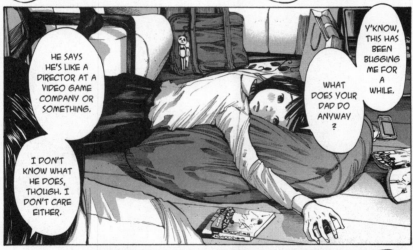

HE SAYS HE'S LIKE A DIRECTOR AT A VIDEO GAME COMPANY OR SOMETHING.

I DON'T KNOW WHAT HE DOES, THOUGH. I DON'T CARE EITHER.

WHAT DOES YOUR DAD DO ANYWAY?

Y'KNOW, THIS HAS BEEN BUGGING ME FOR A WHILE.

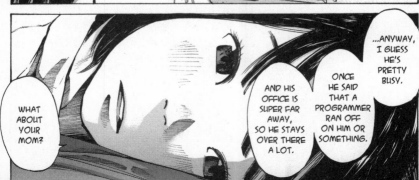

WHAT ABOUT YOUR MOM?

AND HIS OFFICE IS SUPER FAR AWAY, SO HE STAYS OVER THERE A LOT.

ONCE HE SAID THAT A PROGRAMMER RAN OFF ON HIM OR SOMETHING.

...ANYWAY, I GUESS HE'S PRETTY BUSY.

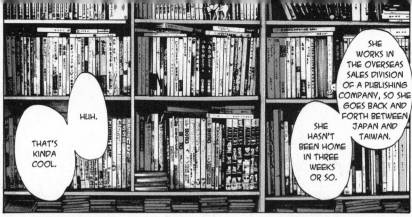

SHE WORKS IN THE OVERSEAS SALES DIVISION OF A PUBLISHING COMPANY, SO SHE GOES BACK AND FORTH BETWEEN JAPAN AND TAIWAN.

SHE HASN'T BEEN HOME IN THREE WEEKS OR SO.

HUH.

THAT'S KINDA COOL.

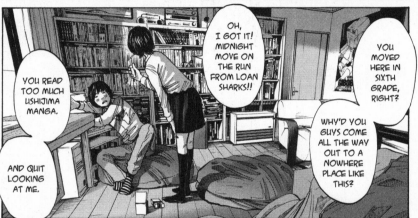

YOU READ TOO MUCH USHIJIMA MANGA.

AND QUIT LOOKING AT ME.

OH, I GOT IT! MIDNIGHT MOVE ON THE RUN FROM LOAN SHARKS!!

YOU MOVED HERE IN SIXTH GRADE, RIGHT?

WHY'D YOU GUYS COME ALL THE WAY OUT TO A NOWHERE PLACE LIKE THIS?

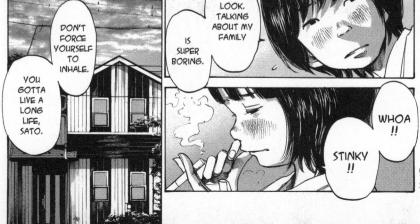

DON'T FORCE YOURSELF TO INHALE.

YOU GOTTA LIVE A LONG LIFE, SATO.

IS SUPER BORING.

LOOK. TALKING ABOUT MY FAMILY

WHOA!!

STINKY!!

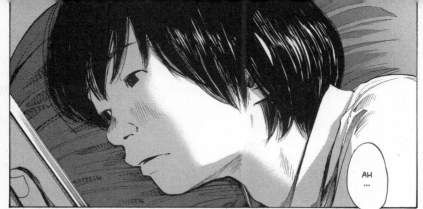

AH
...

IT'S ALREADY FIVE-THIRTY.

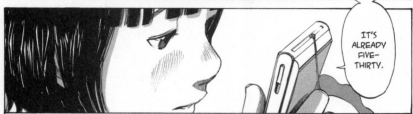

SO LIKE...

ARE YOUR PARENTS GONNA BE SUSPICIOUS OR ANYTHING IF YOU COME HOME LATE?

THE DAYS ARE GETTING LONGER, HUH?

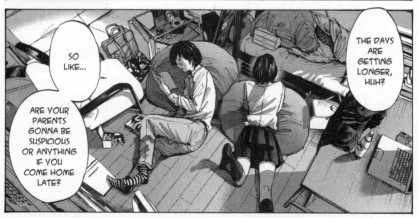

DANG. I'D BE CRYING IF I WAS YOUR DAD.

I TOLD THEM I'D BE LATE 'CAUSE I HAVE PRACTICE.

IT'S FINE.

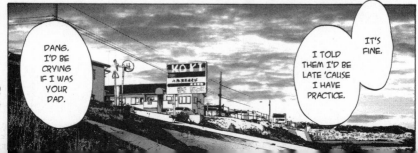

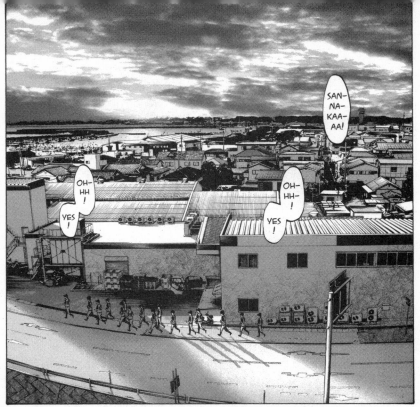

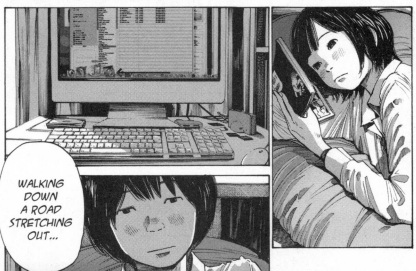

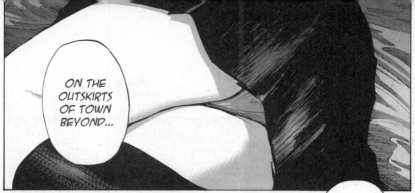

ON THE OUTSKIRTS OF TOWN BEYOND...

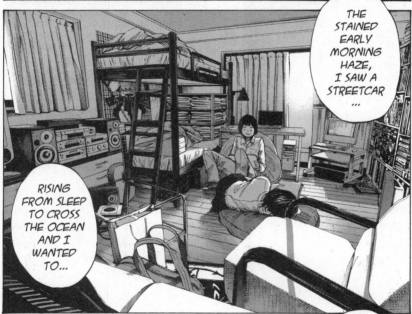

THE STAINED EARLY MORNING HAZE, I SAW A STREETCAR...

RISING FROM SLEEP TO CROSS THE OCEAN AND I WANTED TO...

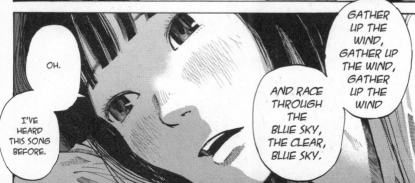

GATHER UP THE WIND, GATHER UP THE WIND, GATHER UP THE WIND

OH.

AND RACE THROUGH THE BLUE SKY, THE CLEAR, BLUE SKY.

I'VE HEARD THIS SONG BEFORE.

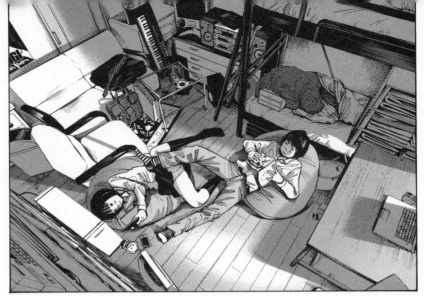

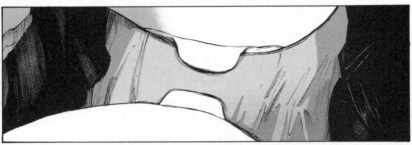

THEN WHAT'D YOU COME OVER HERE FOR?

I HAVE MY PERIOD, SO WE CAN'T TODAY.

OKAY, I'LL GO HOME.

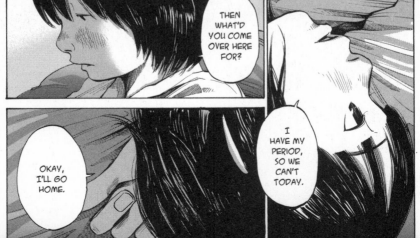

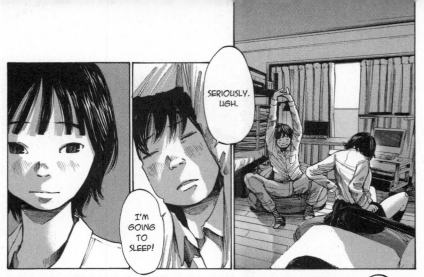

SERIOUSLY, UGH.

I'M GOING TO SLEEP!

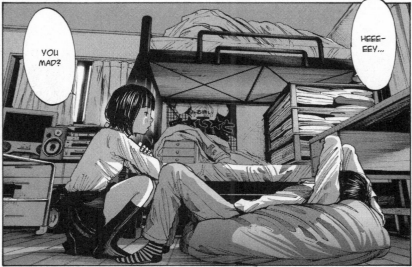

YOU MAD?

HEEE-EEY...

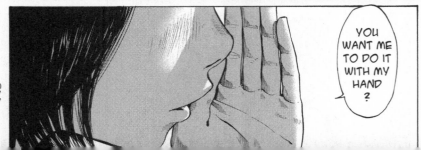

YOU WANT ME TO DO IT WITH MY HAND?

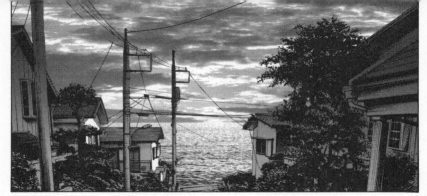

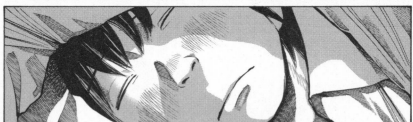

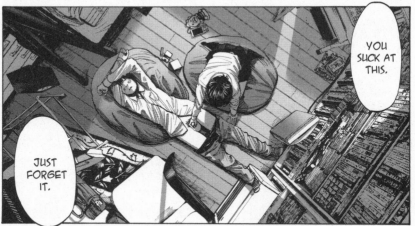

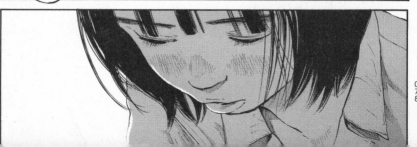

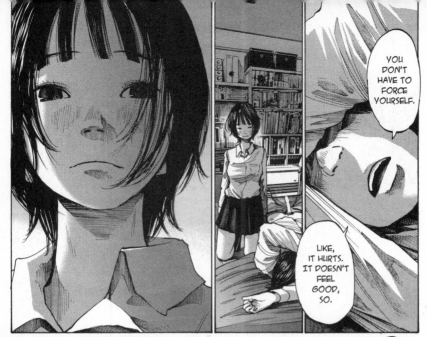

YOU DON'T HAVE TO FORCE YOURSELF.

LIKE, IT HURTS, IT DOESN'T FEEL GOOD, SO.

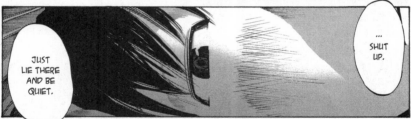

JUST LIE THERE AND BE QUIET.

... SHUT UP.

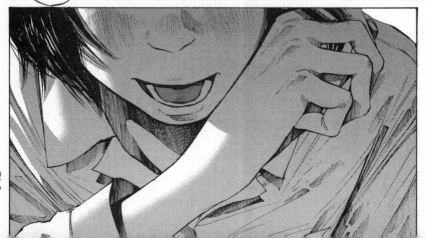

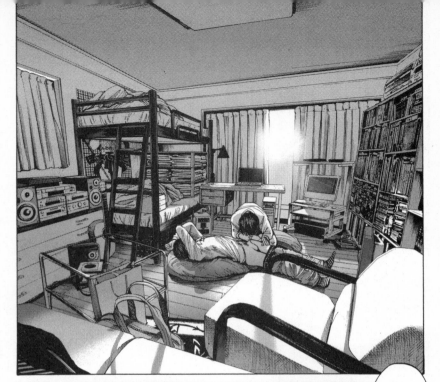

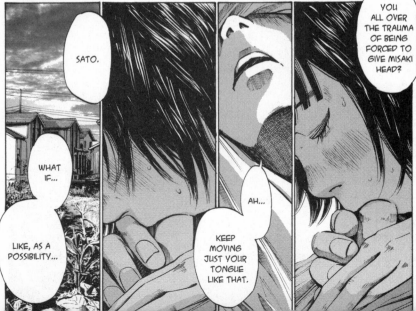

YOU ALL OVER THE TRAUMA OF BEING FORCED TO GIVE MISAKI HEAD?

SATO.

WHAT IF...

LIKE, AS A POSSIBILITY...

AH...

KEEP MOVING JUST YOUR TONGUE LIKE THAT.

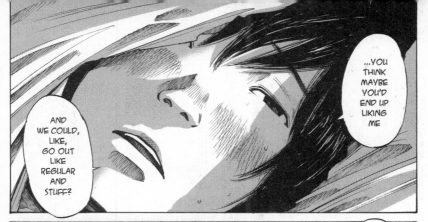

...YOU THINK MAYBE YOU'D END UP LIKING ME

AND WE COULD, LIKE, GO OUT LIKE REGULAR AND STUFF?

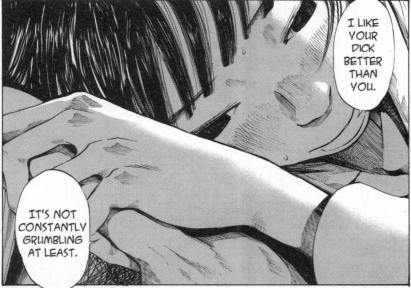

I LIKE YOUR DICK BETTER THAN YOU.

IT'S NOT CONSTANTLY GRUMBLING AT LEAST.

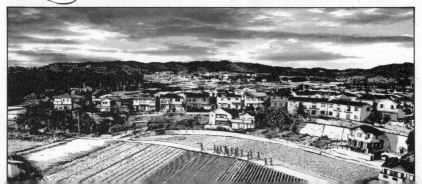

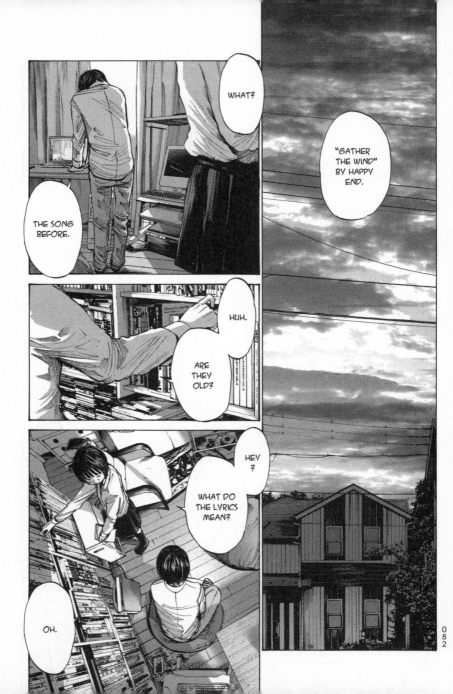

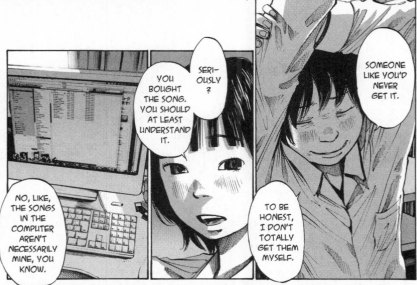

SERI-OUSLY?

YOU BOUGHT THE SONG. YOU SHOULD AT LEAST UNDERSTAND IT.

SOMEONE LIKE YOU'D NEVER GET IT.

NO, LIKE, THE SONGS IN THE COMPUTER AREN'T NECESSARILY MINE, YOU KNOW.

TO BE HONEST, I DON'T TOTALLY GET THEM MYSELF.

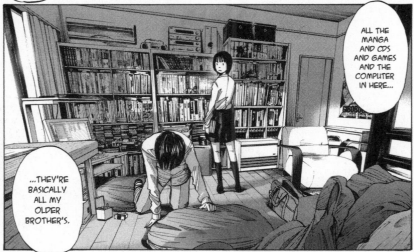

ALL THE MANGA AND CDS AND GAMES AND THE COMPUTER IN HERE...

...THEY'RE BASICALLY ALL MY OLDER BROTHER'S.

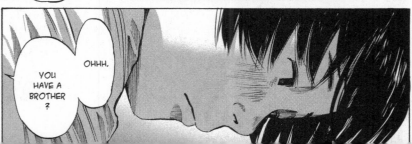

OHHH.

YOU HAVE A BROTHER?

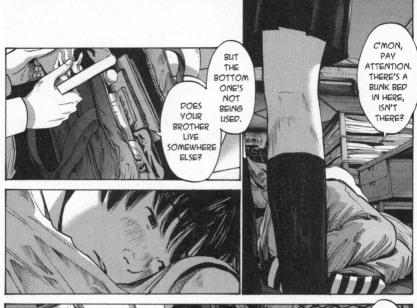

DOES YOUR BROTHER LIVE SOMEWHERE ELSE?

BUT THE BOTTOM ONE'S NOT BEING USED.

C'MON, PAY ATTENTION. THERE'S A BUNK BED IN HERE, ISN'T THERE?

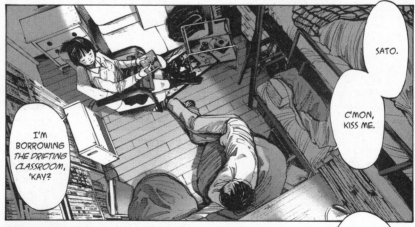

I'M BORROWING *THE DRIFTING CLASSROOM,* 'KAY?

SATO.

C'MON, KISS ME.

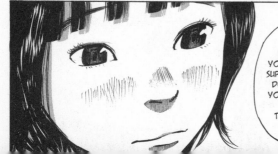

Y'KNOW, IT'S TOTALLY FINE IF YOU JUST COME OVER TO READ MANGA.

BUT, LIKE, YOUR FAMILY'S SUPER NORMAL. DON'T MAKE YOUR PARENTS WORRY TOO MUCH.

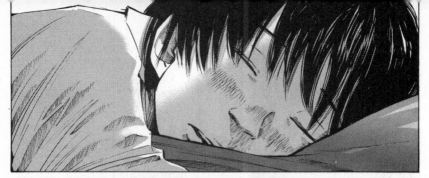

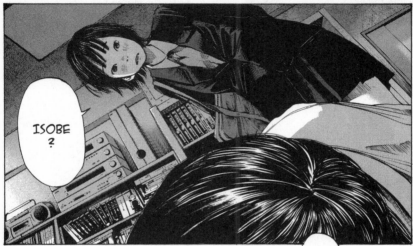

ISOBE
?

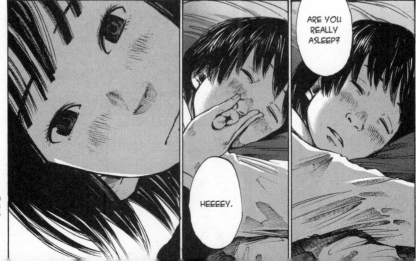

ARE YOU
REALLY
ASLEEP?

HEEEEY.

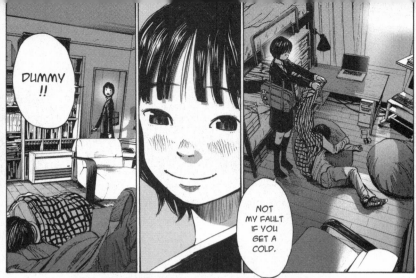

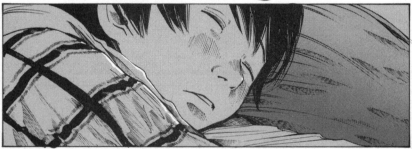

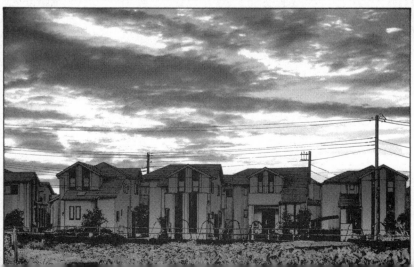

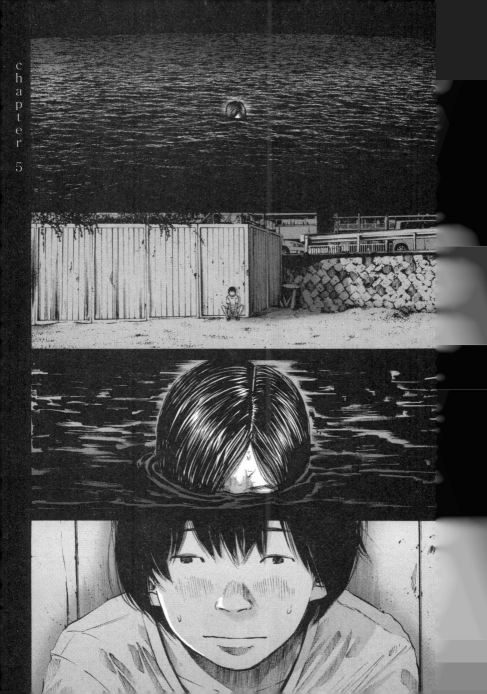

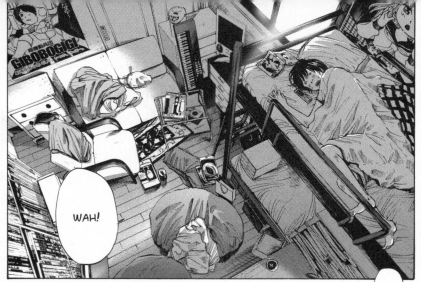

WAH!

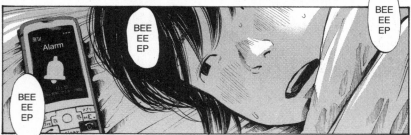

BEE
EE
EP

BEE
EE
EP

BEE
EE
EP

Alarm

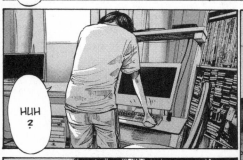

HUH
?

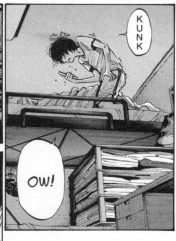

KUNK

OW!

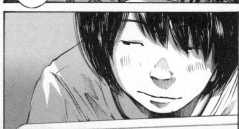

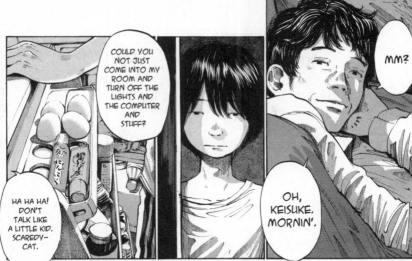

COULD YOU NOT JUST COME INTO MY ROOM AND TURN OFF THE LIGHTS AND THE COMPUTER AND STUFF?

MM?

HA HA HA! DON'T TALK LIKE A LITTLE KID, SCAREDY-CAT.

OH, KEISUKE. MORNIN'.

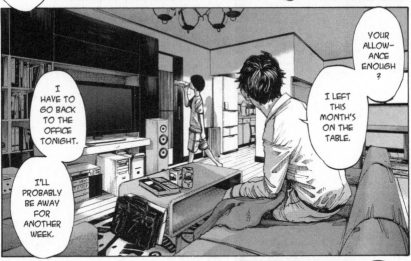

I HAVE TO GO BACK TO THE OFFICE TONIGHT.

I'LL PROBABLY BE AWAY FOR ANOTHER WEEK.

YOUR ALLOW-ANCE ENOUGH?

I LEFT THIS MONTH'S ON THE TABLE.

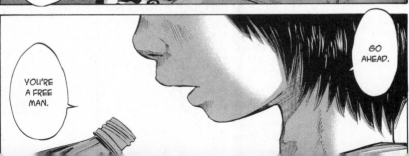

GO AHEAD.

YOU'RE A FREE MAN.

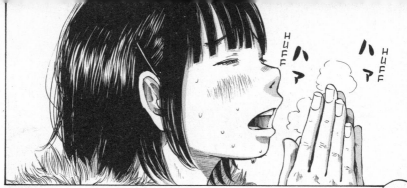

HUFF ハァ HUFF ハァ HUFF

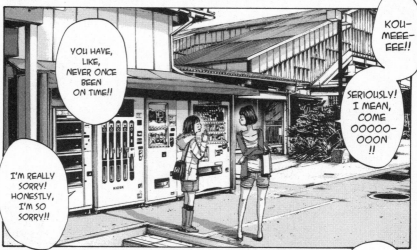

KOU-MEEE-EEE!!

SERIOUSLY! I MEAN, COME OOOOO-OOON!!

YOU HAVE, LIKE, NEVER ONCE BEEN ON TIME!!

I'M REALLY SORRY! HONESTLY, I'M SO SORRY!!

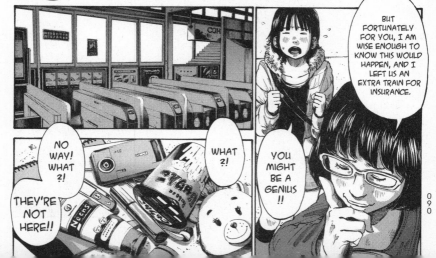

BUT FORTUNATELY FOR YOU, I AM WISE ENOUGH TO KNOW THIS WOULD HAPPEN, AND I LEFT US AN EXTRA TRAIN FOR INSURANCE.

NO WAY! WHAT?!

THEY'RE NOT HERE!!

WHAT ?!

YOU MIGHT BE A GENIUS !!

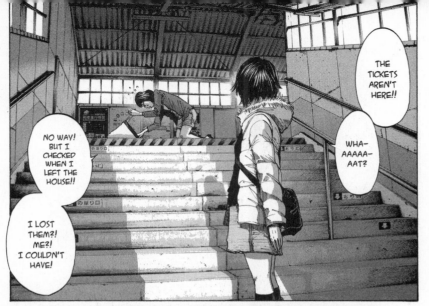

THE TICKETS AREN'T HERE!!

NO WAY! BUT I CHECKED WHEN I LEFT THE HOUSE!!

WHA-AAAAA-AAT?

I LOST THEM?! ME?! I COULDN'T HAVE!

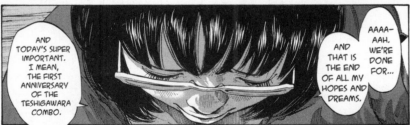

AND TODAY'S SUPER IMPORTANT. I MEAN, THE FIRST ANNIVERSARY OF THE TESHIGAWARA COMBO.

AND THAT IS THE END OF ALL MY HOPES AND DREAMS.

AAAAA-AAH. WE'RE DONE FOR...

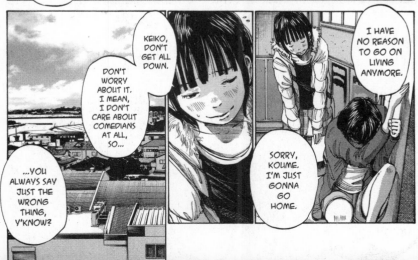

KEIKO, DON'T GET ALL DOWN.

DON'T WORRY ABOUT IT. I MEAN, I DON'T CARE ABOUT COMEDIANS AT ALL, SO...

I HAVE NO REASON TO GO ON LIVING ANYMORE.

...YOU ALWAYS SAY JUST THE WRONG THING, Y'KNOW?

SORRY, KOUME. I'M JUST GONNA GO HOME.

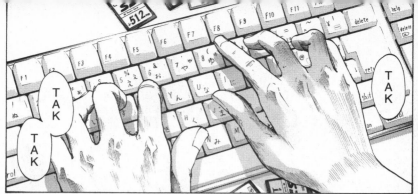

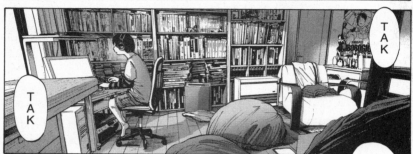

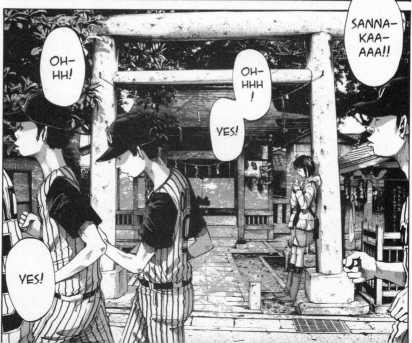

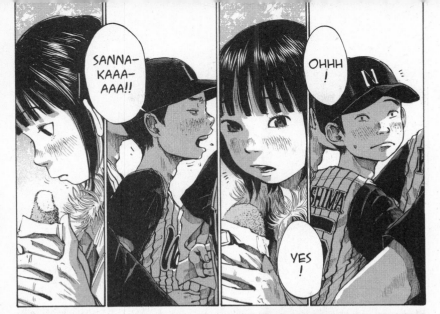

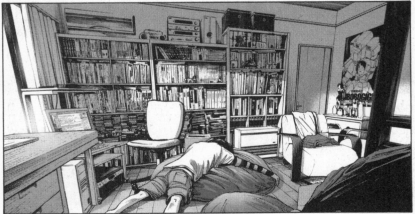

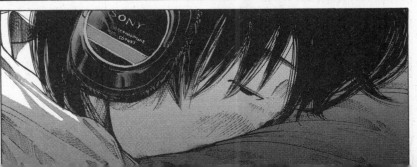

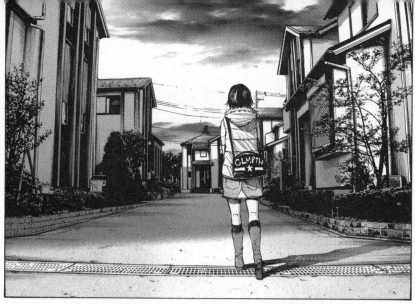

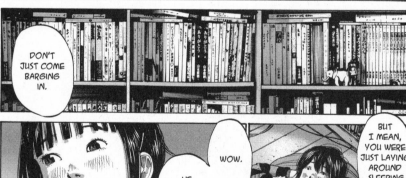

DON'T JUST COME BARGING IN.

HE CAME HOME. THAT'S WEIRD.

WOW.

BUT I MEAN, YOU WERE JUST LAYING AROUND SLEEPING ANYWAY?

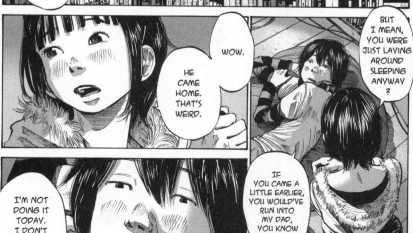

I'M NOT DOING IT TODAY. I DON'T FEEL LIKE IT.

IF YOU CAME A LITTLE EARLIER, YOU WOULD'VE RUN INTO MY DAD, YOU KNOW?

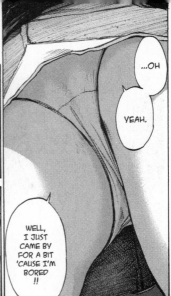

...OH

YEAH.

WELL, I JUST CAME BY FOR A BIT 'CAUSE I'M BORED!!

ANYWAY, LOOK. CHECK IT OUT!

MY DAD GOT ME A DIGITAL CAMERA FOR A PASSING PRESENT.

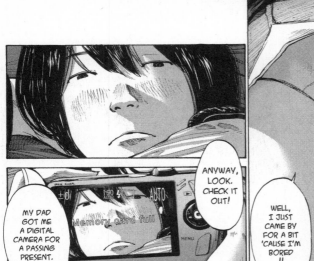

Memory card full

±0 ISO 4 AUTO
MENU

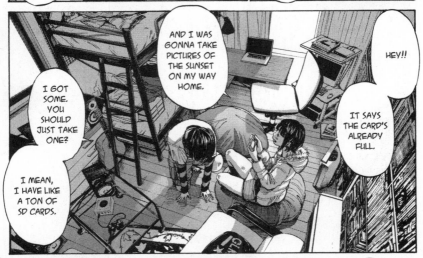

AND I WAS GONNA TAKE PICTURES OF THE SUNSET ON MY WAY HOME.

HEY!!

IT SAYS THE CARD'S ALREADY FULL.

I GOT SOME. YOU SHOULD JUST TAKE ONE?

I MEAN, I HAVE LIKE A TON OF SD CARDS.

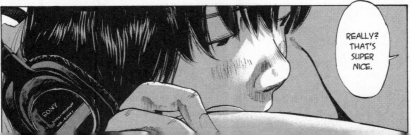

REALLY? THAT'S SUPER NICE.

SONY

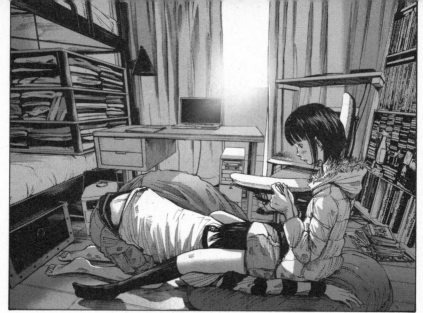

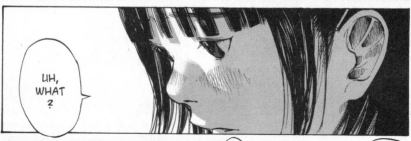

UH, WHAT?

... YEAH.

SORRY.

MM— MM.

I KNOW I SHOULD JUST SHUT UP AND I'M GETTING SUPER ANNOYING, SO THIS IS THE LAST TIME I'LL ASK.

YOU DON'T FEEL LIKE YOU COULD EVER LIKE ME?

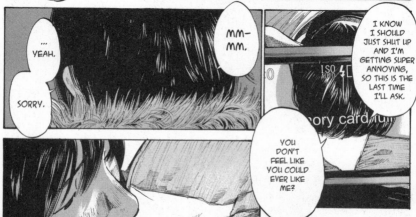

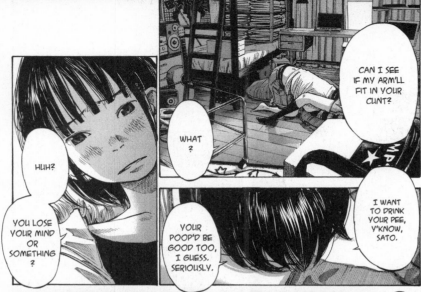

CAN I SEE
IF MY ARM'LL
FIT IN YOUR
CUNT?

WHAT
?

HUH?

YOU LOSE
YOUR MIND
OR
SOMETHING
?

YOUR
POOP'D BE
GOOD TOO,
I GUESS.
SERIOUSLY.

I WANT
TO DRINK
YOUR PEE,
Y'KNOW,
SATO.

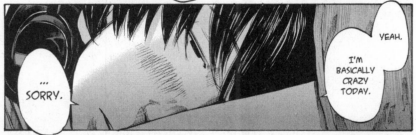

...
SORRY.

YEAH.

I'M
BASICALLY
CRAZY
TODAY.

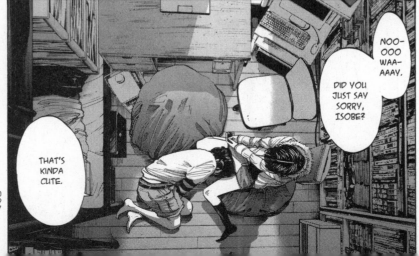

NOO-
OOO
WAA-
AAAY.

DID YOU
JUST SAY
SORRY,
ISOBE?

THAT'S
KINDA
CUTE.

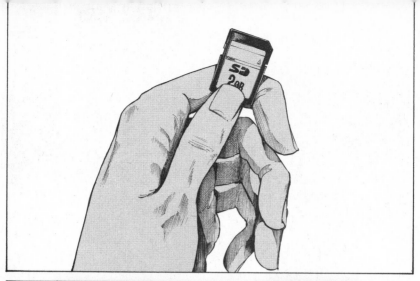

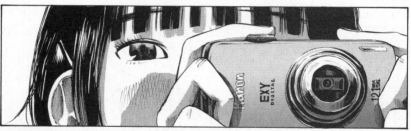

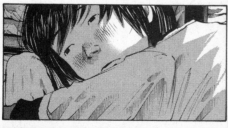

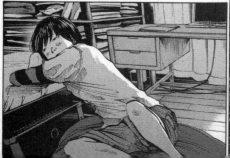

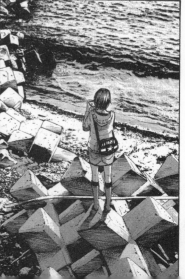

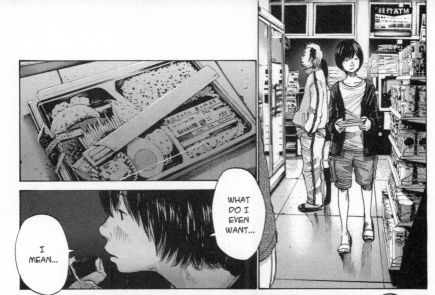

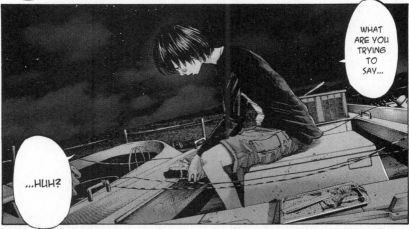

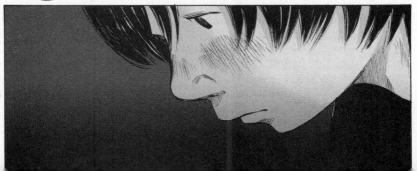

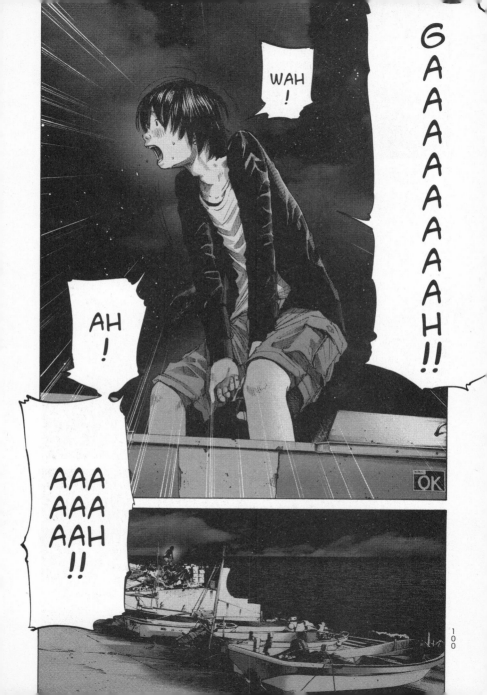

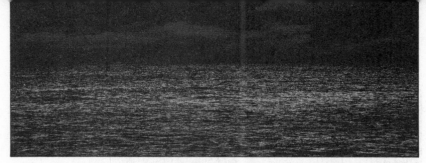

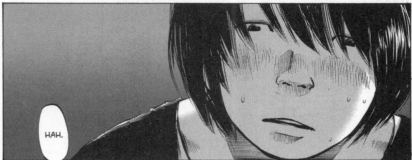

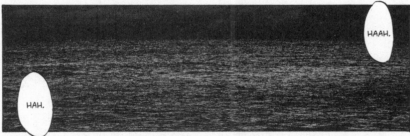

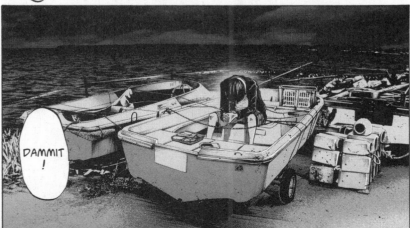

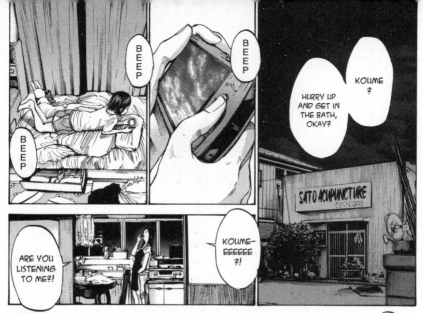

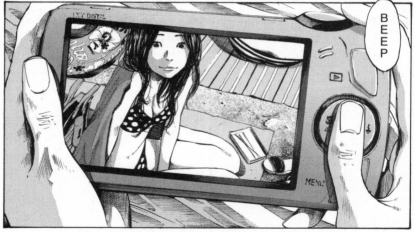

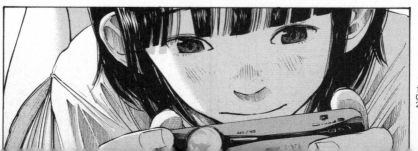

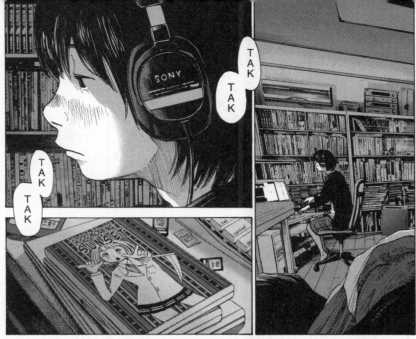

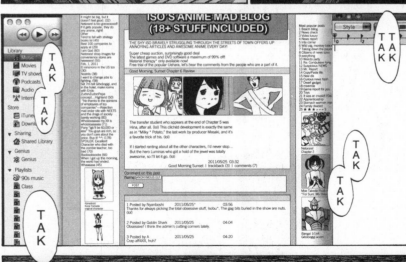

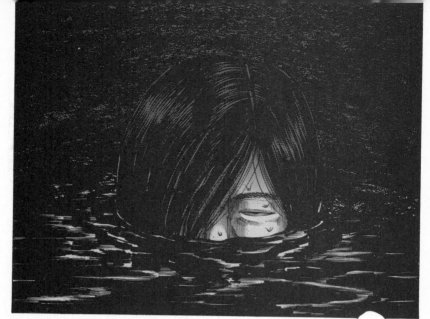

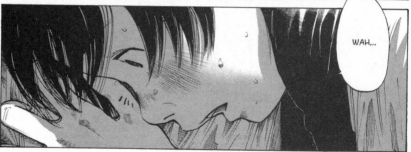

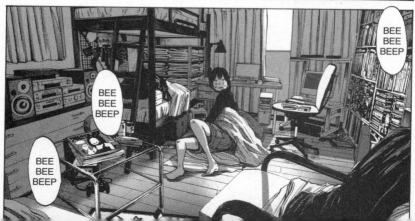

104

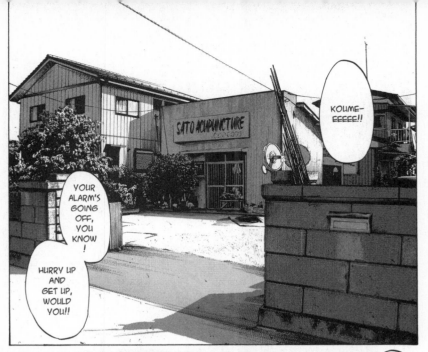

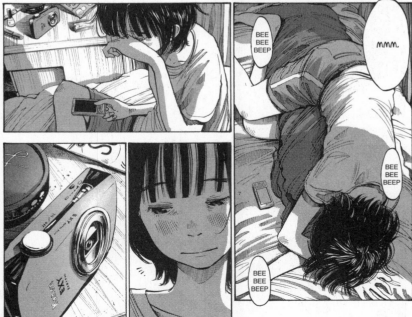

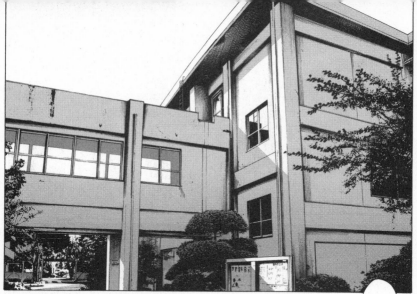

WHOA!

WHAT'S WITH THOSE BAGS?!

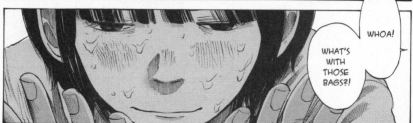

NO SLEEP?

YOU PASSED OUT IN JAPANESE CLASS TOO.

IS IT LOVE?! ARE YOU LOVESICK?!

BUT Y'KNOW, YOU DON'T TALK ABOUT MISAKI ANYMORE.

WHAT'S GOING ON WITH HIM LATELY?

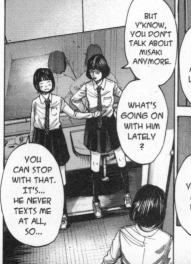

YOU CAN STOP WITH THAT. IT'S... HE NEVER TEXTS ME AT ALL, SO...

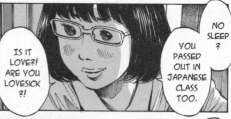

YOU'RE NOT, HUH?

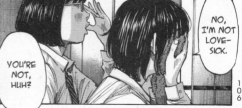

NO, I'M NOT LOVESICK.

106

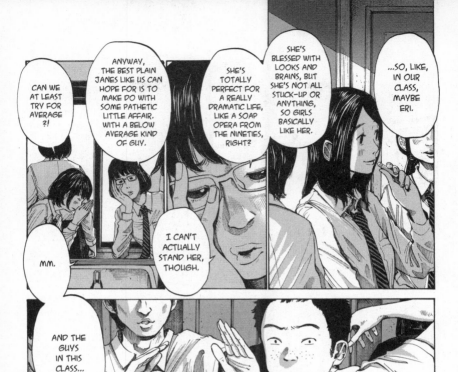

CAN WE AT LEAST TRY FOR AVERAGE?!

ANYWAY, THE BEST PLAIN JANES LIKE US CAN HOPE FOR IS TO MAKE DO WITH SOME PATHETIC LITTLE AFFAIR. WITH A BELOW AVERAGE KIND OF GUY.

SHE'S TOTALLY PERFECT FOR A REALLY DRAMATIC LIFE, LIKE A SOAP OPERA FROM THE NINETIES, RIGHT?

SHE'S BLESSED WITH LOOKS AND BRAINS, BUT SHE'S NOT ALL STUCK-UP OR ANYTHING, SO GIRLS BASICALLY LIKE HER.

...SO, LIKE, IN OUR CLASS, MAYBE ERI.

MM.

I CAN'T ACTUALLY STAND HER, THOUGH.

AND THE GUYS IN THIS CLASS...

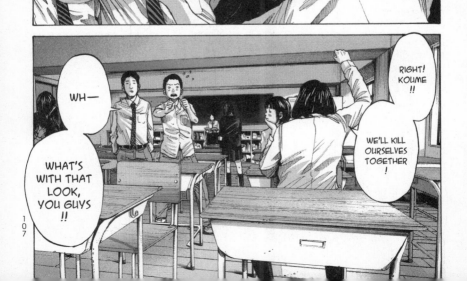

WH—

WHAT'S WITH THAT LOOK, YOU GUYS!!

RIGHT! KOUME!!

WE'LL KILL OURSELVES TOGETHER!

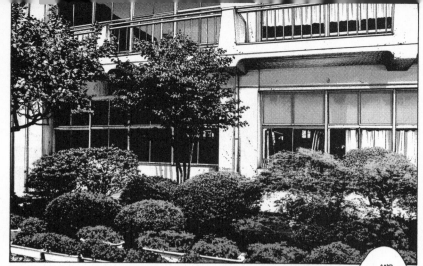

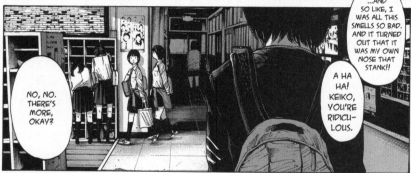

...AND SO LIKE, I WAS ALL THIS SMELLS SO BAD. AND IT TURNED OUT THAT IT WAS MY OWN NOSE THAT STANK!!

A HA HA! KEIKO, YOU'RE RIDICU-LOUS.

NO, NO. THERE'S MORE, OKAY?

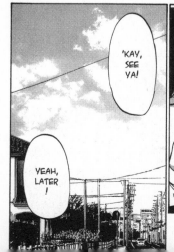

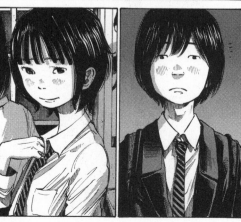

'KAY, SEE YA!

YEAH, LATER!

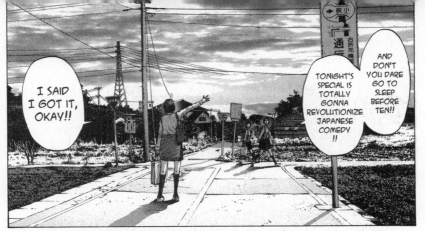

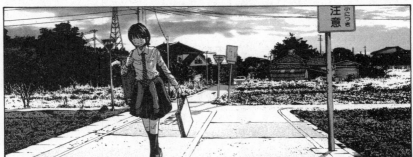

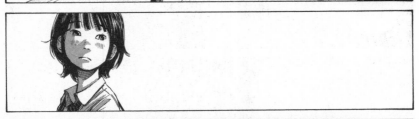

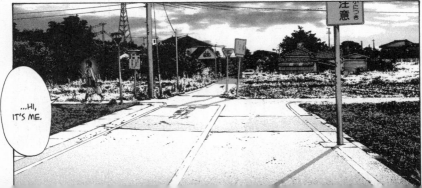

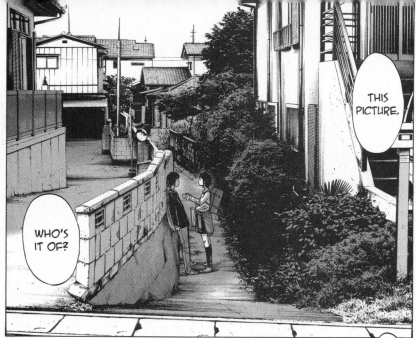

THIS PICTURE.

WHO'S IT OF?

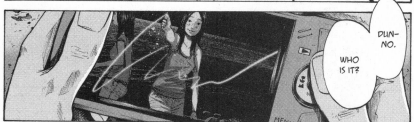

DUN-NO.

WHO IS IT?

RIGHT, RIGHT. THIS THING, HUH?

OHH.

IT WAS ON THE SD CARD YOU GAVE ME.

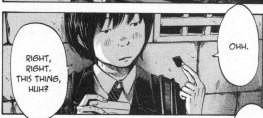

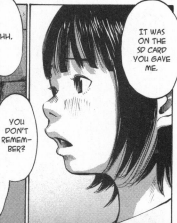

YOU DON'T REMEM-BER?

I PICKED THIS ONE UP ON THE BEACH THAT TIME YOU WERE SOBBING THERE AFTER MISAKI BLEW YOU OFF.

MAYBE SOMEONE WHO CAME TO SET OFF FIREWORKS OR SOMETHING DROPPED IT?

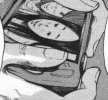

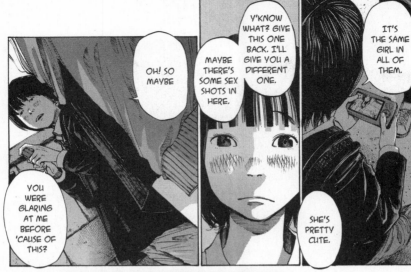

OH! SO MAYBE

MAYBE THERE'S SOME SEX SHOTS IN HERE.

Y'KNOW WHAT? GIVE THIS ONE BACK. I'LL GIVE YOU A DIFFERENT ONE.

IT'S THE SAME GIRL IN ALL OF THEM.

YOU WERE GLARING AT ME BEFORE 'CAUSE OF THIS?

SHE'S PRETTY CUTE.

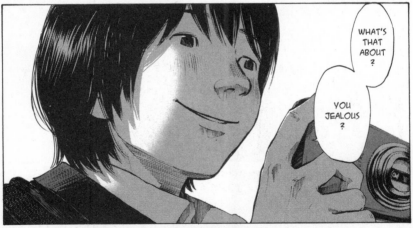

WHAT'S THAT ABOUT ?

YOU JEALOUS ?

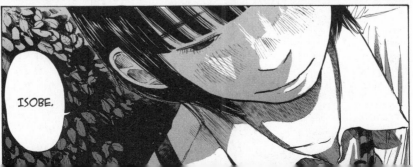

ISOBE.

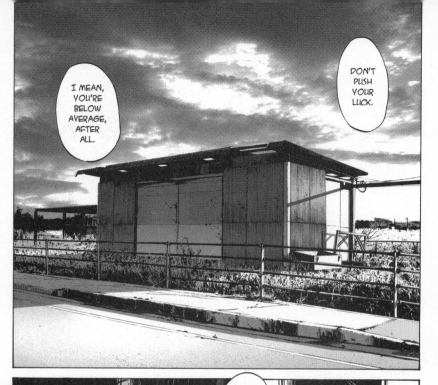

I MEAN, YOU'RE BELOW AVERAGE, AFTER ALL.

DON'T PUSH YOUR LUCK.

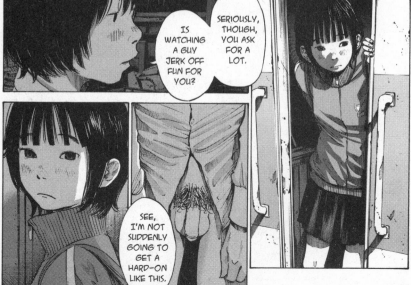

IS WATCHING A GUY JERK OFF FUN FOR YOU?

SERIOUSLY, THOUGH, YOU ASK FOR A LOT.

SEE, I'M NOT SUDDENLY GOING TO GET A HARD-ON LIKE THIS.

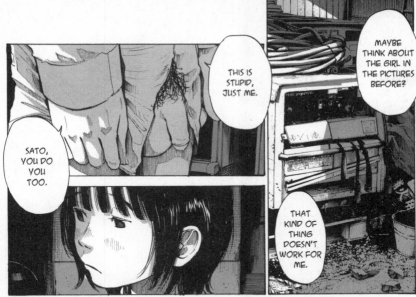

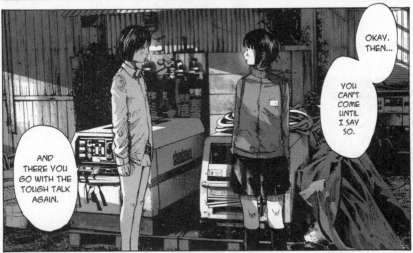

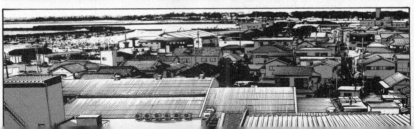

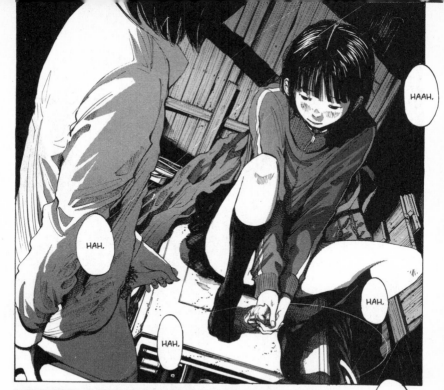

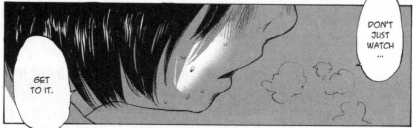

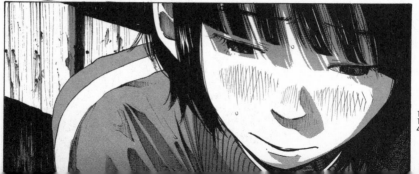

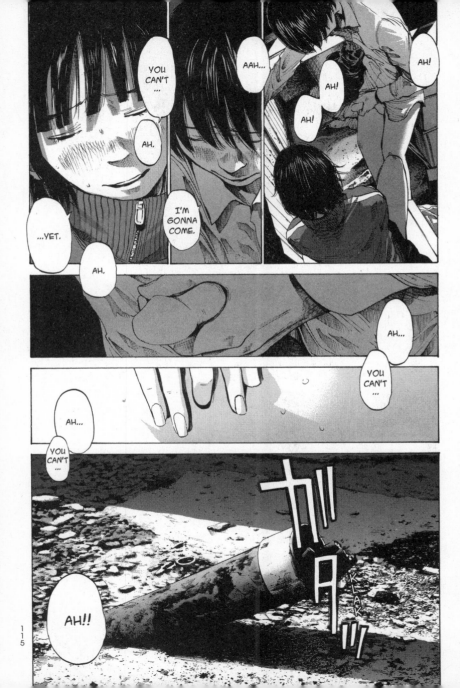

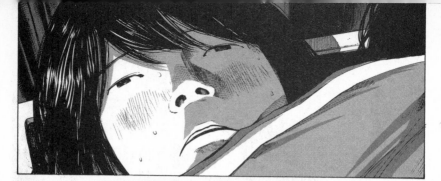

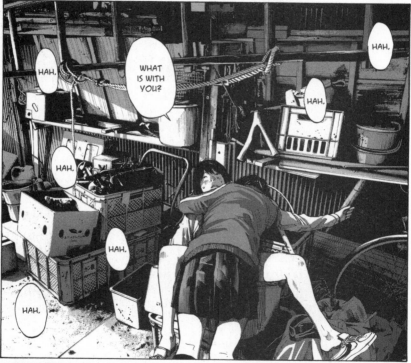

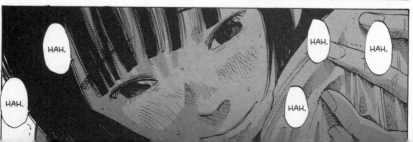

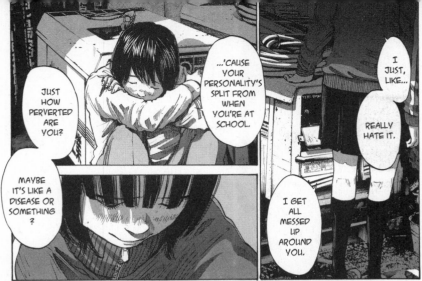

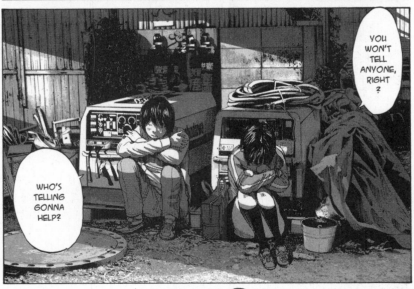

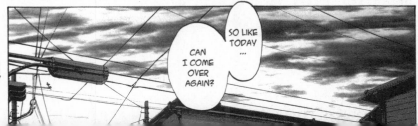

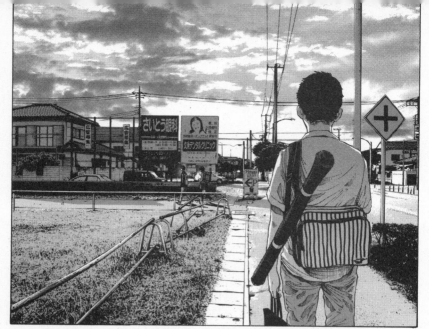

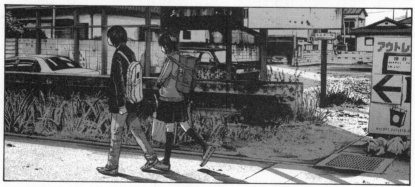

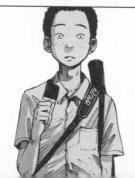

A

Girl

on the

Shore

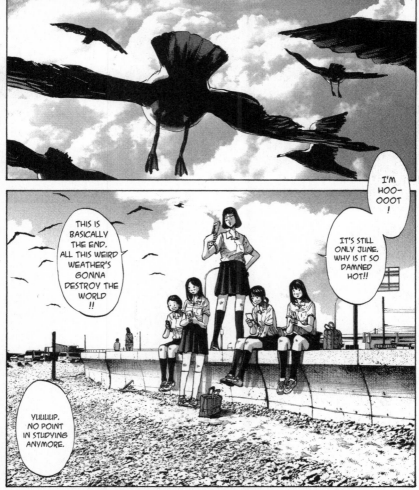

chapter 7

THIS IS BASICALLY THE END. ALL THIS WEIRD WEATHER'S GONNA DESTROY THE WORLD !!

I'M HOO-OOOT !

IT'S STILL ONLY JUNE. WHY IS IT SO DAMNED HOT!!

YUUUUP. NO POINT IN STUDYING ANYMORE.

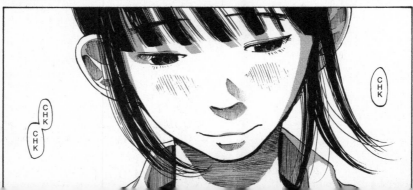

CHK

CHK

CHK

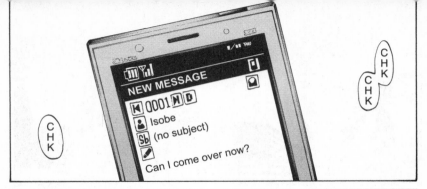

MAKE SURE YOU READ THE FLYER I GAVE YOU, 'KAY?!

'KAY.

INBOX
1001
Isobe
Re
Bring coffee.

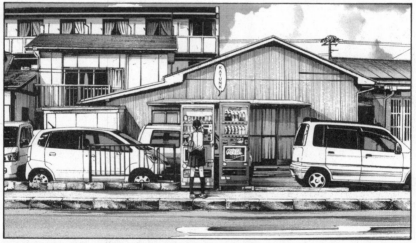

I'M HERE.

GAH!

YOU DOING YOUR SECRET BLOG THING AGAIN?

WHY CAN'T YOU JUST LET ME SEE IT?

NO WAY. YOU'D TOTALLY HATE IT.

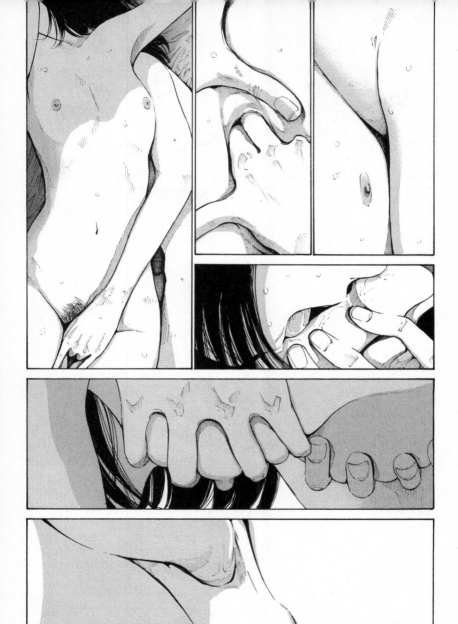

AND
KASHIMA SAYS
HE'S GONNA GO
TO HIGH SCHOOL
ON A SPORTS
SCHOLARSHIP,
SO HE DOESN'T
HAVE TO
STUDY.

SO, LIKE,
THE BASEBALL
TEAM WON
THE SOUTH
PREFECTURAL
FINALS...

YOU
SKIPPED
SCHOOL
TODAY,
DIDN'T
YOU?

I HATE
THAT GUY.
HE NEVER
SHUTS UP.

SO ARE YOU
GONNA TURN
INTO AN
OTAKU
SHUT-IN?

...'COURSE
NOT.

TODAY
WAS JUST
GONNA BE
CHECKING
ANSWERS
FROM THE
MID-TERMS
ANYWAY.

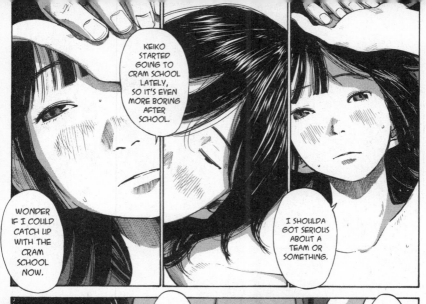

KEIKO STARTED GOING TO CRAM SCHOOL LATELY, SO IT'S EVEN MORE BORING AFTER SCHOOL.

WONDER IF I COULD CATCH UP WITH THE CRAM SCHOOL NOW.

I SHOULDA GOT SERIOUS ABOUT A TEAM OR SOMETHING.

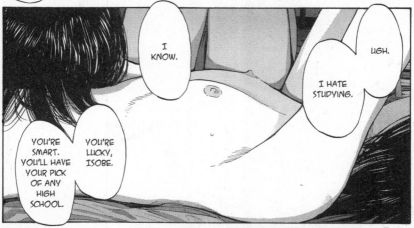

I KNOW.

UGH.

I HATE STUDYING.

YOU'RE SMART. YOU'LL HAVE YOUR PICK OF ANY HIGH SCHOOL.

YOU'RE LUCKY, ISOBE.

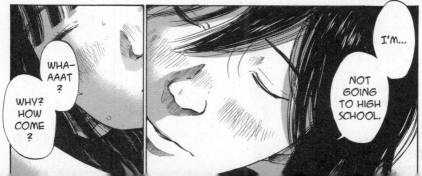

I'M...

WHA--AAAT?

WHY? HOW COME?

NOT GOING TO HIGH SCHOOL.

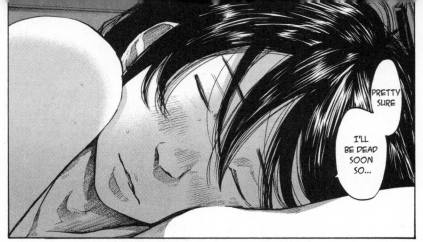

PRETTY SURE

I'LL BE DEAD SOON SO...

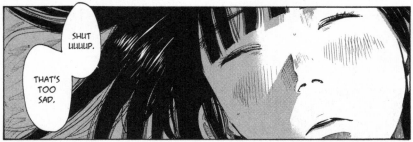

SHUT UUUUP.

THAT'S TOO SAD.

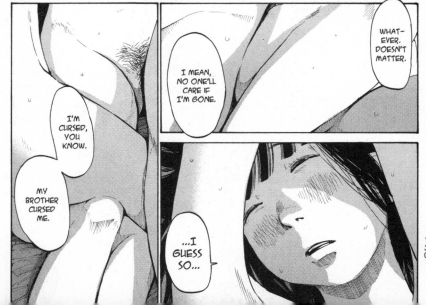

I MEAN, NO ONE'LL CARE IF I'M GONE.

WHAT- EVER. DOESN'T MATTER.

I'M CURSED, YOU KNOW.

MY BROTHER CURSED ME.

...I GUESS SO...

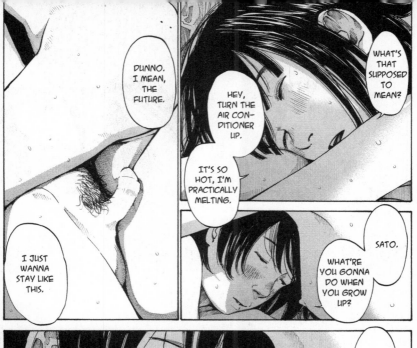

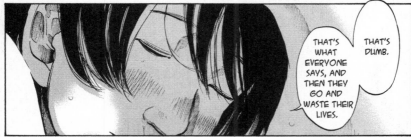

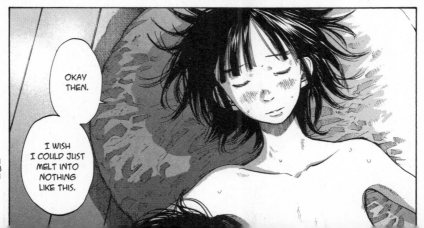

131

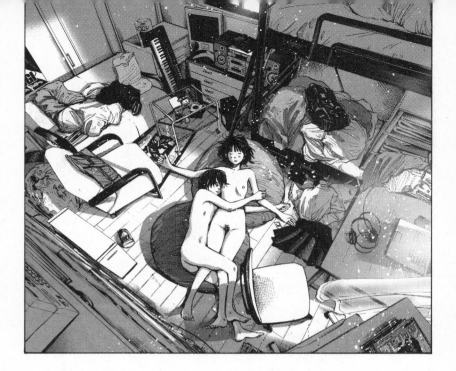

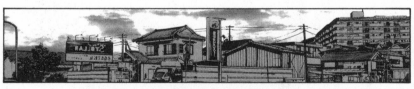

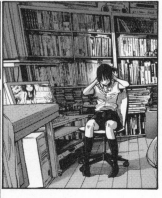

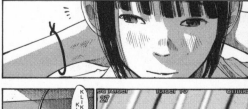

KLIK
KLIK

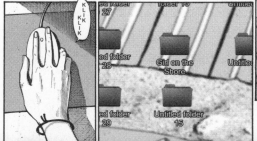

ed folder
27

folder 15

Untitle

ed folder
28

Girl on the
Shore

Untitle

ed folder
29

Untitled folder
15

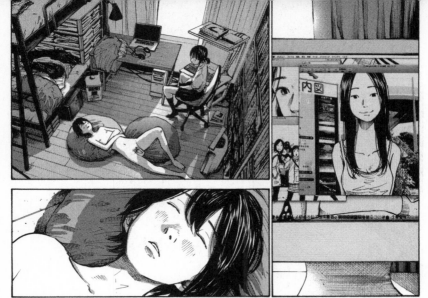

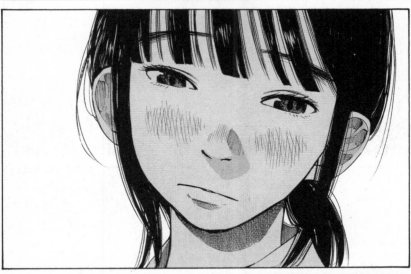

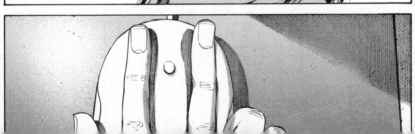

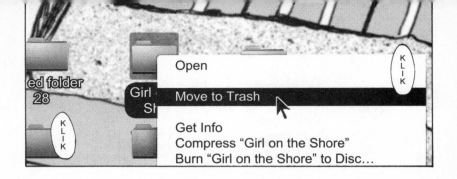

Open   KLIK

Move to Trash

Get Info
Compress "Girl on the Shore"
Burn "Girl on the Shore" to Disc…

ed folder
28

Girl o
Sh

KLIK

KLIK

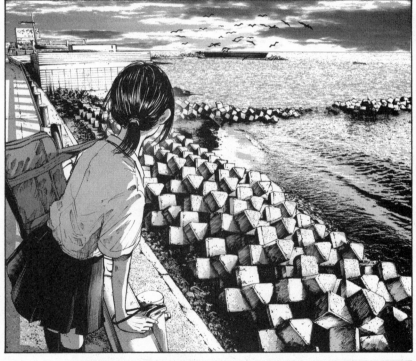

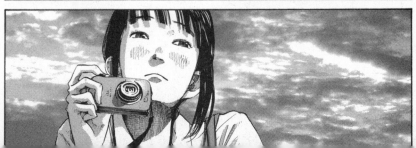

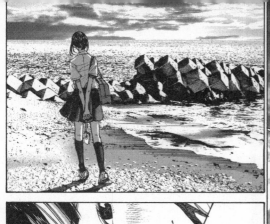

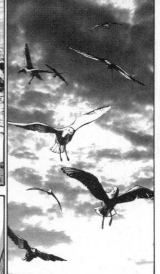

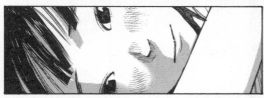

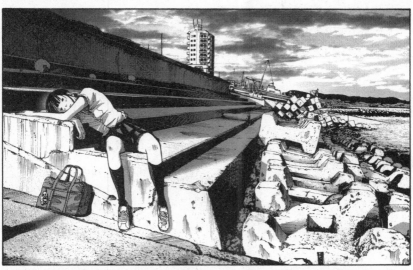

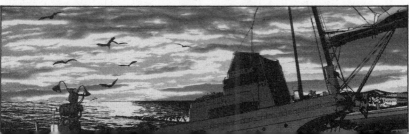

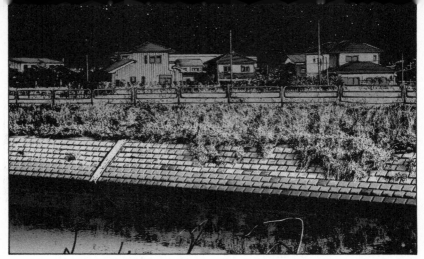

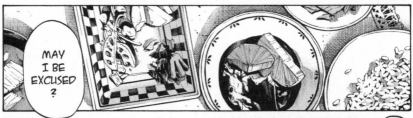

MAY
I BE
EXCUSED
?

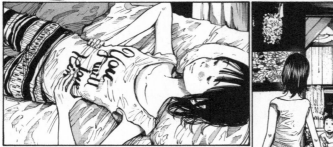

WHAT?
YOU'RE
DONE
ALREADY,
KOUME
?

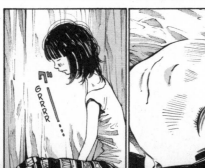

GRRRR
.....

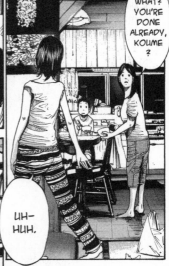

UH-
HUH.

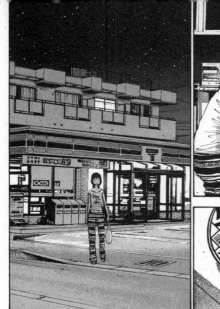

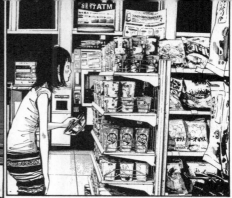

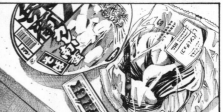

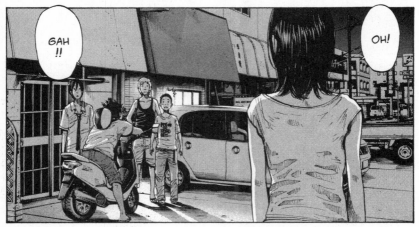

GAH
!!

OH!

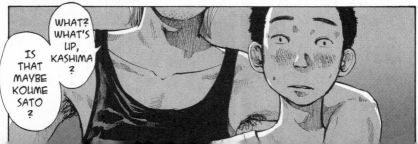

WHAT?
WHAT'S
UP,
KASHIMA
?

IS
THAT
MAYBE
KOUME
SATO
?

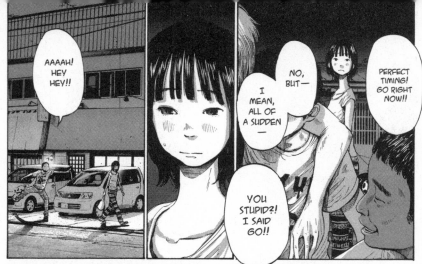

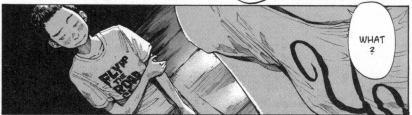

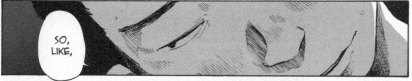

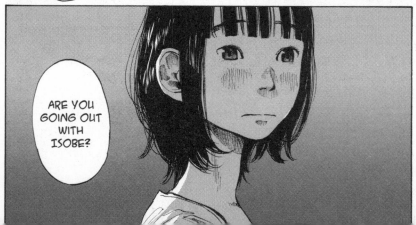

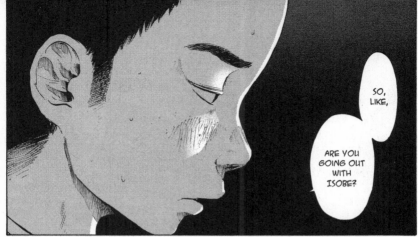

SO, LIKE,

ARE YOU GOING OUT WITH ISOBE?

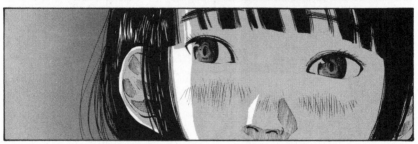

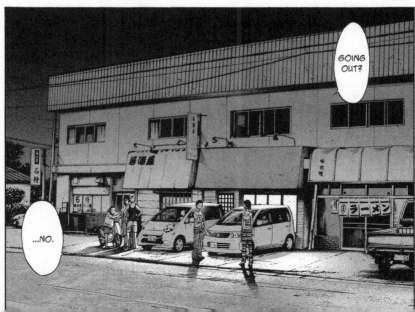

GOING OUT?

...NO.

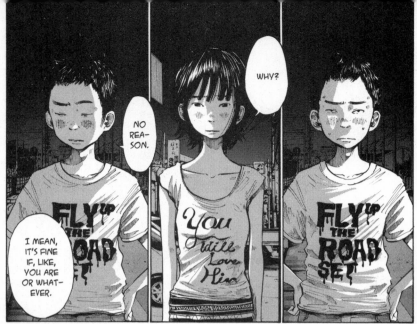

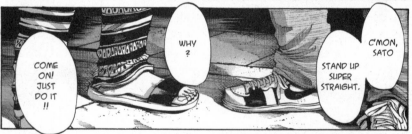

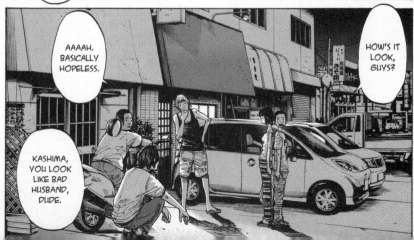

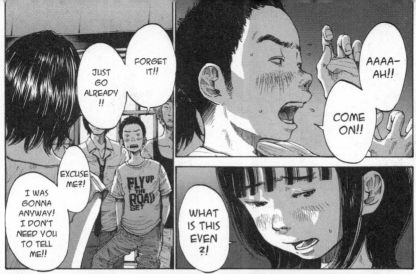

JUST GO ALREADY!!

FORGET IT!!

AAAA-AH!!

COME ON!!

EXCUSE ME?!

I WAS GONNA ANYWAY! I DON'T NEED YOU TO TELL ME!!

WHAT IS THIS EVEN?!

FLY UP THE ROAD SET

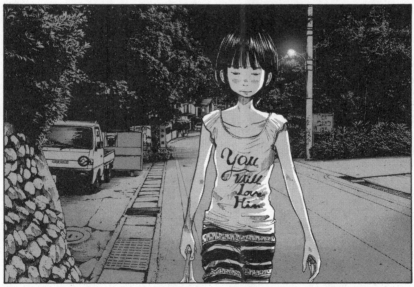

...WHAT WAS THAT EVEN, GOD—

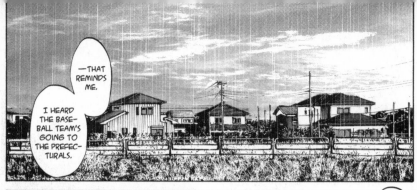
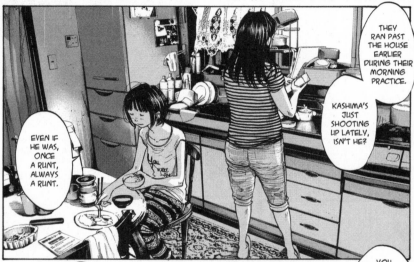
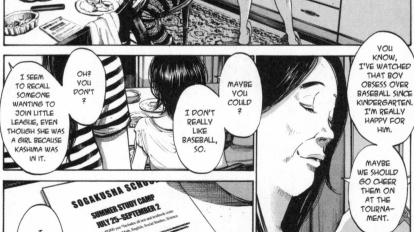

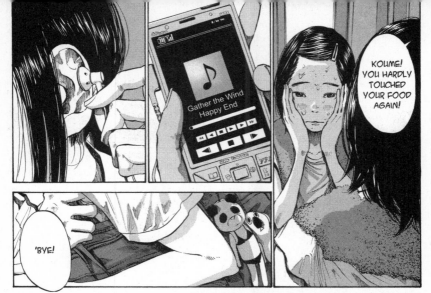

KOUME! YOU HARDLY TOUCHED YOUR FOOD AGAIN!

Gather the Wind
Happy End

'BYE!

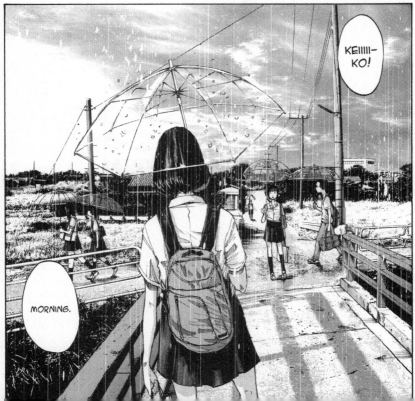

KEIIIIII‐KO!

MORNING.

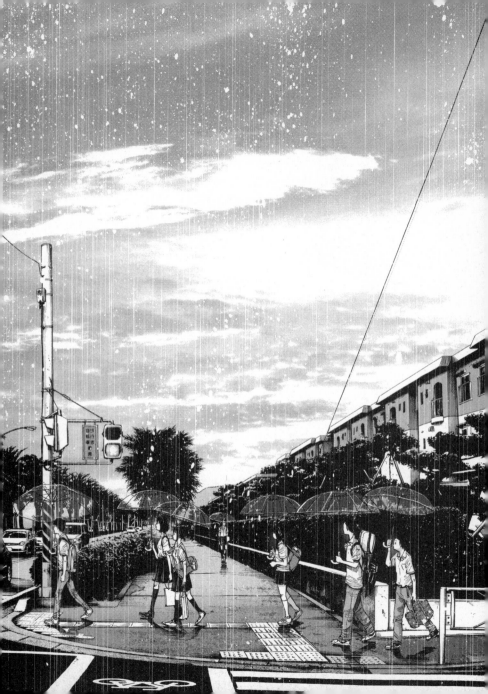

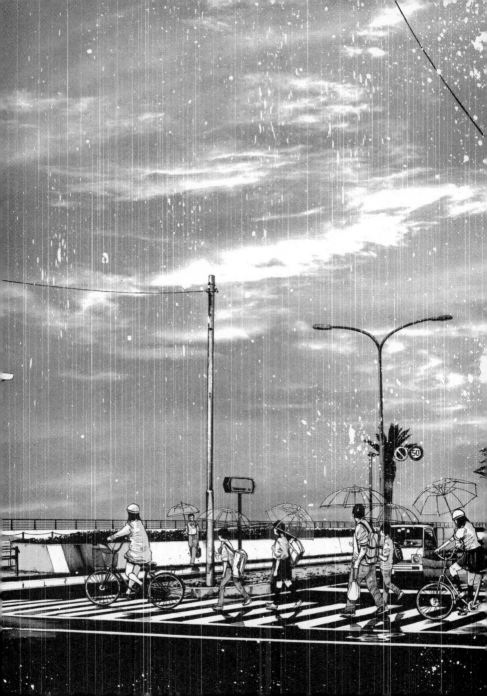

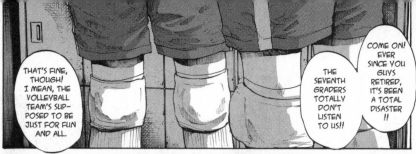

THAT'S FINE, THOUGH! I MEAN, THE VOLLEYBALL TEAM'S SUPPOSED TO BE JUST FOR FUN AND ALL.

THE SEVENTH GRADERS TOTALLY DON'T LISTEN TO US!!

COME ON! EVER SINCE YOU GUYS RETIRED, IT'S BEEN A TOTAL DISASTER !!

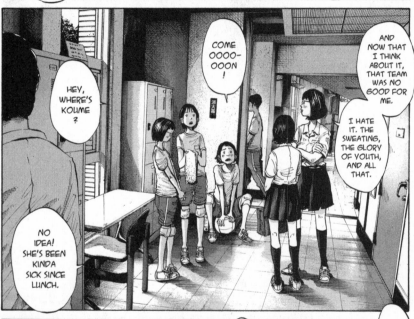

HEY, WHERE'S KOUME ?

COME OOOO-OOON !

AND NOW THAT I THINK ABOUT IT, THAT TEAM WAS NO GOOD FOR ME.

I HATE IT. THE SWEATING, THE GLORY OF YOUTH, AND ALL THAT.

NO IDEA! SHE'S BEEN KINDA SICK SINCE LUNCH.

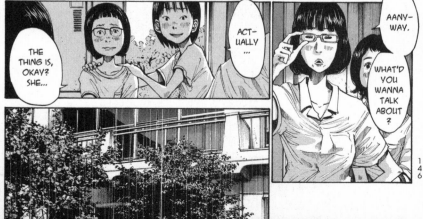

THE THING IS, OKAY? SHE...

ACTUALLY ...

AANY-WAY.

WHAT'D YOU WANNA TALK ABOUT ?

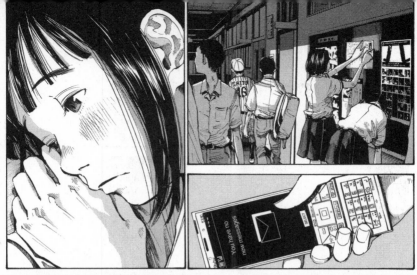

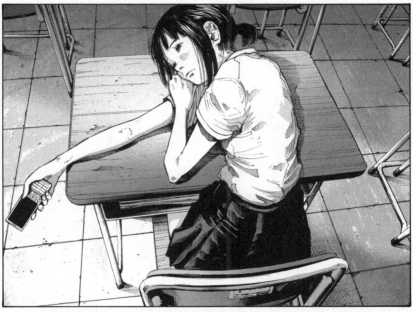

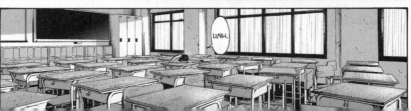

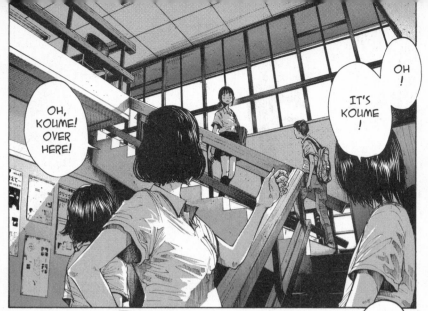

OH
!

IT'S
KOUME
!

OH,
KOUME!
OVER
HERE!

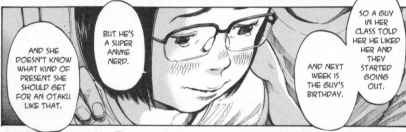

AND SHE
DOESN'T KNOW
WHAT KIND OF
PRESENT SHE
SHOULD GET
FOR AN OTAKU
LIKE THAT.

BUT HE'S
A SUPER
ANIME
NERD.

SO A GUY
IN HER
CLASS TOLD
HER HE LIKED
HER AND
THEY
STARTED
GOING
OUT.

AND NEXT
WEEK IS
THE GUY'S
BIRTHDAY.

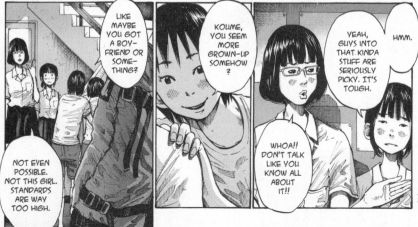

LIKE
MAYBE
YOU GOT
A BOY-
FRIEND OR
SOME-
THING?

KOUME,
YOU SEEM
MORE
GROWN-UP
SOMEHOW
?

YEAH,
GUYS INTO
THAT KINDA
STUFF ARE
SERIOUSLY
PICKY. IT'S
TOUGH.

HMM.

NOT EVEN
POSSIBLE.
NOT THIS GIRL.
STANDARDS
ARE WAY
TOO HIGH.

WHOA!!
DON'T TALK
LIKE YOU
KNOW ALL
ABOUT
IT!!

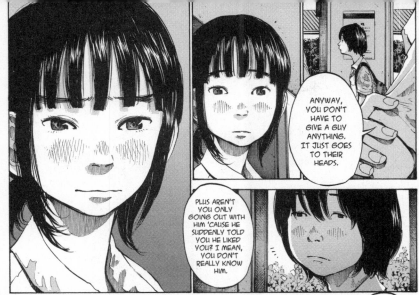

ANYWAY, YOU DON'T HAVE TO GIVE A GUY ANYTHING. IT JUST GOES TO THEIR HEADS.

PLUS AREN'T YOU ONLY GOING OUT WITH HIM 'CAUSE HE SUDDENLY TOLD YOU HE LIKED YOU? I MEAN, YOU DON'T REALLY KNOW HIM.

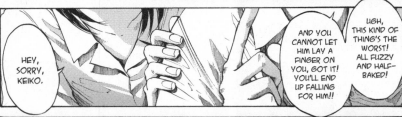

AND YOU CANNOT LET HIM LAY A FINGER ON YOU, GOT IT! YOU'LL END UP FALLING FOR HIM!!

UGH, THIS KIND OF THING'S THE WORST! ALL FUZZY AND HALF-BAKED!

HEY, SORRY, KEIKO.

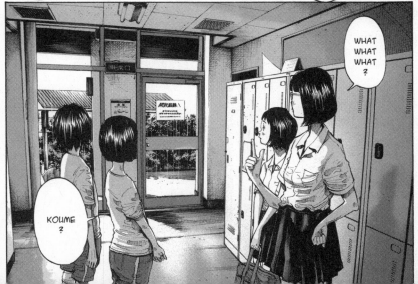

WHAT WHAT WHAT ?

KOUME ?

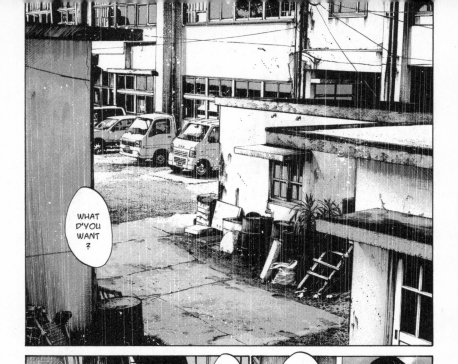

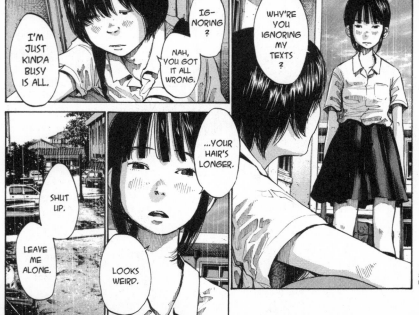

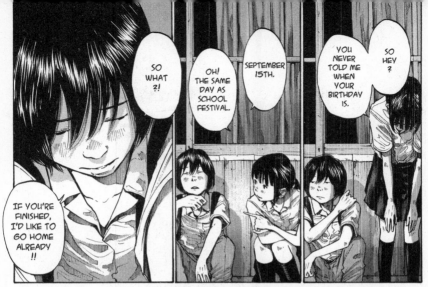

SO
HEY
?

YOU
NEVER
TOLD ME
WHEN
YOUR
BIRTHDAY
IS.

SEPTEMBER
15TH.

OH!
THE SAME
DAY AS
SCHOOL
FESTIVAL.

SO
WHAT
?!

IF YOU'RE
FINISHED,
I'D LIKE TO
GO HOME
ALREADY
!!

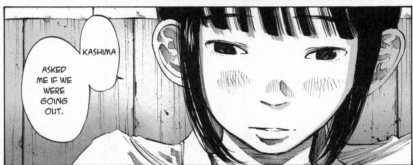

KASHIMA
ASKED
ME IF WE
WERE
GOING
OUT.

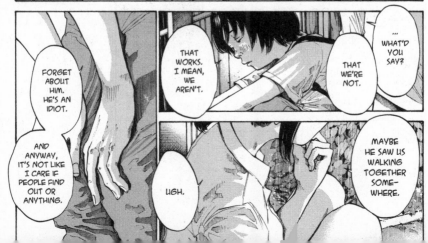

...
WHAT'D
YOU
SAY?

THAT
WE'RE
NOT.

THAT
WORKS.
I MEAN,
WE
AREN'T.

FORGET
ABOUT
HIM.
HE'S AN
IDIOT.

AND
ANYWAY,
IT'S NOT LIKE
I CARE IF
PEOPLE FIND
OUT OR
ANYTHING.

UGH.

MAYBE
HE SAW US
WALKING
TOGETHER
SOME-
WHERE.

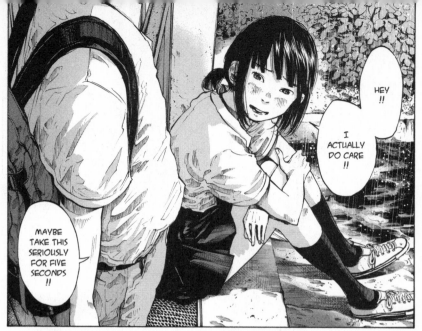

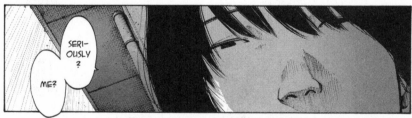

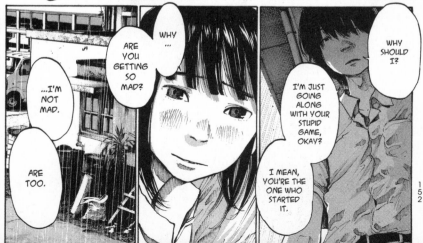

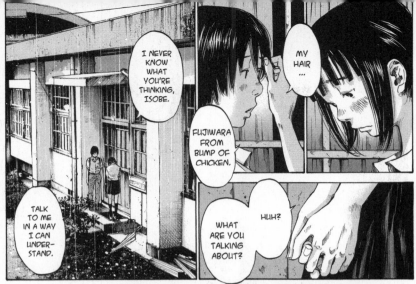

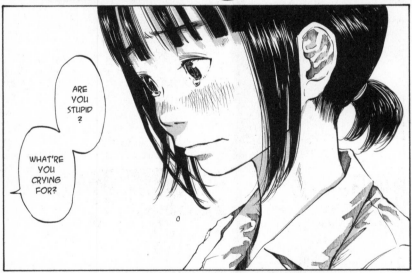

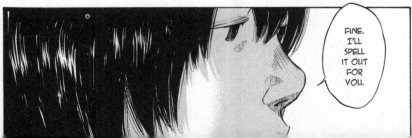

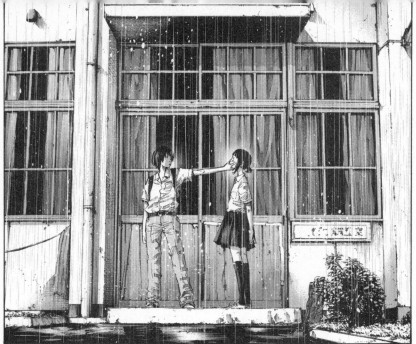

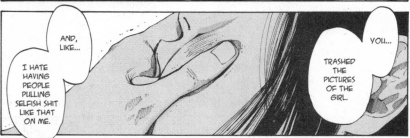

AND,
LIKE...

I HATE
HAVING
PEOPLE
PULLING
SELFISH SHIT
LIKE THAT
ON ME.

YOU...

TRASHED
THE
PICTURES
OF THE
GIRL.

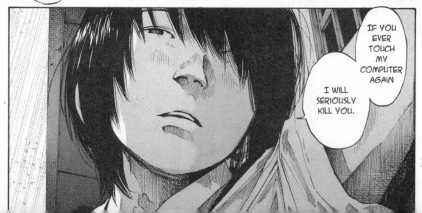

IF YOU
EVER
TOUCH
MY
COMPUTER
AGAIN

I WILL
SERIOUSLY
KILL YOU.

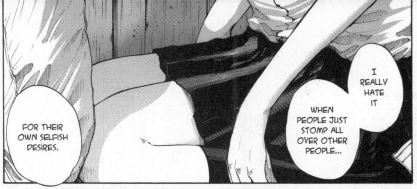

I REALLY HATE IT

WHEN PEOPLE JUST STOMP ALL OVER OTHER PEOPLE...

FOR THEIR OWN SELFISH DESIRES.

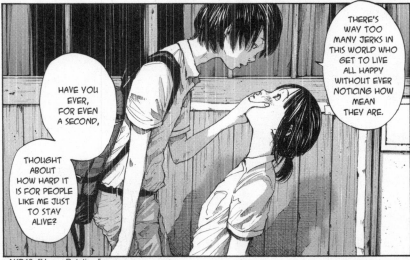

THERE'S WAY TOO MANY JERKS IN THIS WORLD WHO GET TO LIVE ALL HAPPY WITHOUT EVER NOTICING HOW MEAN THEY ARE.

HAVE YOU EVER, FOR EVEN A SECOND,

THOUGHT ABOUT HOW HARD IT IS FOR PEOPLE LIKE ME JUST TO STAY ALIVE?

* AKB48, "Heavy Rotation."

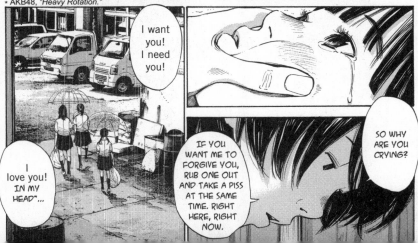

I want you! I need you!

I love you! IN MY HEAD"...

IF YOU WANT ME TO FORGIVE YOU, RUB ONE OUT AND TAKE A PISS AT THE SAME TIME. RIGHT HERE, RIGHT NOW.

SO WHY ARE YOU CRYING?

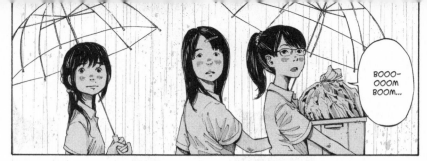

BOOO-OOOM BOOM...

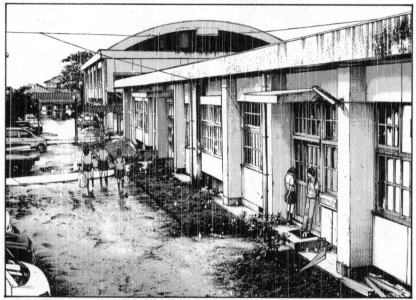

DID YOU FUCK AROUND WITH ANY-THING ELSE ON MY COMPUTER?

DID YOU LOOK AT THE BLOG POST I WAS WRITING?

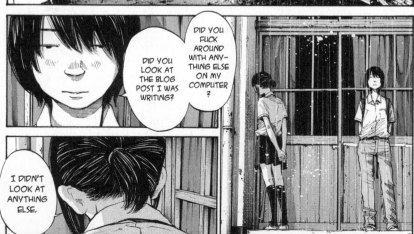

I DIDN'T LOOK AT ANYTHING ELSE.

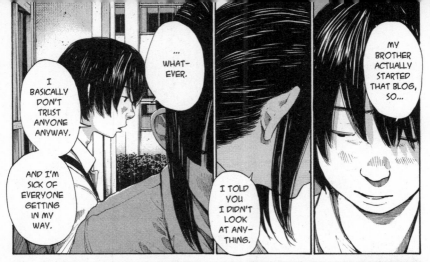

I BASICALLY DON'T TRUST ANYONE ANYWAY.

...WHAT-EVER.

MY BROTHER ACTUALLY STARTED THAT BLOG, SO...

AND I'M SICK OF EVERYONE GETTING IN MY WAY.

I TOLD YOU I DIDN'T LOOK AT ANY-THING.

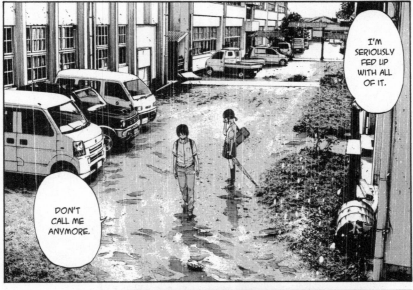

I'M SERIOUSLY FED UP WITH ALL OF IT.

DON'T CALL ME ANYMORE.

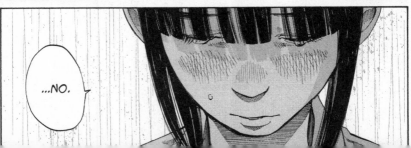

...NO.

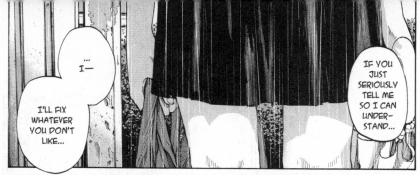

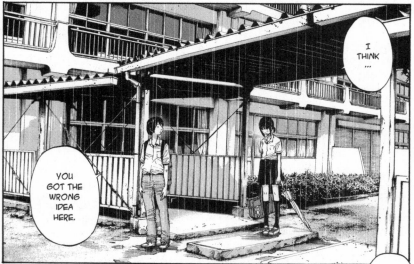

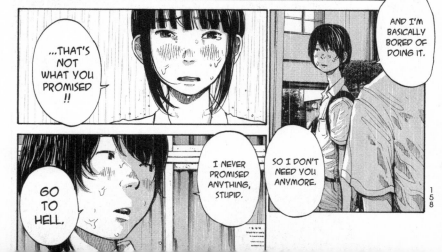

158

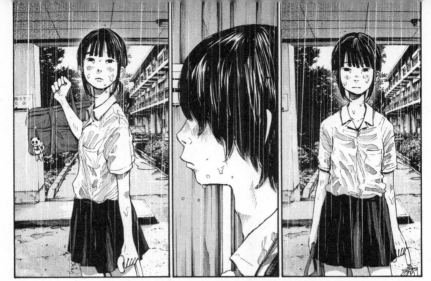

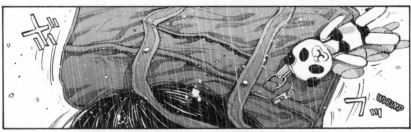

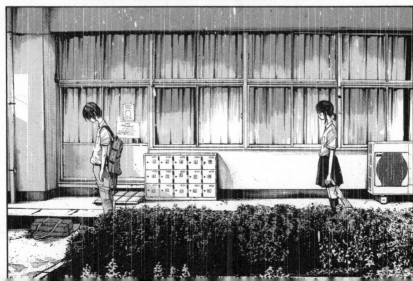

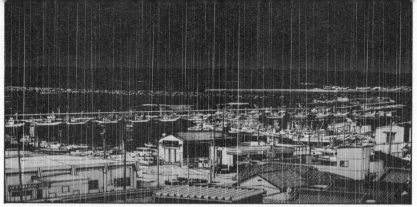

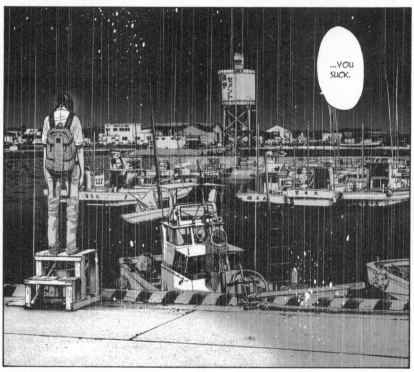

...YOU SUCK.

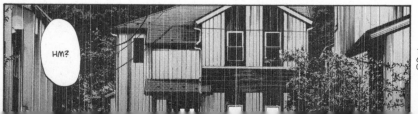

HM?

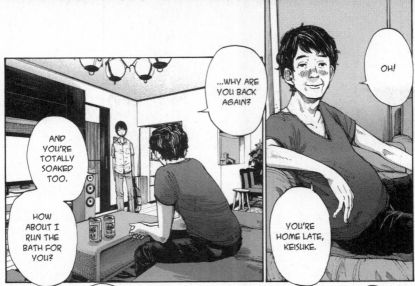

...WHY ARE YOU BACK AGAIN?

OH!

AND YOU'RE TOTALLY SOAKED TOO.

HOW ABOUT I RUN THE BATH FOR YOU?

YOU'RE HOME LATE, KEISUKE.

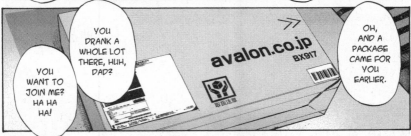

YOU DRANK A WHOLE LOT THERE, HUH, DAD?

YOU WANT TO JOIN ME? HA HA HA!

avalon.co.jp
BX917

OH, AND A PACKAGE CAME FOR YOU EARLIER.

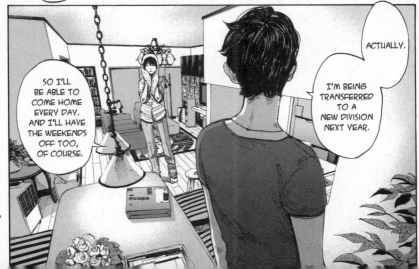

SO I'LL BE ABLE TO COME HOME EVERY DAY. AND I'LL HAVE THE WEEKENDS OFF TOO, OF COURSE.

ACTUALLY.

I'M BEING TRANSFERRED TO A NEW DIVISION NEXT YEAR.

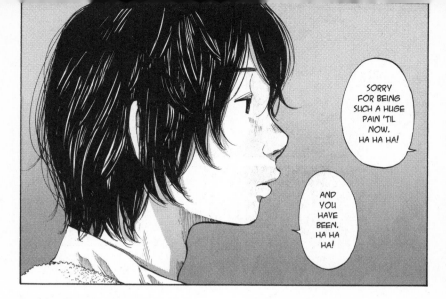

SORRY FOR BEING SUCH A HUGE PAIN 'TIL NOW. HA HA HA!

AND YOU HAVE BEEN. HA HA HA!

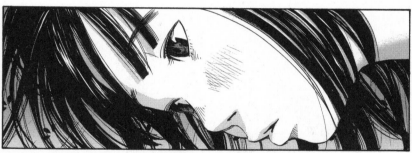

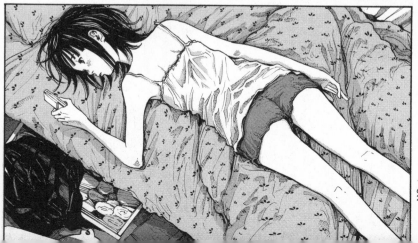

162

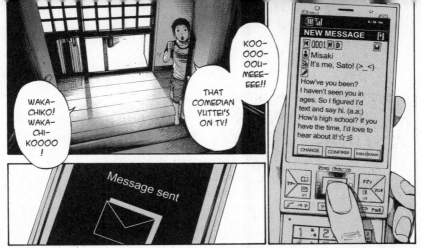

WAKA-CHIKO! WAKA-CHI-KOOOO!

KOO-OOO-OOU-MEEE-EEE!!

THAT COMEDIAN YUTTEI'S ON TV!

NEW MESSAGE

0001

Misaki

It's me, Sato! (>_<)

How've you been? I haven't seen you in ages. So I figured I'd text and say hi. (a.a;) How's high school? If you have the time, I'd love to hear about it! ☆彡

CHANGE   CONFIRM   KANJI/KANA

Message sent

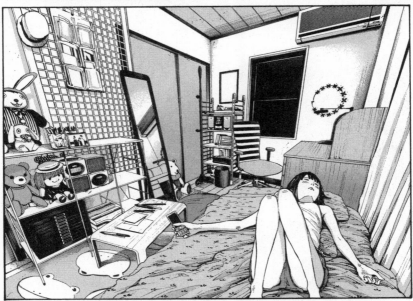

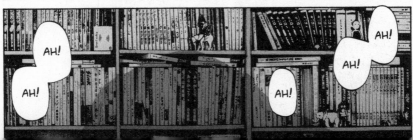

AH!

AH!

AH!

AH!

AH!

163

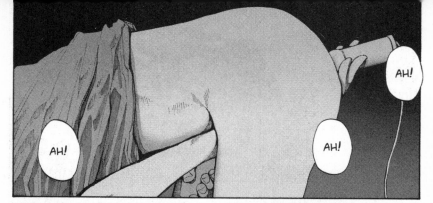

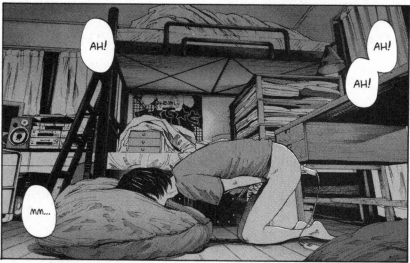

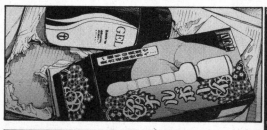

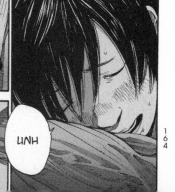

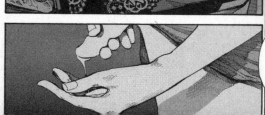

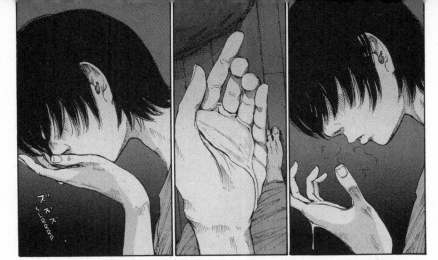

ズズズ
しゅるるる

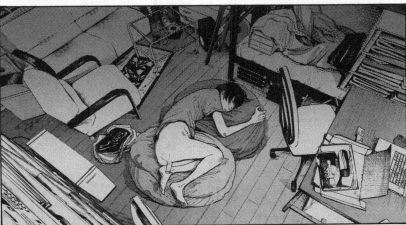

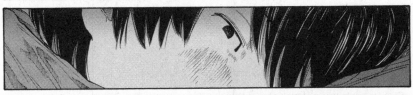

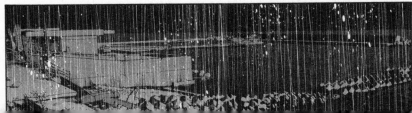

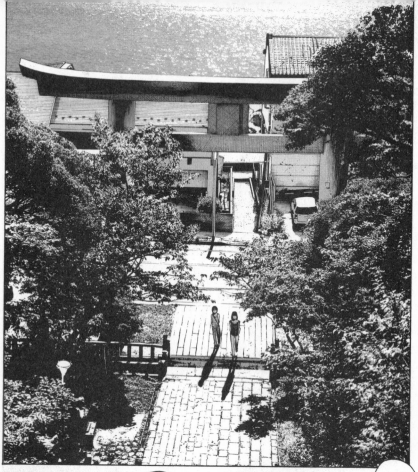

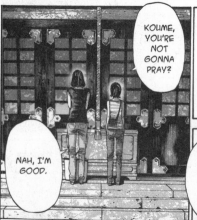

KOUME, YOU'RE NOT GONNA PRAY?

NAH, I'M GOOD.

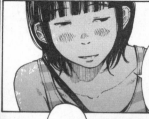

YOU'RE SUPER SERIOUS ABOUT THIS..

WHAT ARE YOU PRAYING SO HARD FOR?

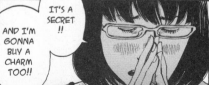

IT'S A SECRET !!

AND I'M GONNA BUY A CHARM TOO!!

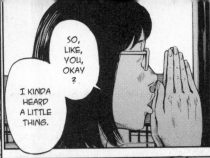

SO, LIKE, YOU, OKAY?

I KINDA HEARD A LITTLE THING.

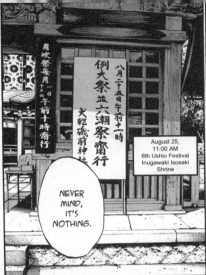

August 25, 11:00 AM
6th Ushio Festival Inugawaki Isosaki Shrine

NEVER MIND, IT'S NOTHING.

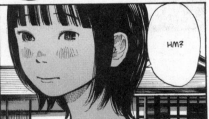

HM?

YOU'RE ALWAYS GONNA BE A GOOD KID, RIGHT?

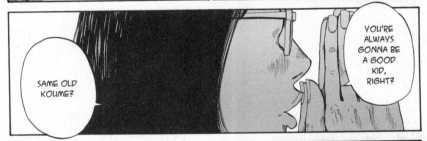

SAME OLD KOUME?

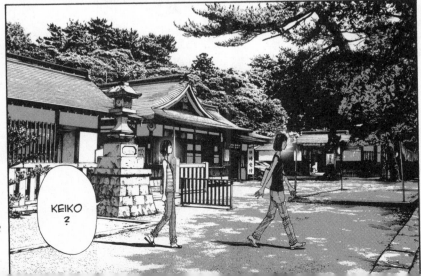

KEIKO?

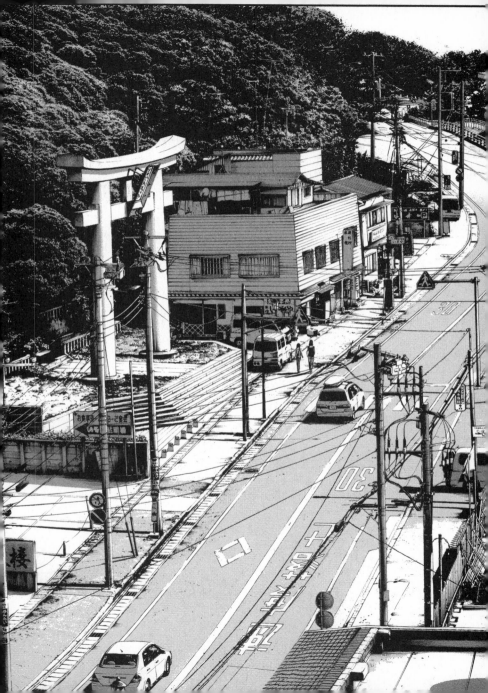

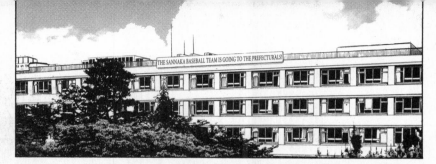

THE SANNAKA BASEBALL TEAM IS GOING TO THE PREFECTURALS!

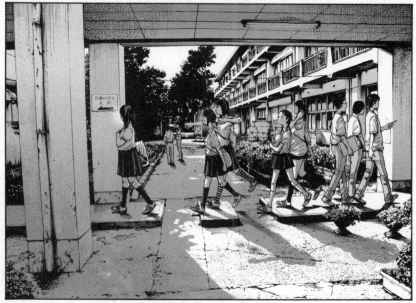

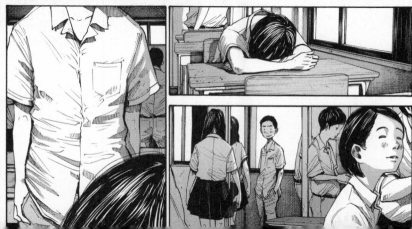

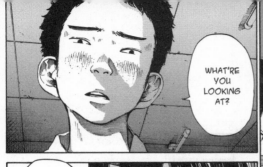

WHAT'RE YOU LOOKING AT?

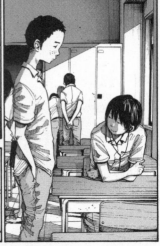

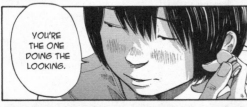

YOU'RE THE ONE DOING THE LOOKING.

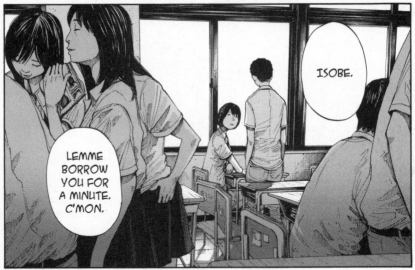

ISOBE.

LEMME BORROW YOU FOR A MINUTE. C'MON.

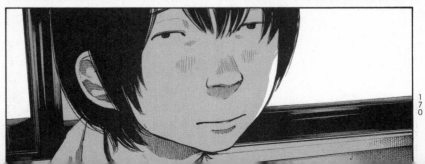

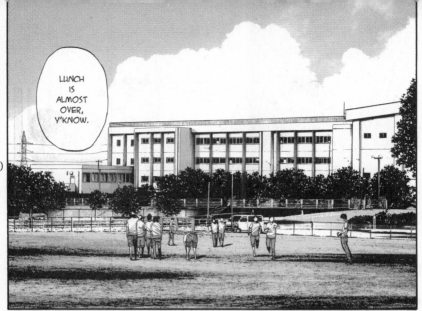

LUNCH IS ALMOST OVER, Y'KNOW.

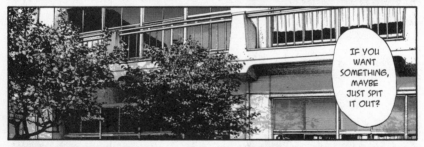

IF YOU WANT SOMETHING, MAYBE JUST SPIT IT OUT?

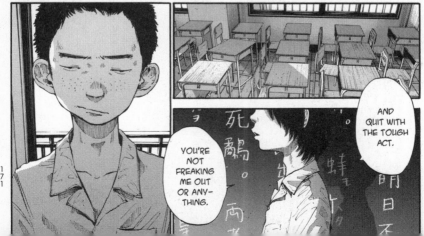

YOU'RE NOT FREAKING ME OUT OR ANY-THING.

AND QUIT WITH THE TOUGH ACT.

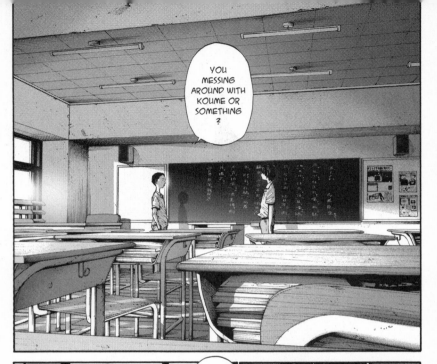

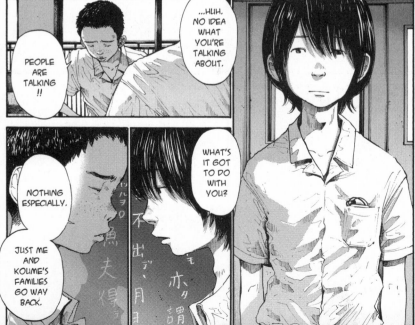

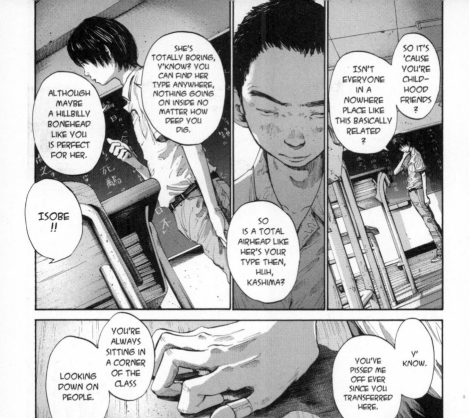

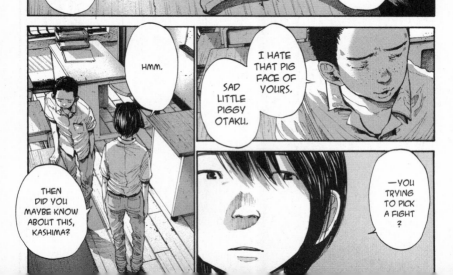

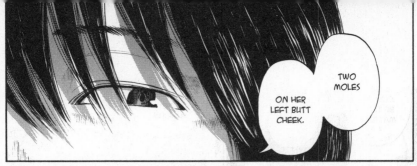

TWO MOLES

ON HER LEFT BUTT CHEEK.

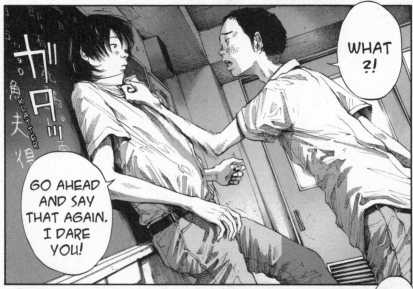

WHAT ?!

GO AHEAD AND SAY THAT AGAIN. I DARE YOU!

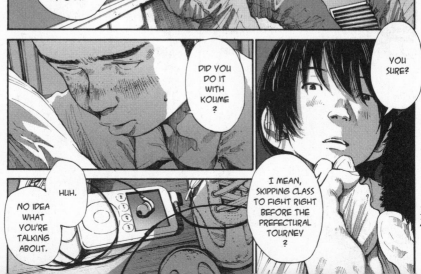

DID YOU DO IT WITH KOUME ?

YOU SURE?

HUH.

NO IDEA WHAT YOU'RE TALKING ABOUT.

I MEAN, SKIPPING CLASS TO FIGHT RIGHT BEFORE THE PREFECTURAL TOURNEY ?

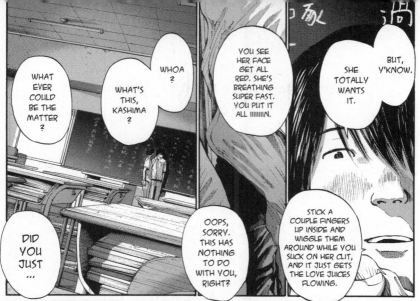

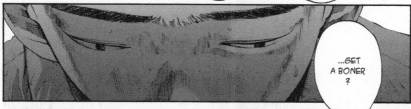

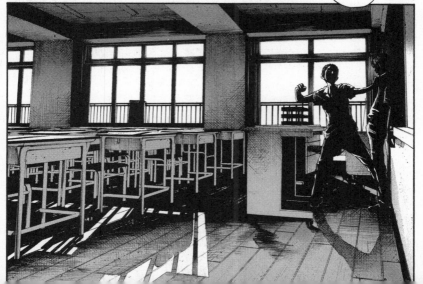

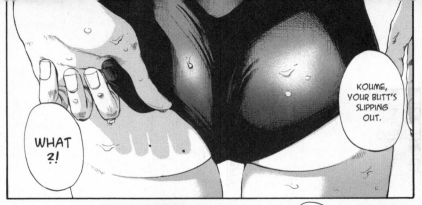

KOUME, YOUR BUTT'S SLIPPING OUT.

WHAT?!

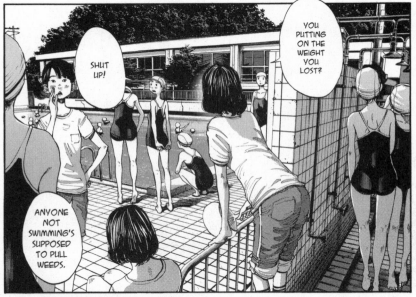

SHUT UP!

YOU PUTTING ON THE WEIGHT YOU LOST?

ANYONE NOT SWIMMING'S SUPPOSED TO PULL WEEDS.

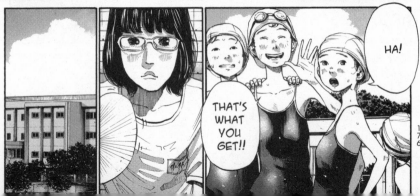

THAT'S WHAT YOU GET!!

HA!

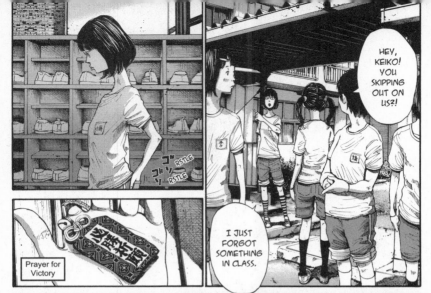

HEY, KEIKO! YOU SKIPPING OUT ON US?!

Prayer for Victory

ゴソ RSTLE
ゴソ RSTLE

I JUST FORGOT SOMETHING IN CLASS.

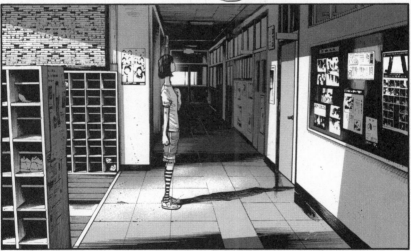

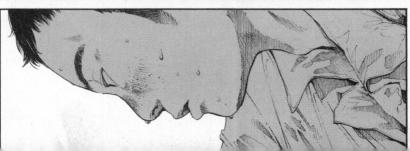

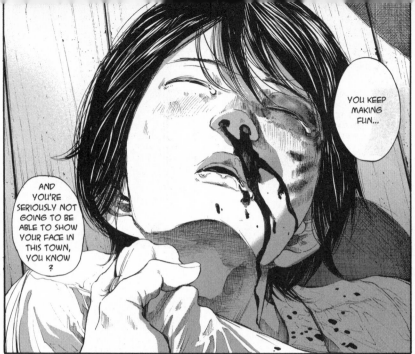

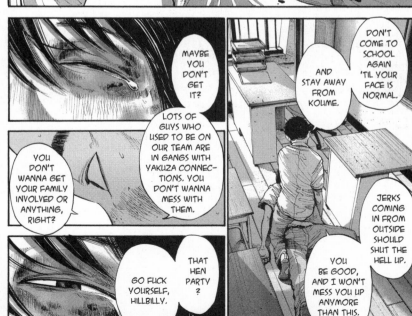

178

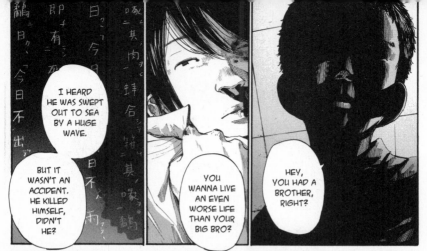

I HEARD HE WAS SWEPT OUT TO SEA BY A HUGE WAVE.

BUT IT WASN'T AN ACCIDENT. HE KILLED HIMSELF, DIDN'T HE?

YOU WANNA LIVE AN EVEN WORSE LIFE THAN YOUR BIG BRO?

HEY, YOU HAD A BROTHER, RIGHT?

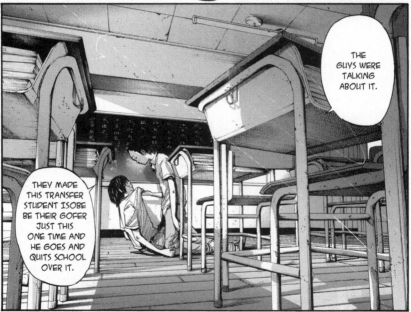

THE GUYS WERE TALKING ABOUT IT.

THEY MADE THIS TRANSFER STUDENT ISOBE BE THEIR GOFER JUST THIS ONE TIME AND HE GOES AND QUITS SCHOOL OVER IT.

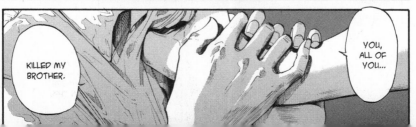

KILLED MY BROTHER.

YOU, ALL OF YOU...

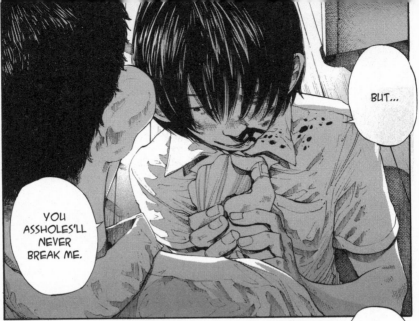

BUT...

YOU ASSHOLES'LL NEVER BREAK ME.

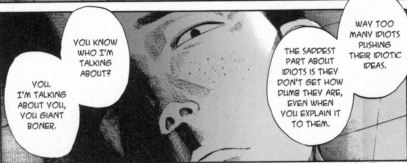

YOU KNOW WHO I'M TALKING ABOUT?

YOU. I'M TALKING ABOUT YOU, YOU GIANT BONER.

THE SADDEST PART ABOUT IDIOTS IS THEY DON'T GET HOW DUMB THEY ARE, EVEN WHEN YOU EXPLAIN IT TO THEM.

WAY TOO MANY IDIOTS PUSHING THEIR IDIOTIC IDEAS.

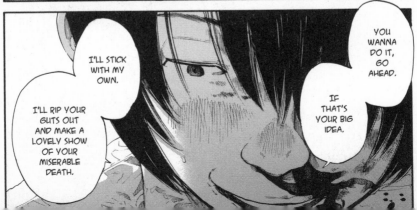

I'LL STICK WITH MY OWN.

I'LL RIP YOUR GUTS OUT AND MAKE A LOVELY SHOW OF YOUR MISERABLE DEATH.

YOU WANNA DO IT, GO AHEAD.

IF THAT'S YOUR BIG IDEA.

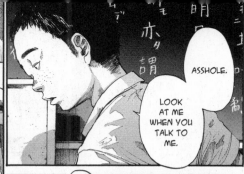
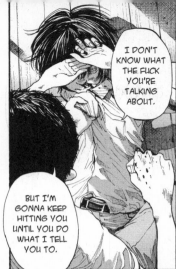
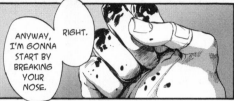
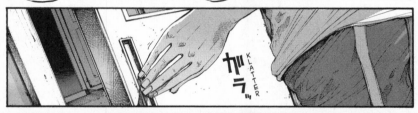
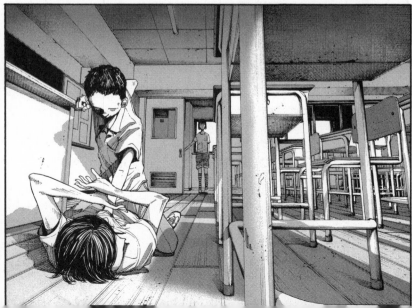

181

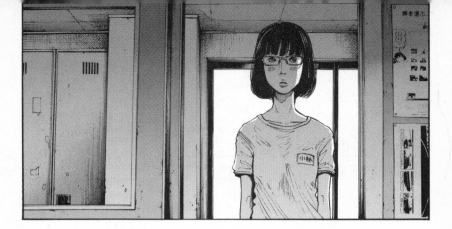

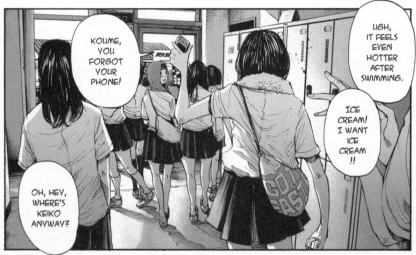

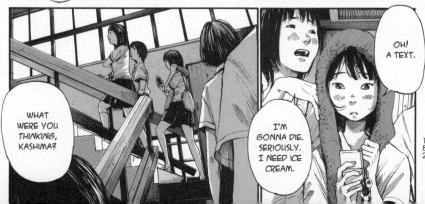

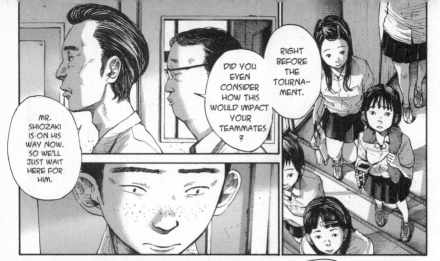

MR. SHIOZAKI IS ON HIS WAY NOW, SO WE'LL JUST WAIT HERE FOR HIM.

DID YOU EVEN CONSIDER HOW THIS WOULD IMPACT YOUR TEAMMATES?

RIGHT BEFORE THE TOURNAMENT.

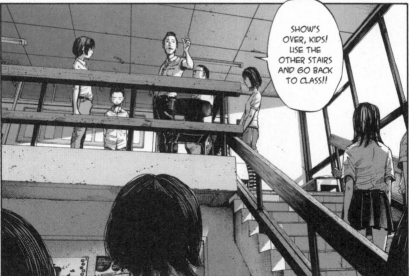

SHOW'S OVER, KIDS! USE THE OTHER STAIRS AND GO BACK TO CLASS!!

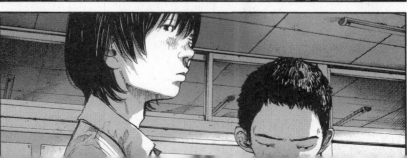

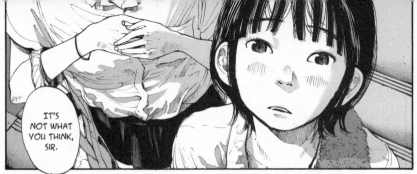

IT'S NOT WHAT YOU THINK, SIR.

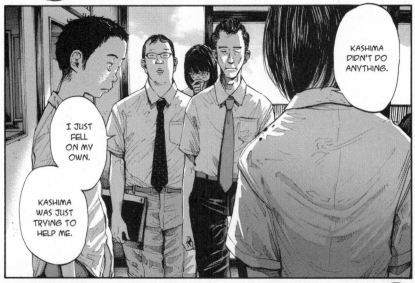

KASHIMA DIDN'T DO ANYTHING.

I JUST FELL ON MY OWN.

KASHIMA WAS JUST TRYING TO HELP ME.

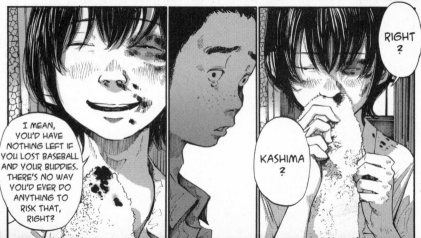

RIGHT?

KASHIMA?

I MEAN, YOU'D HAVE NOTHING LEFT IF YOU LOST BASEBALL AND YOUR BUDDIES. THERE'S NO WAY YOU'D EVER DO ANYTHING TO RISK THAT, RIGHT?

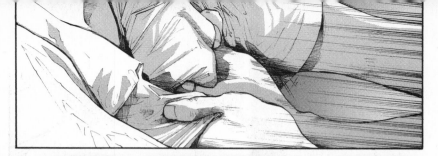

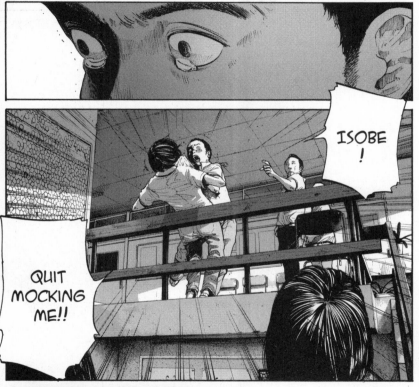

ISOBE
!

QUIT
MOCKING
ME!!

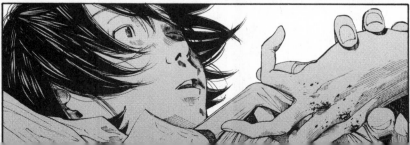

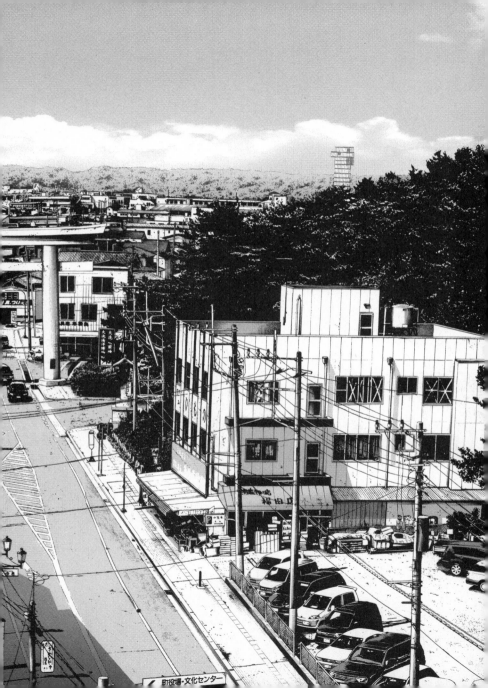

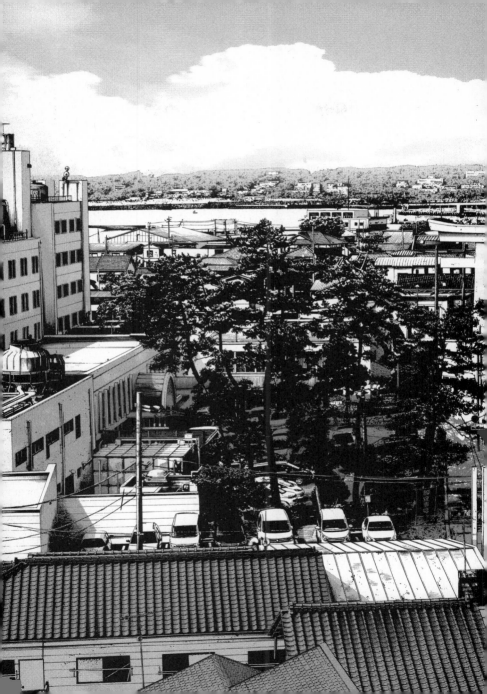

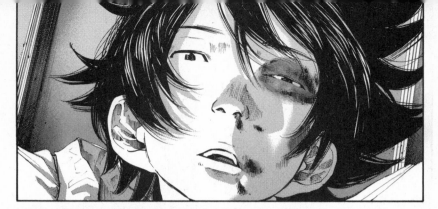

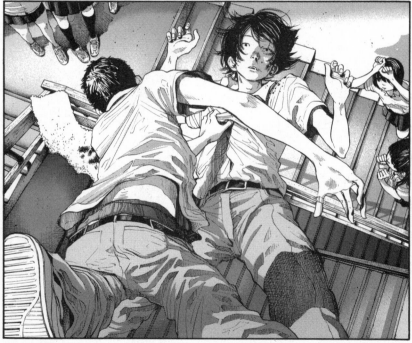

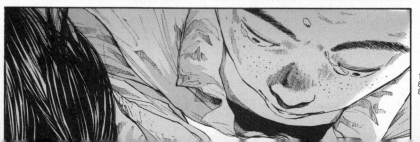

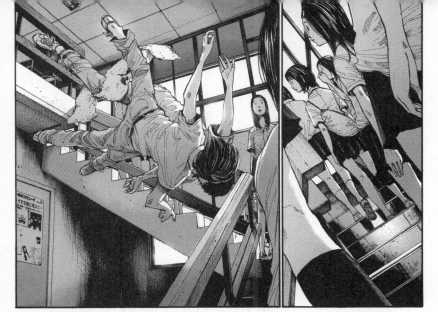

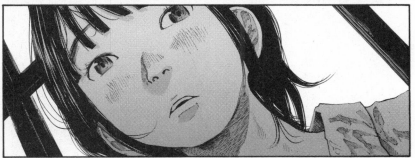

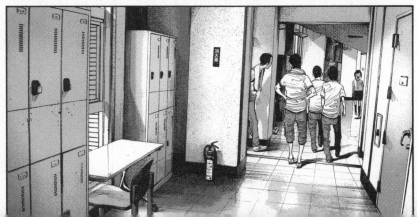

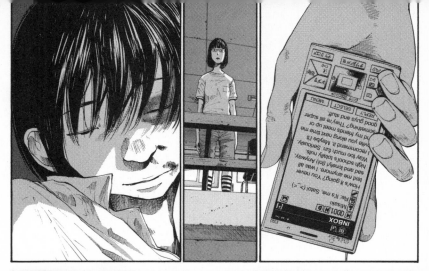

Misaki
Re: it's me, Sato! (ゝ∀<)

How's it going? you never
text me anymore. I was all
sad and lonely (lol) Anyway,
high school's totally nuts.
Way too much fun. Seriously
I recommend it. Maybe I'll
invite you along next time or
and my friends meet up or
something? They're all super
good guys and stuff.

INBOX
□□01
▶◀ REPLY   SELECT   MENU

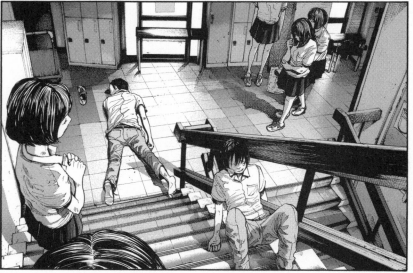

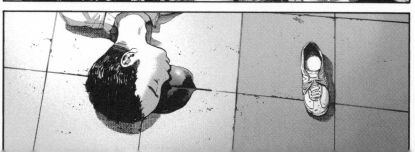

190

A

Girl

on the

Shore

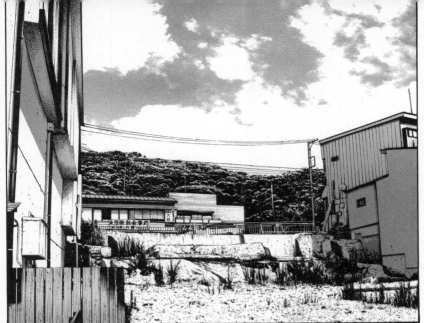

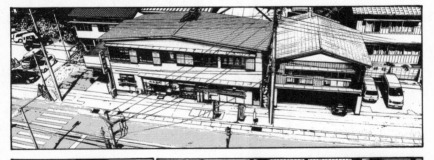

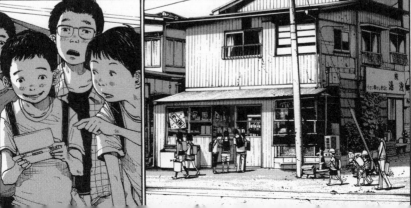

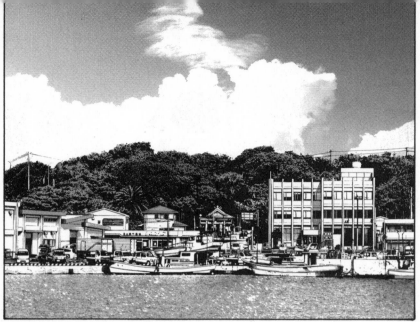

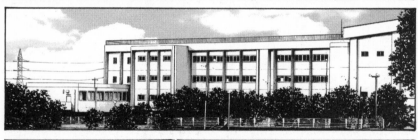

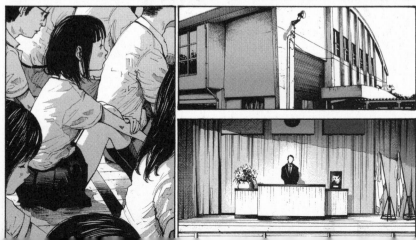

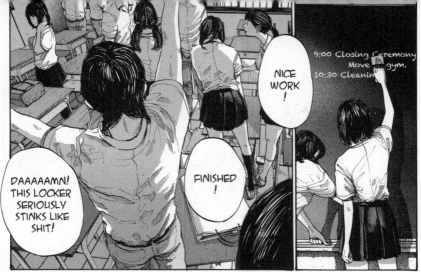

9:00 Closing Ceremony
Move to gym.
10:30 Cleaning

NICE WORK!

FINISHED!

DAAAAAMN! THIS LOCKER SERIOUSLY STINKS LIKE SHIT!

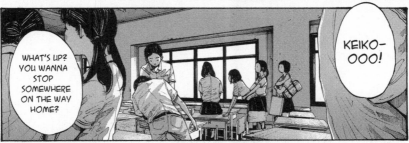

WHAT'S UP? YOU WANNA STOP SOMEWHERE ON THE WAY HOME?

KEIKO-OOO!

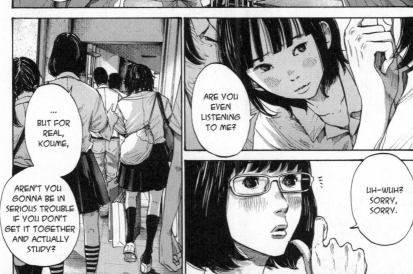

... BUT FOR REAL, KOUME,

ARE YOU EVEN LISTENING TO ME?

AREN'T YOU GONNA BE IN SERIOUS TROUBLE IF YOU DON'T GET IT TOGETHER AND ACTUALLY STUDY?

UH-WUH? SORRY, SORRY.

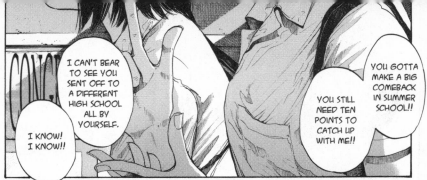

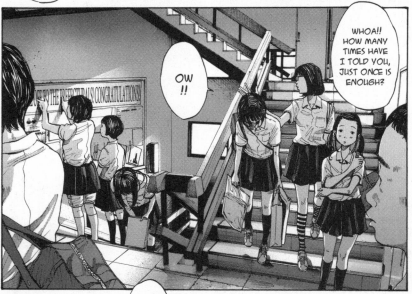

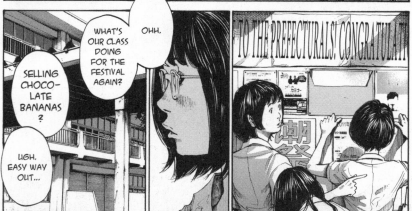

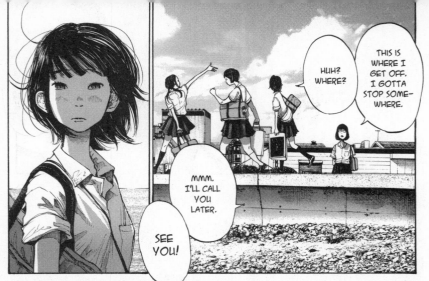

HUH? WHERE?

THIS IS WHERE I GET OFF. I GOTTA STOP SOME- WHERE.

MMM. I'LL CALL YOU LATER.

SEE YOU!

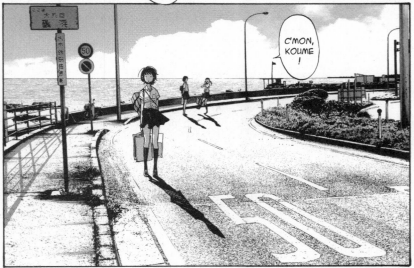

C'MON, KOUME !

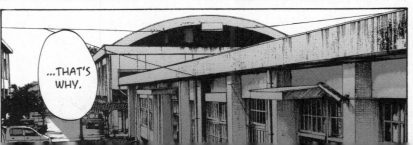

...THAT'S WHY.

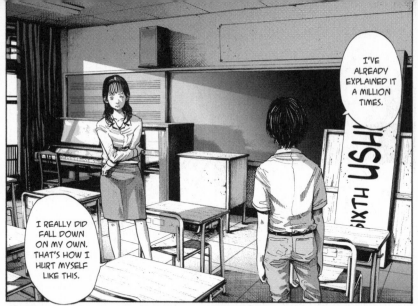

I'VE ALREADY EXPLAINED IT A MILLION TIMES.

I REALLY DID FALL DOWN ON MY OWN. THAT'S HOW I HURT MYSELF LIKE THIS.

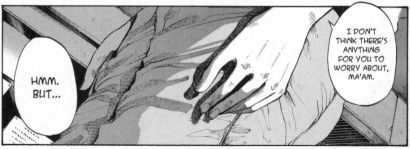

HMM, BUT...

I DON'T THINK THERE'S ANYTHING FOR YOU TO WORRY ABOUT, MA'AM.

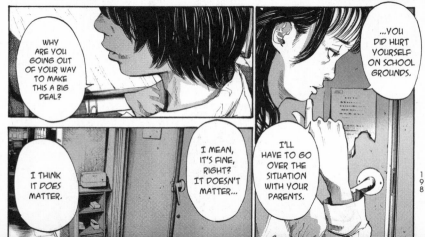

WHY ARE YOU GOING OUT OF YOUR WAY TO MAKE THIS A BIG DEAL?

...YOU DID HURT YOURSELF ON SCHOOL GROUNDS.

I THINK IT DOES MATTER.

I MEAN, IT'S FINE, RIGHT? IT DOESN'T MATTER...

I'LL HAVE TO GO OVER THE SITUATION WITH YOUR PARENTS.

198

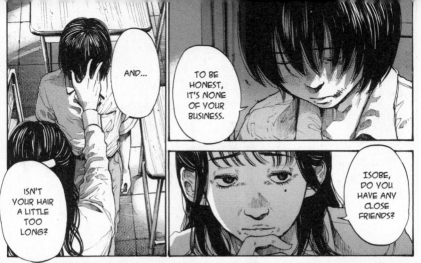

AND...

TO BE HONEST, IT'S NONE OF YOUR BUSINESS.

ISN'T YOUR HAIR A LITTLE TOO LONG?

ISOBE, DO YOU HAVE ANY CLOSE FRIENDS?

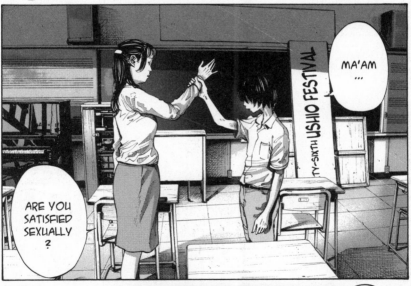

MA'AM...

ARE YOU SATISFIED SEXUALLY?

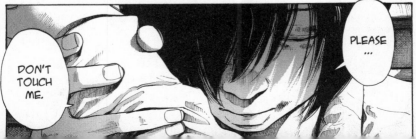

PLEASE...

DON'T TOUCH ME.

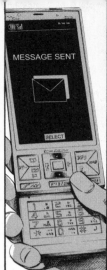

MESSAGE SENT

SELECT

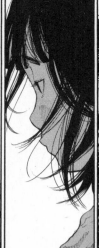

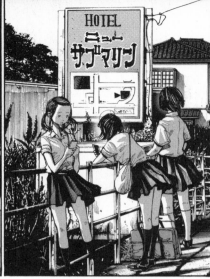

HOTEL
サブマリン

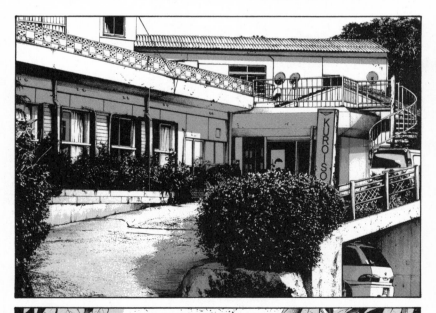

KUROISO

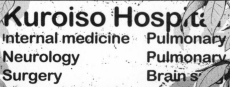

Kuroiso Hospital

Internal medicine   Pulmonary
Neurology   Pulmonary
Surgery   Brain s
Orthopedic surger

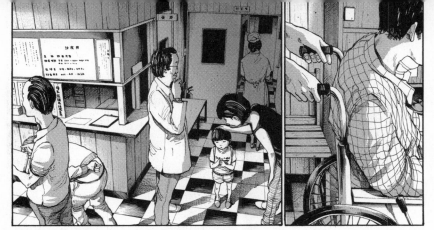

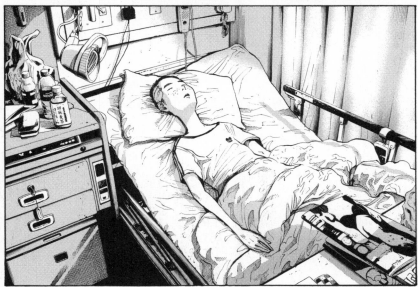

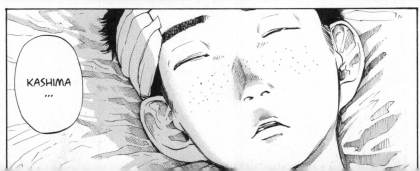

KASHIMA
...

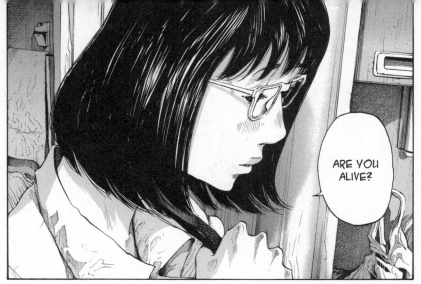

ARE YOU ALIVE?

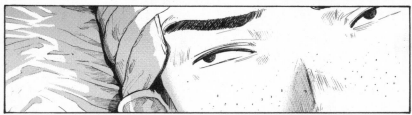

AND I FIGURED YOU'D BE BORED.

HERE.

MY GRANDMA'S IN THE HOSPITAL HERE.

YOU ALONE?

YEAH.

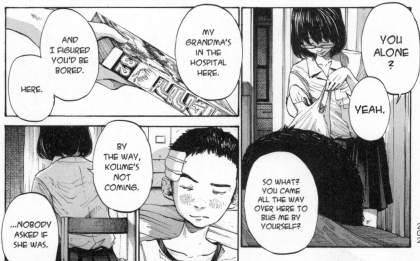

BY THE WAY, KOUME'S NOT COMING.

...NOBODY ASKED IF SHE WAS.

SO WHAT? YOU CAME ALL THE WAY OVER HERE TO BUG ME BY YOURSELF?

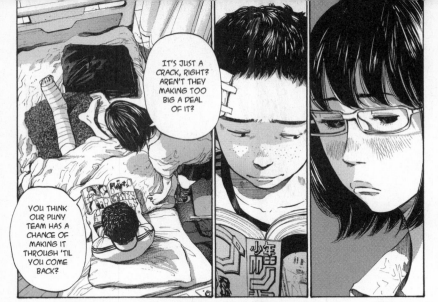

IT'S JUST A CRACK, RIGHT? AREN'T THEY MAKING TOO BIG A DEAL OF IT?

YOU THINK OUR PUNY TEAM HAS A CHANCE OF MAKING IT THROUGH 'TIL YOU COME BACK?

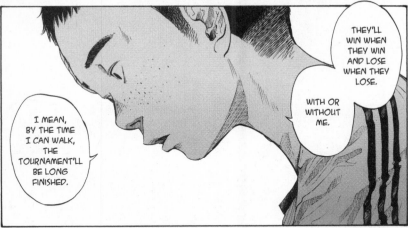

THEY'LL WIN WHEN THEY WIN AND LOSE WHEN THEY LOSE.

WITH OR WITHOUT ME.

I MEAN, BY THE TIME I CAN WALK, THE TOURNAMENT'LL BE LONG FINISHED.

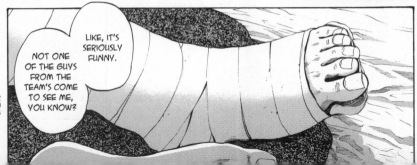

LIKE, IT'S SERIOUSLY FUNNY.

NOT ONE OF THE GUYS FROM THE TEAM'S COME TO SEE ME, YOU KNOW?

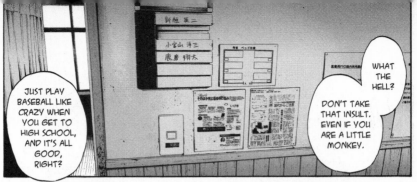

JUST PLAY BASEBALL LIKE CRAZY WHEN YOU GET TO HIGH SCHOOL, AND IT'S ALL GOOD, RIGHT?

WHAT THE HELL?

DON'T TAKE THAT INSULT. EVEN IF YOU ARE A LITTLE MONKEY.

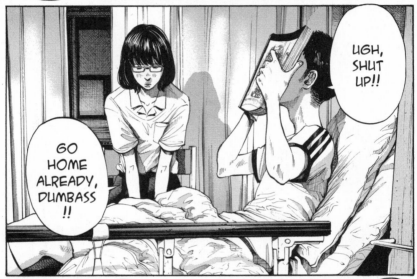

UGH, SHUT UP!!

GO HOME ALREADY, DUMBASS!!

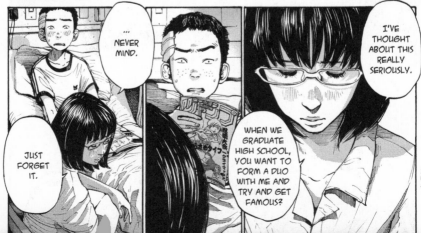

... NEVER MIND.

I'VE THOUGHT ABOUT THIS REALLY SERIOUSLY.

JUST FORGET IT.

WHEN WE GRADUATE HIGH SCHOOL, YOU WANT TO FORM A DUO WITH ME AND TRY AND GET FAMOUS?

204

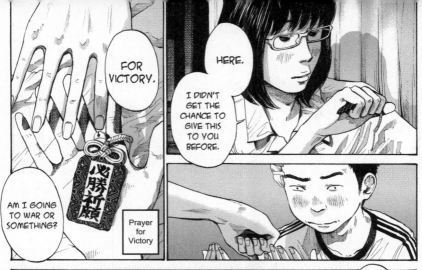

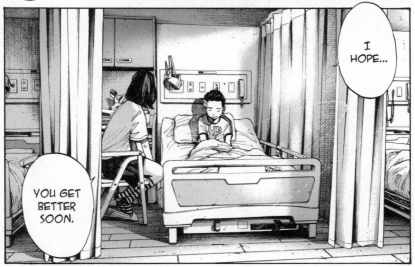

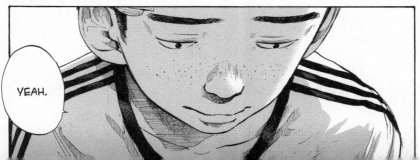

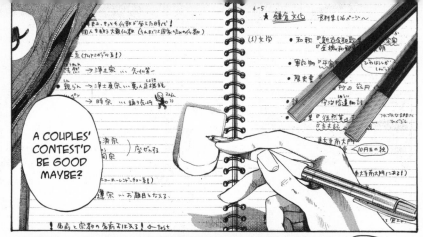

A COUPLES' CONTEST'D BE GOOD MAYBE?

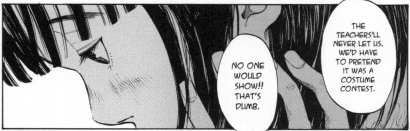

THE TEACHERS'LL NEVER LET US. WE'D HAVE TO PRETEND IT WAS A COSTUME CONTEST.

NO ONE WOULD SHOW!! THAT'S DUMB.

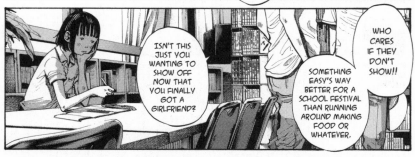

ISN'T THIS JUST YOU WANTING TO SHOW OFF NOW THAT YOU FINALLY GOT A GIRLFRIEND?

WHO CARES IF THEY DON'T SHOW!!

SOMETHING EASY'S WAY BETTER FOR A SCHOOL FESTIVAL THAN RUNNING AROUND MAKING FOOD OR WHATEVER.

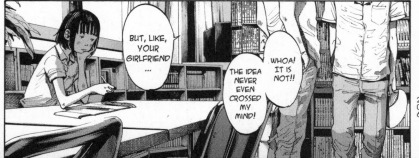

BUT, LIKE, YOUR GIRLFRIEND...

WHOA! IT IS NOT!!

THE IDEA NEVER EVEN CROSSED MY MIND!

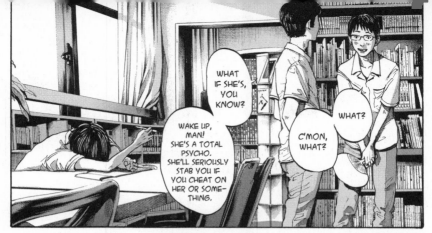

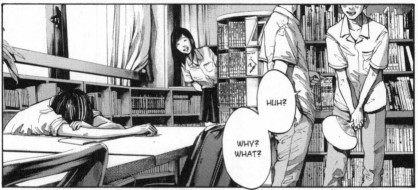

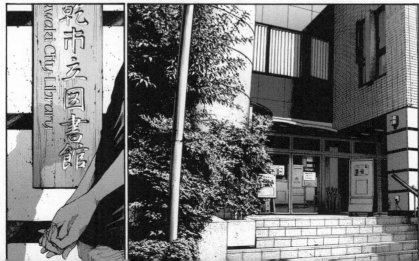

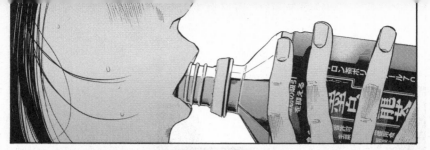

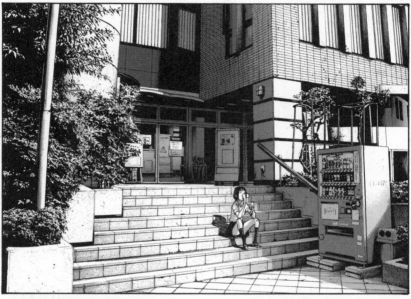

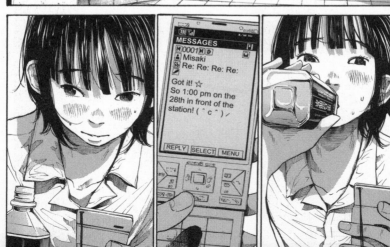

MESSAGES

Misaki
Re: Re: Re: Re:

Got it! ☆
So 1:00 pm on the
28th in front of the
station! (ﾟｃﾟ)/

REPLY SELECT MENU

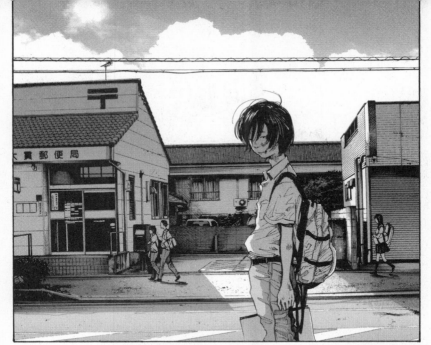

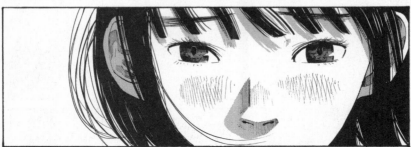

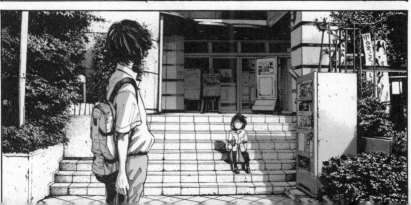

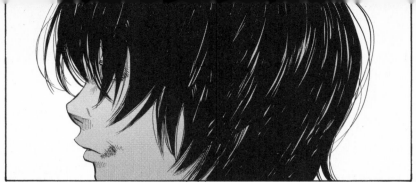

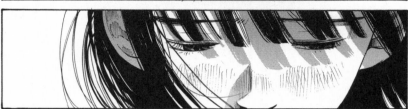

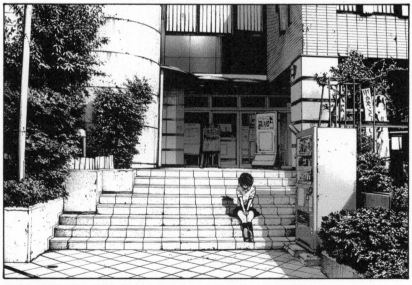

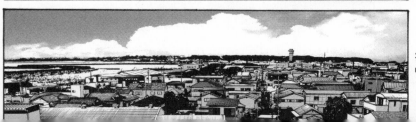

A

Girl

on the

Shore

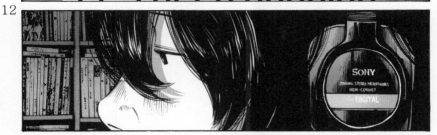

1 Posted by Goblin Sha

I'm onto you, you kn

Tt's been bugging

c
h
a
p
t
e
r

12

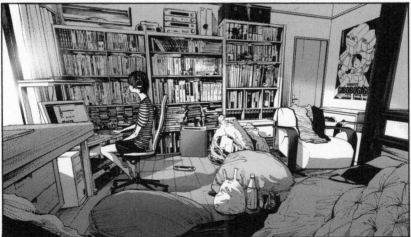

This month's popular posts

1 Apparently, the economy's in serious trouble (242)
2 48-year-old woman: "Surprised by her sleeping boyfriend! Titled "Fireworks and You and the Buddhist Priest" —> finger blow off (206)
3 Reader Warning: This is a naturally magic film... (205)
4 Famous cosplayer Falcon Kishimoto banished? (164)
5 Mountain danger: NASA releases underwater images (133)
6 Japan Owata: Leader of net terror response group trying to attack

Name: ANONYMOUS ELF

Post

Comments

Posted by Goblin Shark   2011/08/10   05:22   Reply
I'm onto you, you know? This has been bugging me for a while, actually. It's obvious this blog is getting worse. The number of garbage posts have increased, plus the number of affiliates has also blatantly gone up. You should announce it if there's a new admin now. Who are you?

Posted by Anonymous Elf   2011/08/10   07:23   Reply

3 Video luxury
4 News report
5 Inta corner
6 Wild pig, mon
7 Taking down
8 Citizens of ne
9 everything
10 Weirdo part
11 Re: Compul
12 Suspicious
13 Mr. Report
14 Copy/Paste
15 New di
16 Curious new
17 Dwarf gadge
18 moemoe
19 Game repor
20 Toys
21 It was an in
22 Apprentices
23 Stomach we
24 Family divid
25 ★★★===

Latest posts

1 Nettorare!
Here we go aga

2
1
3

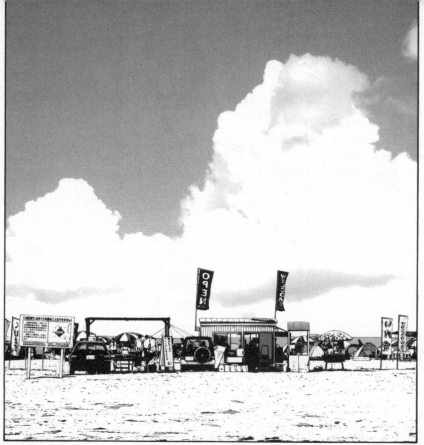

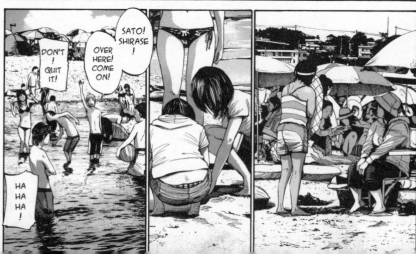

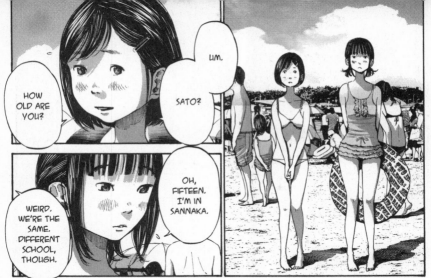

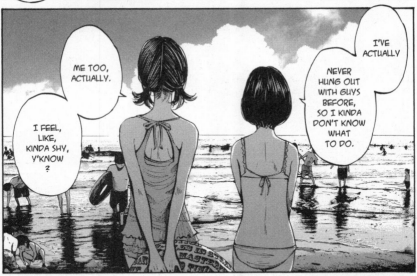

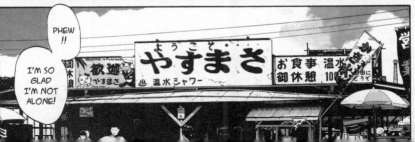

Buddhist Priest" —>
finger blow off (206)
3 Reader Warning: This
is a naturally magic
film... (205)
4 Famous cosplayer
Falcon Kishimoto
banished? (164)
5 Mountain danger:
NASA releases
underwater images
(133)
6 Japan Owata: Leader
of net terror response
group trying to attack
Japan has account
hacked (113)
7 Screaming from old
person somewhere in
apartment building is
amazing (108)
8 Happy Happy:
Cosplay picture
round-up Day 3 (104)
9 Tiny good Android

This has been bugging me for a while, actually.
It's obvious this blog is getting worse. The number
of garbage posts have increased, plus the number of
affiliates has also blatantly gone up. You should announce
it if there's a new admin now. Who are you?

Posted by Anonymous Elf   2011/08/10   07:23   Reply

2 Posted by ISO 2011/08/10   14:35   Reply
>Goblin Shark,
For questions other than post comments,
please use the email form to get in touch.

13 Mr. Repor
14 Copy/Past
15 New di
16 Curious ne
17 Dwarf gad
18 moemoe
19 Game rep
20 Toys
21 It was an i
22 Apprentice
23 Stomach v
24 Family div
25 ★★★ ==

Latest posts
1 Nettorare!
Here we go a
2 Honestly, th
already done
3 Shooting sta
NASA astrona
posted after
4 Tonma, Tsu
sales compar
5 High schoo

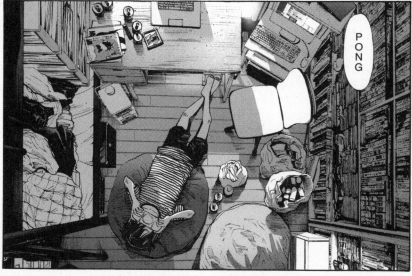

P
O
N
G

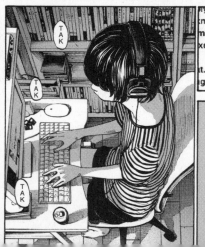

TAK

TAK

TAK

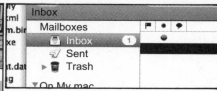

Inbox
Mailboxes
📁 Inbox   1
✉ Sent
🗑 Trash
On My mac

Dear ISO,

I'm sorry to bother you by email. I'm the
person who left the comment earlier. I realize
I might sound a bit like a mother hen, but I'm
worried that some accident or something
happened to the administrator.

If you don't mind my asking, I'd really
appreciate it if you could let me know if
something has happened. My apologies if
I'm asking too much of you. Thank you in
advance.

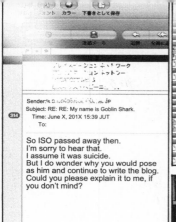

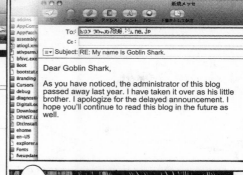

To: [redacted]

Cc:

Subject: RE: My name is Goblin Shark.

Dear Goblin Shark,

As you have noticed, the administrator of this blog passed away last year. I have taken it over as his little brother. I apologize for the delayed announcement. I hope you'll continue to read this blog in the future as well.

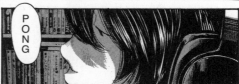

Sender: [redacted] jp
Subject: RE: RE: My name is Goblin Shark.
Time: June X, 201X 15:39 JUT
To:

So ISO passed away then.
I'm sorry to hear that.
I assume it was suicide.
But I do wonder why you would pose as him and continue to write the blog. Could you please explain it to me, if you don't mind?

PONG

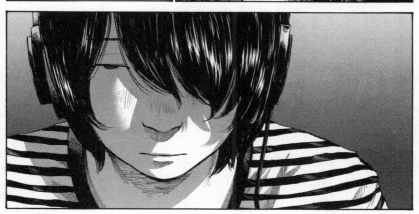

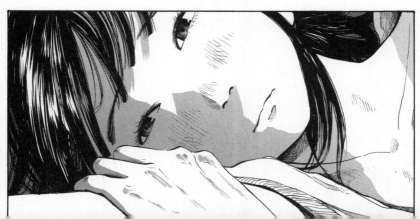

217

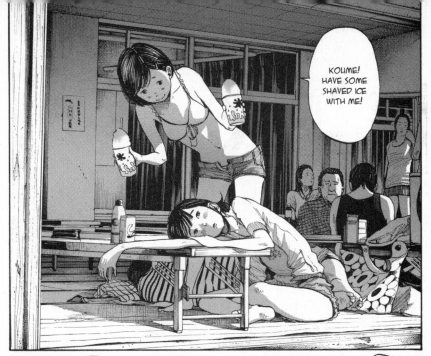

KOUME! HAVE SOME SHAVED ICE WITH ME!

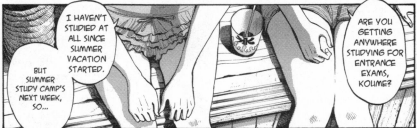

I HAVEN'T STUDIED AT ALL SINCE SUMMER VACATION STARTED.

BUT SUMMER STUDY CAMP'S NEXT WEEK, SO...

ARE YOU GETTING ANYWHERE STUDYING FOR ENTRANCE EXAMS, KOUME?

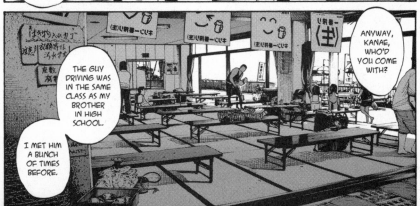

THE GUY DRIVING WAS IN THE SAME CLASS AS MY BROTHER IN HIGH SCHOOL.

I MET HIM A BUNCH OF TIMES BEFORE.

ANYWAY, KANAE, WHO'D YOU COME WITH?

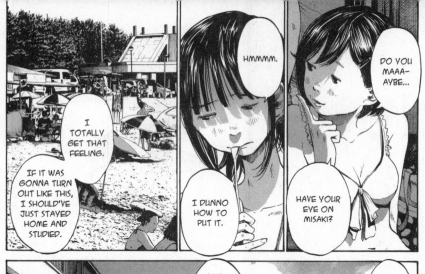

HMMMM.

DO YOU MAAA-AYBE...

I TOTALLY GET THAT FEELING.

IF IT WAS GONNA TURN OUT LIKE THIS, I SHOULD'VE JUST STAYED HOME AND STUDIED.

I DUNNO HOW TO PUT IT.

HAVE YOUR EYE ON MISAKI?

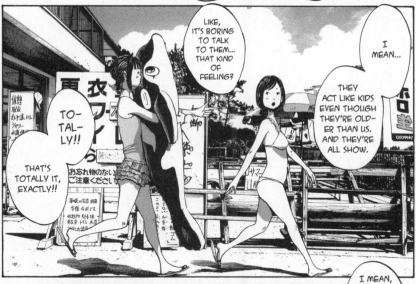

LIKE, IT'S BORING TO TALK TO THEM... THAT KIND OF FEELING?

I MEAN...

TO-TAL-LY!!

THAT'S TOTALLY IT, EXACTLY!!

THEY ACT LIKE KIDS EVEN THOUGH THEY'RE OLD-ER THAN US. AND THEY'RE ALL SHOW.

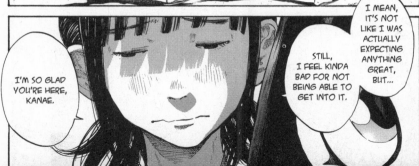

I MEAN, IT'S NOT LIKE I WAS ACTUALLY EXPECTING ANYTHING GREAT, BUT...

STILL, I FEEL KINDA BAD FOR NOT BEING ABLE TO GET INTO IT.

I'M SO GLAD YOU'RE HERE, KANAE.

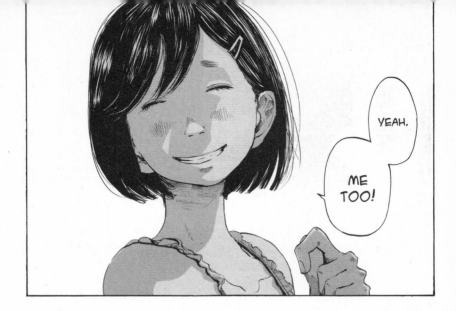

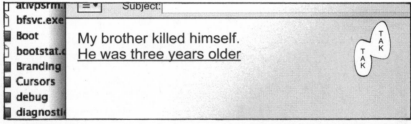

My brother killed himself.
He was three years older than me, and ever since he was born, his leg was kind of bad. Because of that, he tended to miss a lot of school ever since we were kids. In junior high, he was badly bullied and my parents decided to move the whole family from Tokyo to the country, but once he moved onto high school, he tended to lock himself up his room again. My brother was a so-called
But

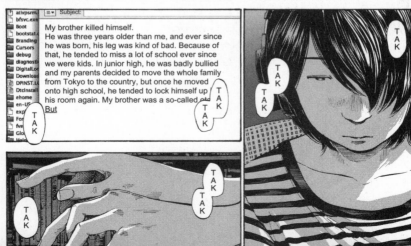

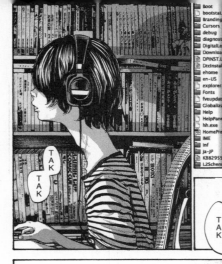

he was born, his leg was kind of bad. Because of that, he tended to miss a lot of school ever since we were kids. In junior high, he was badly bullied and my parents decided to move the whole family from Tokyo to the country, but once he moved onto high school, he tended to lock himself up in his room again. My brother was a so-called otaku. But I can't believe his personality was the problem. In fact, I think he was too nice. He could talk normally with our parents, and even though the two of us shared a room, we never fought.
He was like a good friend.

But

But my brother killed himself.

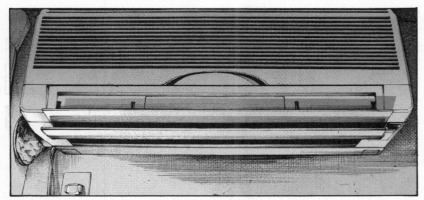

shared a room, we never fought.
He was like a good friend.

But my brother killed himself.
He made sure to save a note on his computer. I deleted it. I didn't want to make my parents sadder for no reason.
The police quickly processed it as an accidental death, thankfully. The day he died, September 15th, is my <u>bir</u>

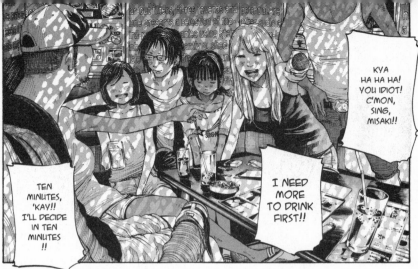

accidential death, thankfully. The day he died, September 15, is my birthday. Is there some kind of meaning in that? At the very least, I guess I'll remember my brother's skinny back on my birthday every year. Maybe he had been sending me some kind of silent SOS, and he was annoyed at me for not getting it.

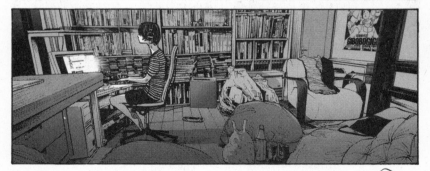

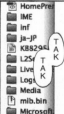

When I think about it now, I think that my dad was just playing the role of the dad, my mom the mom, and their sons the sons, and our relationship was actually one where we never talked about what we really felt.

The only thing my brother was into was running this blog. The back and forth in the comments were his sole communication with the outside world. I was reluctant to stop updating

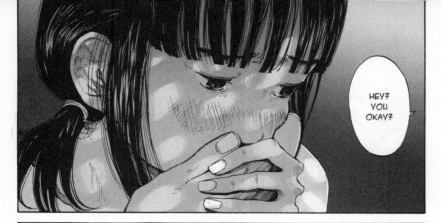

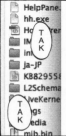

The only thing my brother was into was running this blog. The back and forth in the comments were his sole communication with the outside world. I was reluctant to stop updating it. I hated the idea that his existence would completely disappear if I stopped. More than anything, I was scared I'd have to hold onto his existence all by myself. Then, before I knew it, aimlessly continuing to update the blog had turned into something like my life's work, and I stopped knowing if I was alive or dead myself. I don't know how much longer I can keep doing it.

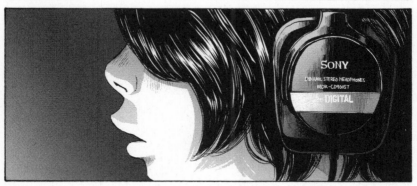

longer I can keep doing it.

I think the trigger for my brother's suicide was bullying. No matter what reasons they had, I will never forgive those guys who disrespected him. I'll never forgive those guys who can't even imagine the pain of another person.
But I'm the one who struck the finishing blow.

I just know

But I'm the one who struck the finishing blow.

I just know that tonight again, my brother will be calling me from outside the window.

Help.|

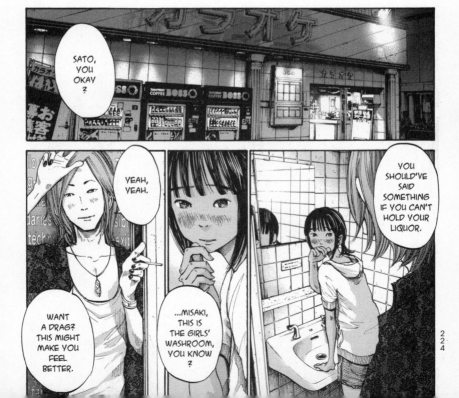

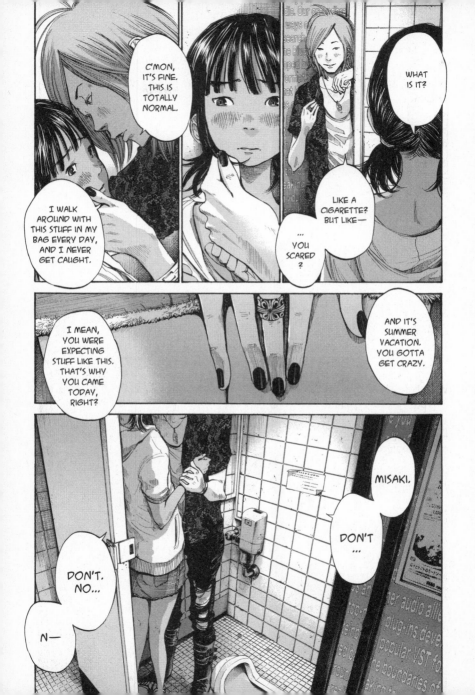

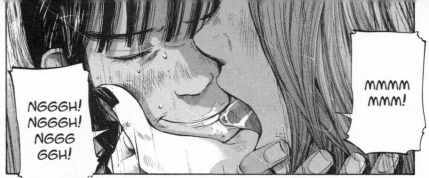

NGGGH!
NGGGH!
NGGG
GGH!

MMMM
MMM!

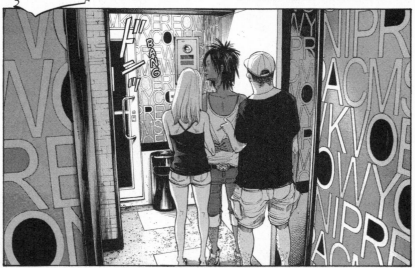

YOU'LL
BUG THE
OTHER
CUSTOMERS,
Y'KNOW
?

YOU
START
SHOUTING
AND...

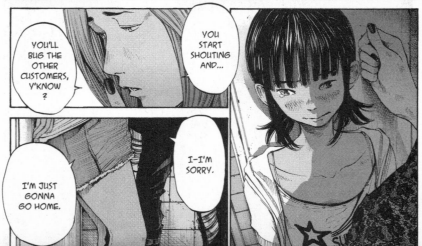

I-I'M
SORRY.

I'M JUST
GONNA
GO HOME.

226

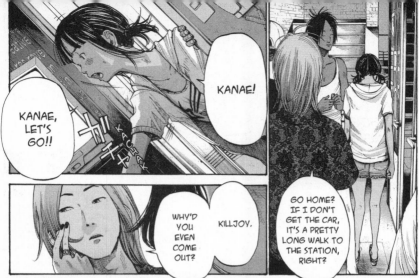

KANAE!

KANAE, LET'S GO!!

GO HOME? IF I DON'T GET THE CAR, IT'S A PRETTY LONG WALK TO THE STATION, RIGHT?

WHY'D YOU EVEN COME OUT?

KILLJOY.

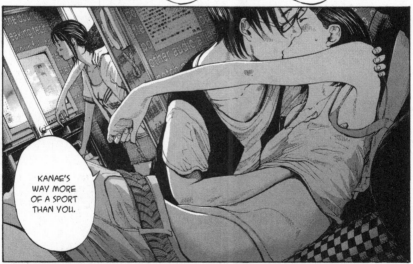

KANAE'S WAY MORE OF A SPORT THAN YOU.

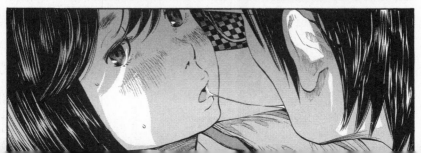

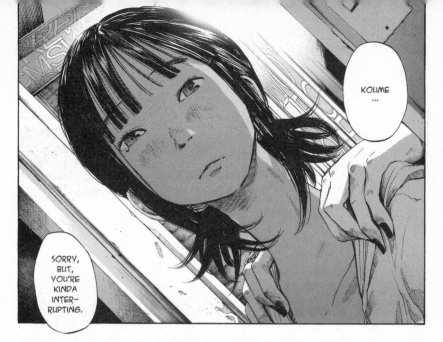

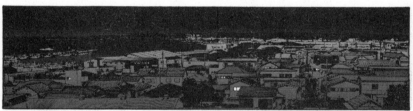

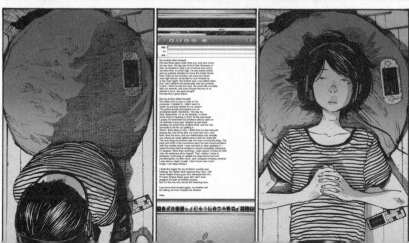

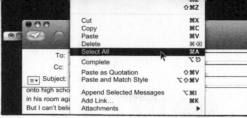
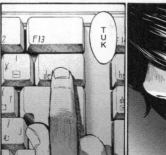
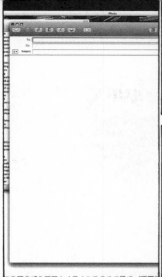
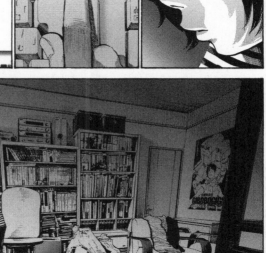

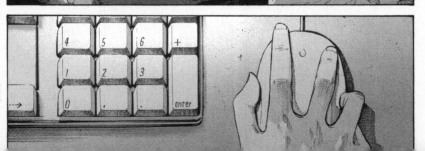

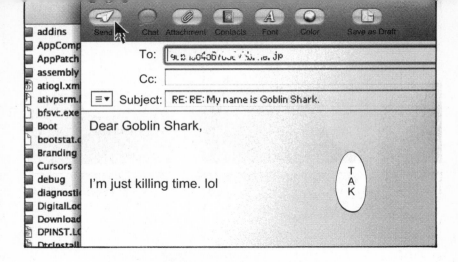

To: 9LB 100406700 'ᴚᵘᵘ .ᴺᵃ. ᴶᴾ

Cc:

Subject: RE: RE: My name is Goblin Shark.

Dear Goblin Shark,

I'm just killing time. lol

TAK

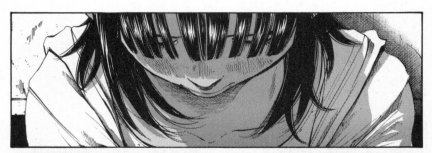

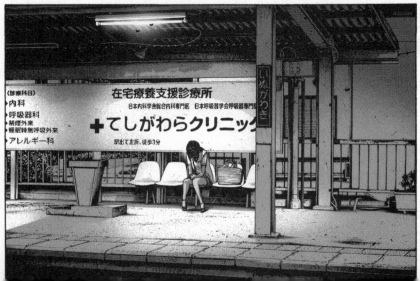

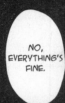

NO,
EVERYTHING'S
FINE.

KOUME,
YOU SEEM
KINDA
BUMMED?

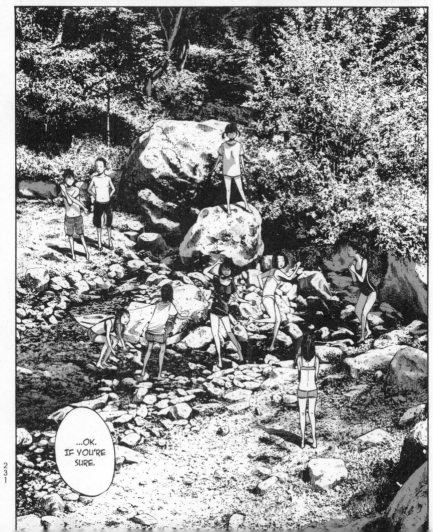

...OK,
IF YOU'RE
SURE.

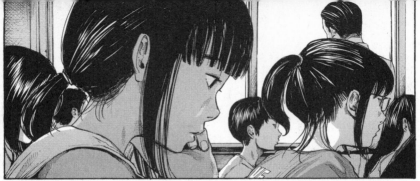

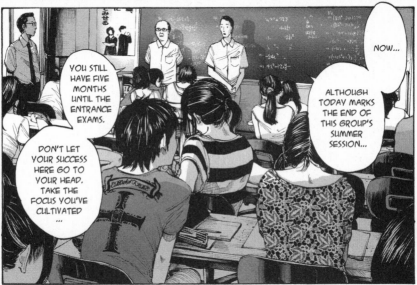

NOW...

ALTHOUGH TODAY MARKS THE END OF THIS GROUP'S SUMMER SESSION...

YOU STILL HAVE FIVE MONTHS UNTIL THE ENTRANCE EXAMS.

DON'T LET YOUR SUCCESS HERE GO TO YOUR HEAD. TAKE THE FOCUS YOU'VE CULTIVATED ...

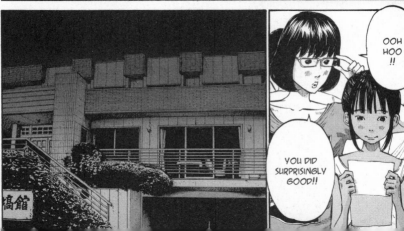

OOH HOO !!

YOU DID SURPRISINGLY GOOD!!

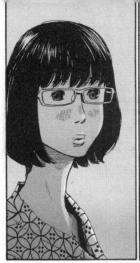
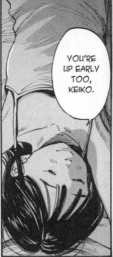
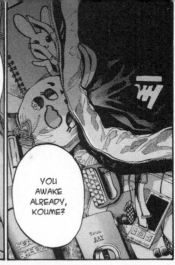

YOU'RE UP EARLY TOO, KEIKO.

YOU AWAKE ALREADY, KOUME?

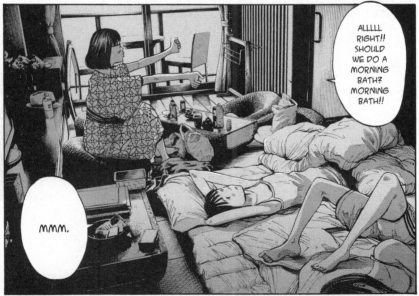

ALLLLL RIGHT!! SHOULD WE DO A MORNING BATH? MORNING BATH!!

MMM.

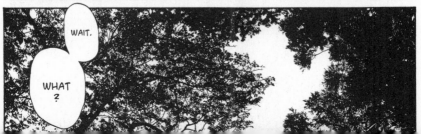

WAIT.

WHAT ?

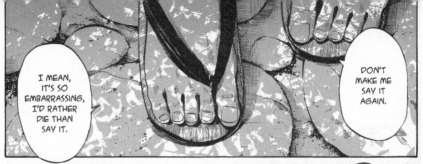

I MEAN, IT'S SO EMBARRASSING, I'D RATHER DIE THAN SAY IT.

DON'T MAKE ME SAY IT AGAIN.

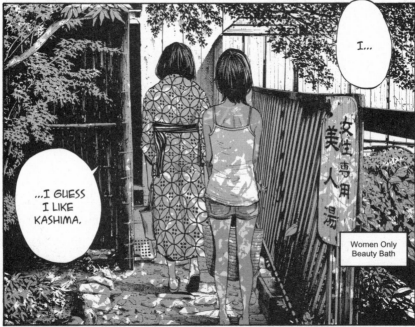

I...

...I GUESS I LIKE KASHIMA.

Women Only Beauty Bath

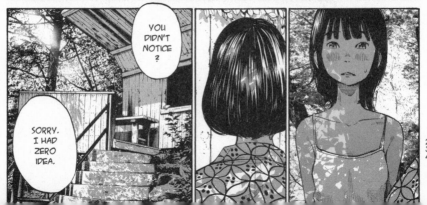

YOU DIDN'T NOTICE?

SORRY. I HAD ZERO IDEA.

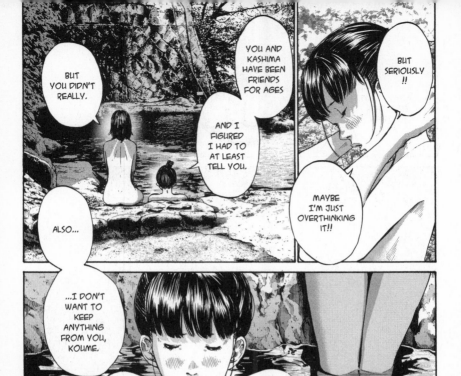

BUT YOU DIDN'T REALLY.

YOU AND KASHIMA HAVE BEEN FRIENDS FOR AGES

AND I FIGURED I HAD TO AT LEAST TELL YOU.

BUT SERIOUSLY!!

MAYBE I'M JUST OVERTHINKING IT!!

ALSO...

...I DON'T WANT TO KEEP ANYTHING FROM YOU, KOUME.

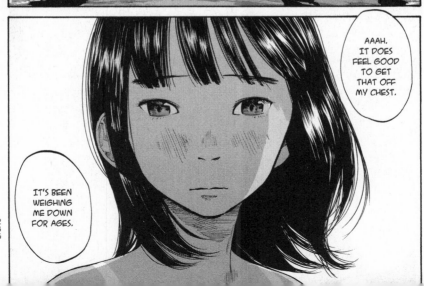

AAAH. IT DOES FEEL GOOD TO GET THAT OFF MY CHEST.

IT'S BEEN WEIGHING ME DOWN FOR AGES.

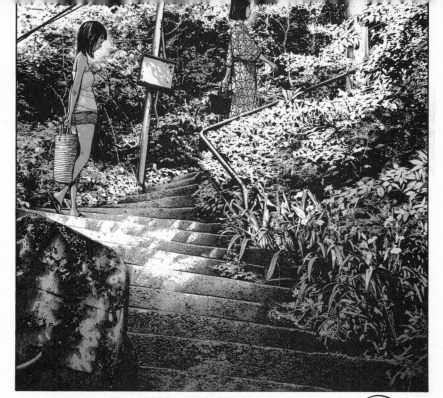

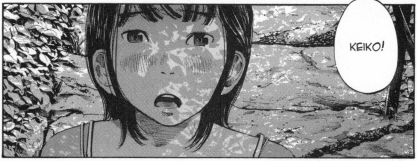

KEIKO!

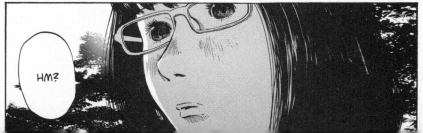

HM?

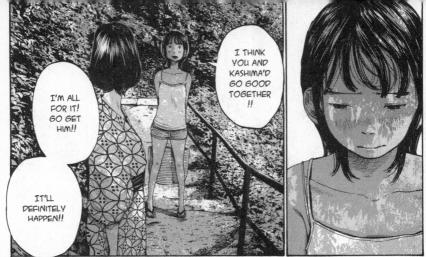

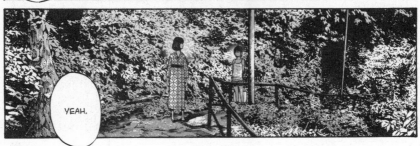

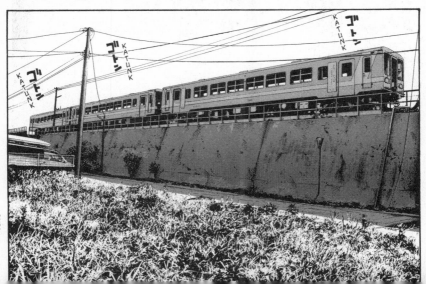

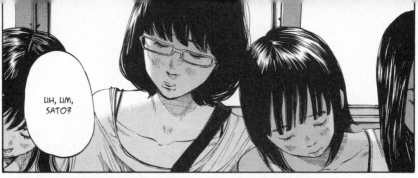

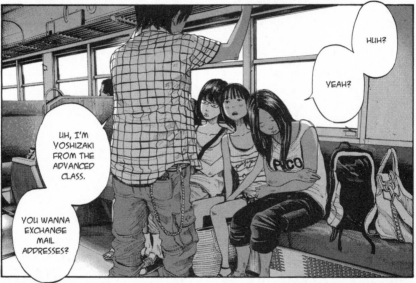

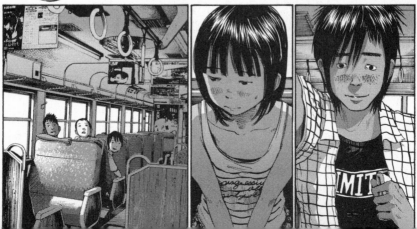

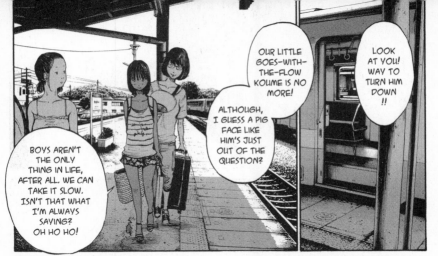

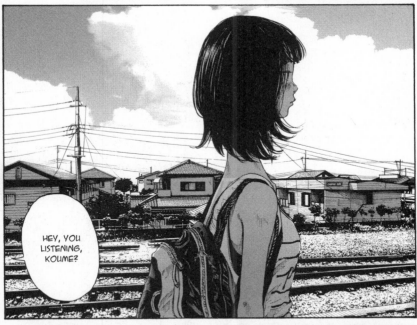

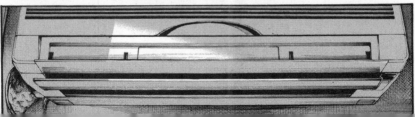

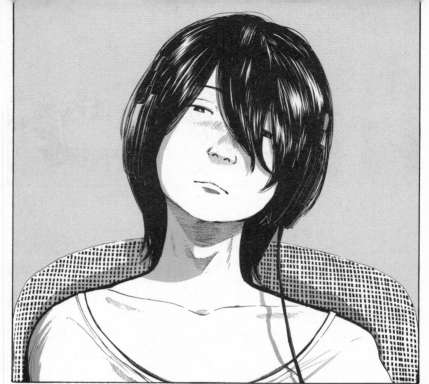

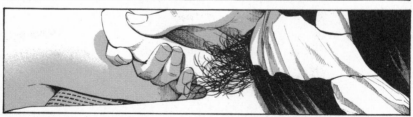

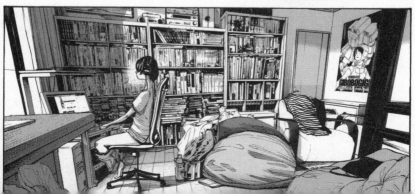

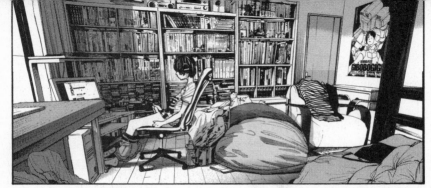

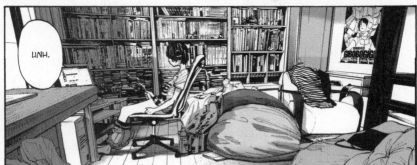

UNH.

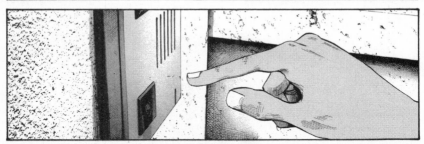

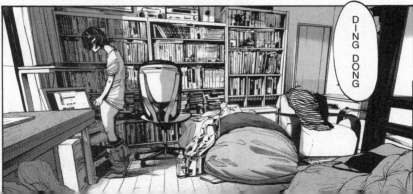

DING DONG

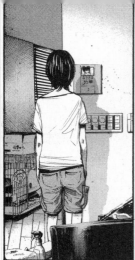
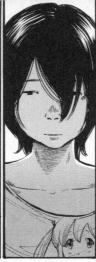
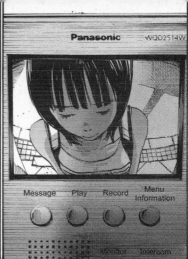

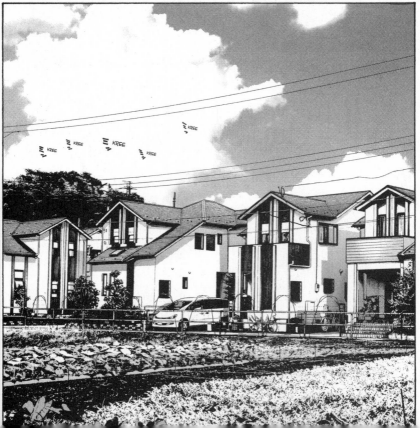

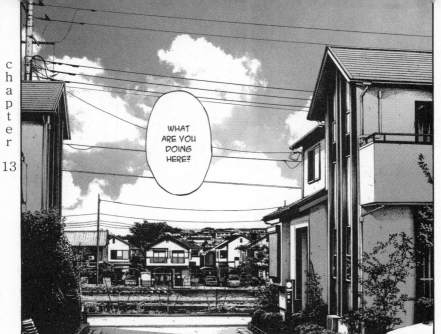

WHAT ARE YOU DOING HERE?

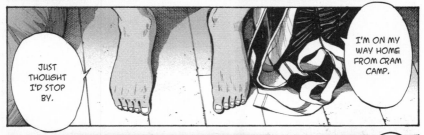

JUST THOUGHT I'D STOP BY.

I'M ON MY WAY HOME FROM CRAM CAMP.

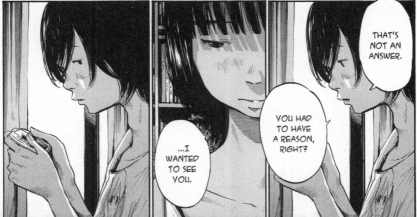

...I WANTED TO SEE YOU.

THAT'S NOT AN ANSWER.

YOU HAD TO HAVE A REASON, RIGHT?

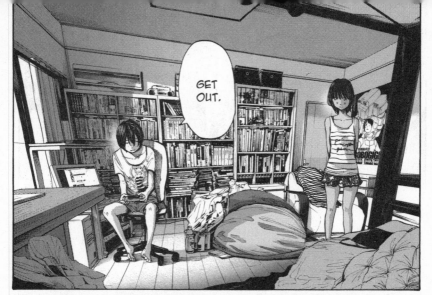

GET OUT.

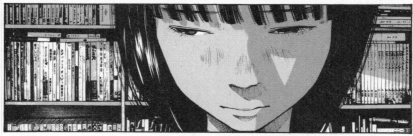

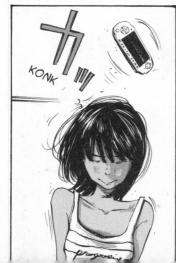

KONK

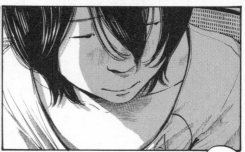

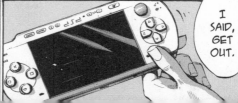

I SAID, GET OUT.

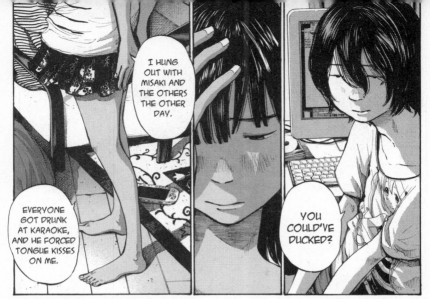

I HUNG OUT WITH MISAKI AND THE OTHERS THE OTHER DAY.

YOU COULD'VE DUCKED?

EVERYONE GOT DRUNK AT KARAOKE, AND HE FORCED TONGUE KISSES ON ME.

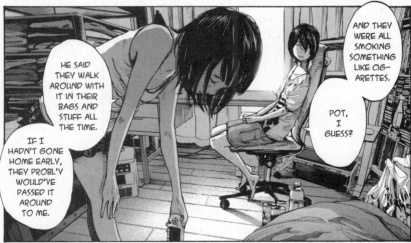

HE SAID THEY WALK AROUND WITH IT IN THEIR BAGS AND STUFF ALL THE TIME.

IF I HADN'T GONE HOME EARLY, THEY PROBL'Y WOULD'VE PASSED IT AROUND TO ME.

AND THEY WERE ALL SMOKING SOMETHING LIKE CIG-ARETTES.

POT, I GUESS?

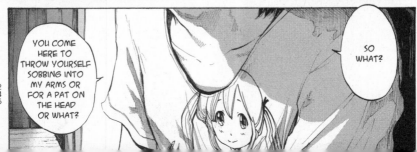

YOU COME HERE TO THROW YOURSELF SOBBING INTO MY ARMS OR FOR A PAT ON THE HEAD OR WHAT?

SO WHAT?

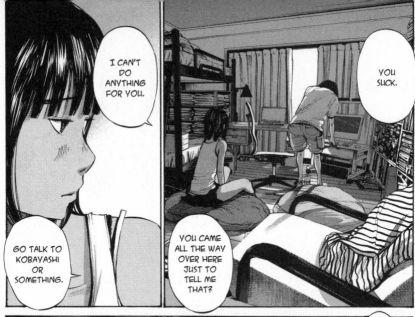

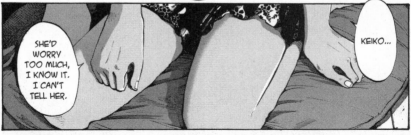

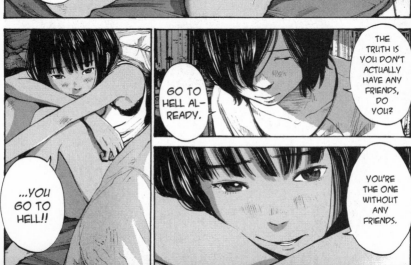

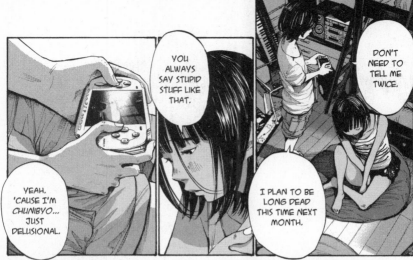

YOU ALWAYS SAY STUPID STUFF LIKE THAT.

DON'T NEED TO TELL ME TWICE.

YEAH. 'CAUSE I'M CHUNIBYO... JUST DELUSIONAL.

I PLAN TO BE LONG DEAD THIS TIME NEXT MONTH.

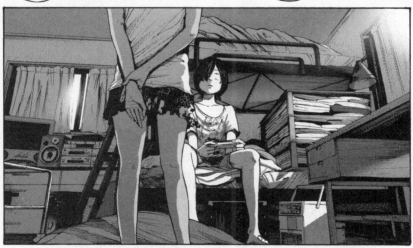

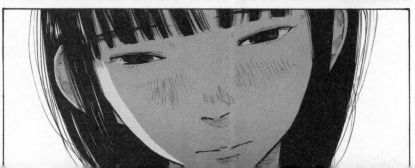

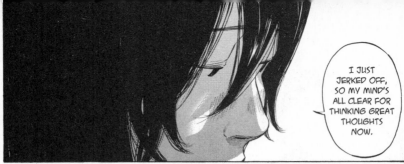

I JUST JERKED OFF, SO MY MIND'S ALL CLEAR FOR THINKING GREAT THOUGHTS NOW.

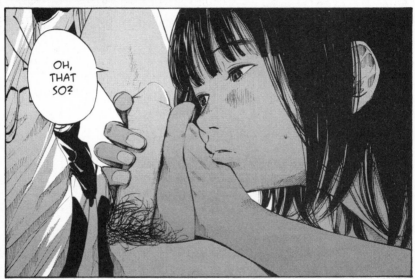

OH, THAT SO?

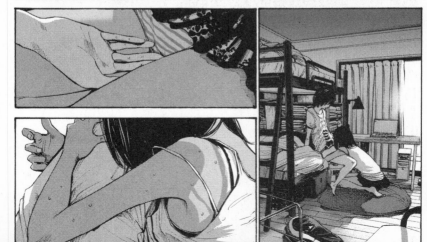

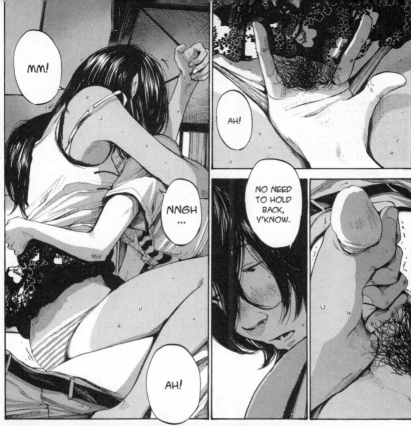

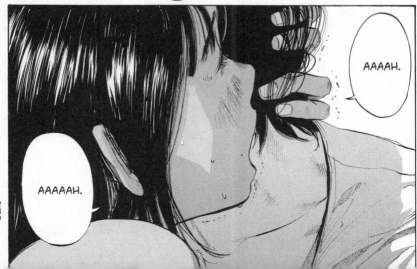

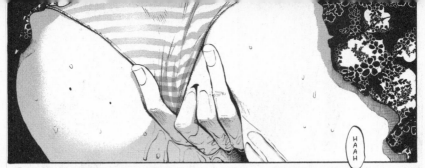

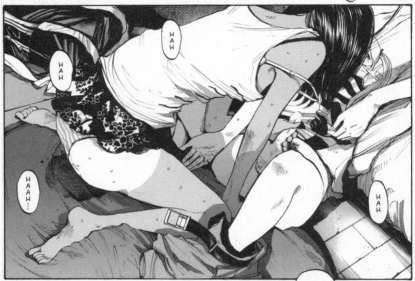

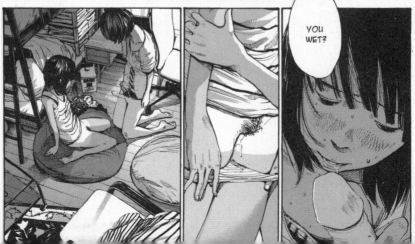

250

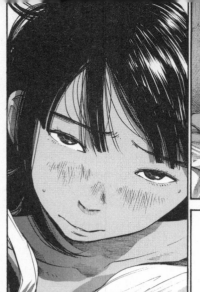
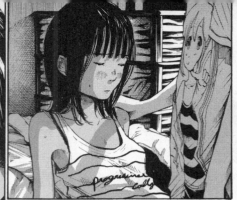
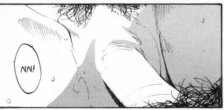

NN!

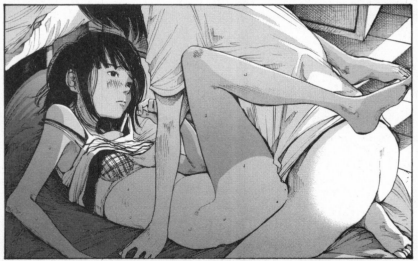

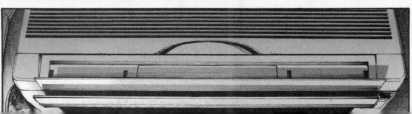

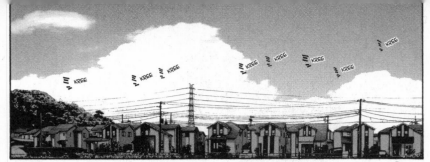

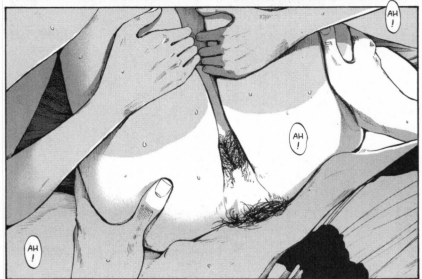

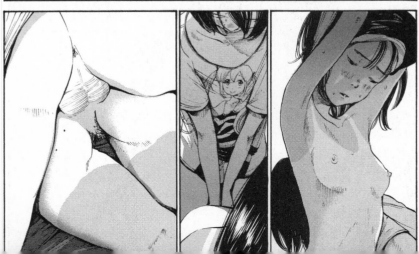

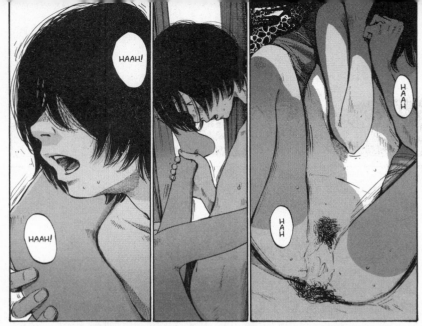

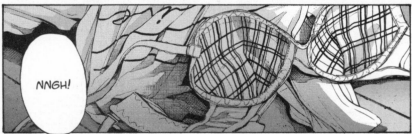

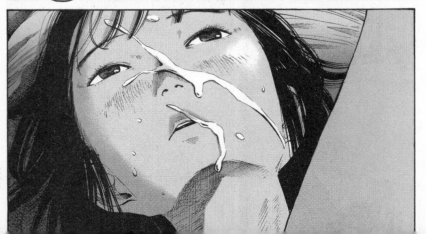

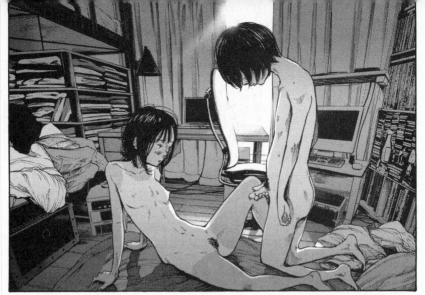

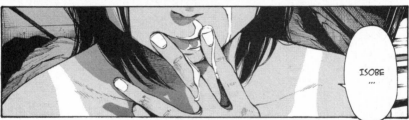

ISOBE
...

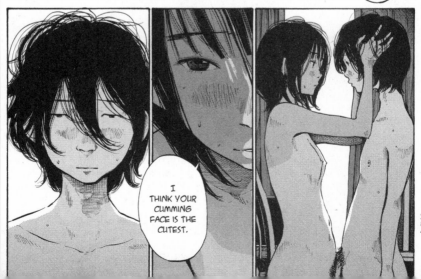

I THINK YOUR CUMMING FACE IS THE CUTEST.

254

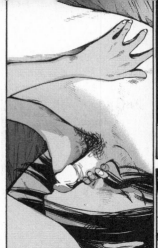
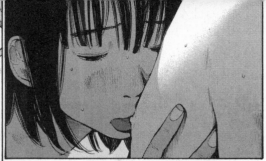
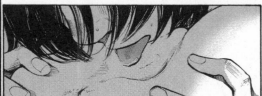
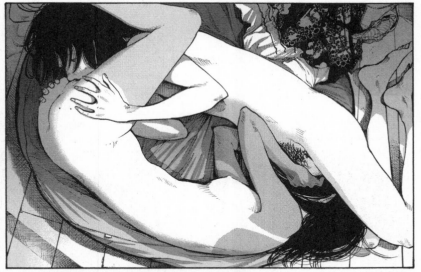
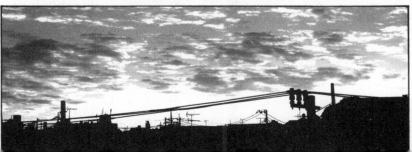

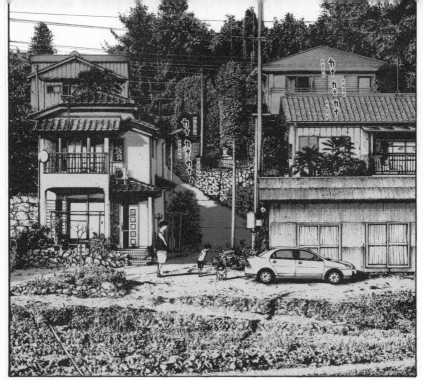

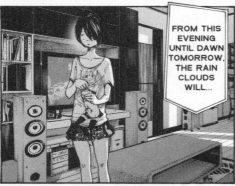

FROM THIS
EVENING
UNTIL DAWN
TOMORROW,
THE RAIN
CLOUDS
WILL...

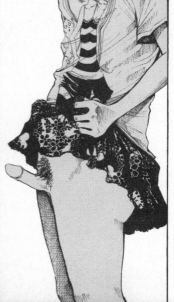

SATO.

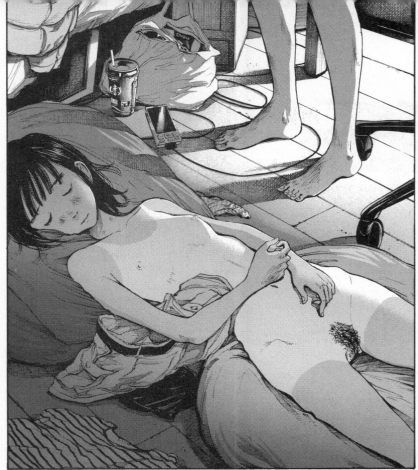

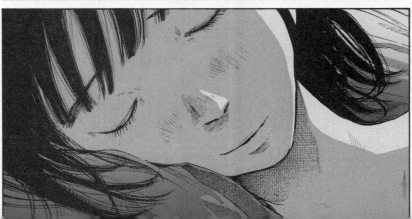

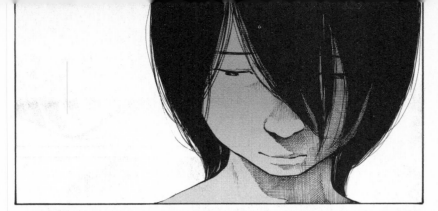

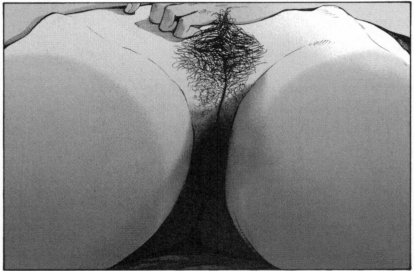

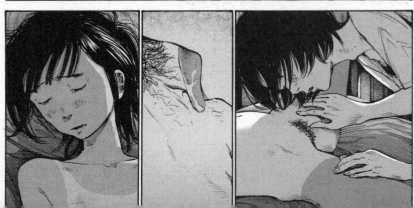

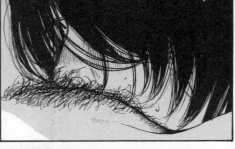

IT'S SIX O'CLOCK.

MY FAMILY'S GONE TO STAY WITH RELATIVES 'TIL TOMORROW.

SO I DON'T NEED TO WORRY ABOUT THE TIME.

'KAY.

THEN STAY OVER.

THAT WAS MY PLAN WHEN I CAME OVER.

AH!

THE RAIN STOP?

NO.

NAH, TOO MUCH OF A HASSLE.

YOU WANNA GO TO THE STORE?

LET'S MAKE SUPPER AFTER.

AH,

AH.

AH!

'KAY. BUT THERE'S LIKE NOTHING IN THE FRIDGE.

NO, GET IT WET FIRST.

SO LIKE, HEY?

COULD YOU PUT A FINGER IN THERE?

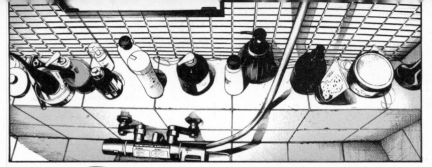

YOU SERIOUSLY DON'T SAY NO TO ANYTHING, HUH?

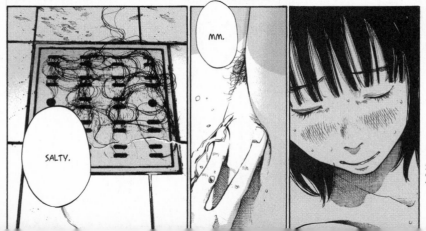

MM.

SALTY.

HEY, ISOBE?

YEAH?

WE JUST DO IT AND DO IT, BUT I KEEP FEELING LIKE IT'S NOT ENOUGH.

WHY, DO YOU THINK?

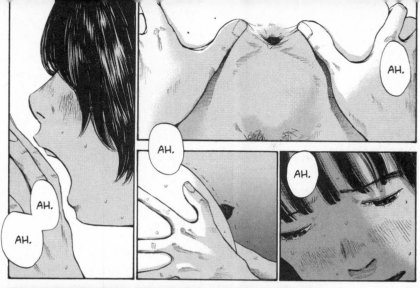

WHY'D YOU TELL ME YOU LIKE ME IN SEVENTH GRADE?

BACK THEN,

YOU WERE TINY, YOU DIDN'T STAND OUT.

YOUR VOICE WAS QUIET, YOU SEEMED SERIOUS.

I WANTED TO BE FRIENDS.

ONCE YOU GO TO HIGH SCHOOL, YOU'LL TOTALLY FORGET TODAY EVEN HAPPENED.

YOU'LL JUST MEET SOME GUY YOU LIKE, AND THEN YOU'LL HAVE SEX LIKE IT WAS YOUR FIRST TIME.

WHAT'S SAD?

IT'S SAD.

SORRY I'M LIKE THIS.

270

ALL YOU NEED TO DO IS GET IT IN YOUR HEAD, AND YOU COULD GET A GUY HARD. AND IF YOU SPREAD YOUR LEGS, MOST OF THEM'D STICK IT IN FOR YOU.

YOU'LL GO SEE SOME DUMB, POPULAR MOVIE WITH THE FIRST GUY YOU DATE, AND YOU'LL CRY.

EVEN THOUGH YOU'VE POOPED A LITTLE IN FRONT OF SOMEONE ELSE.

WISH I COULD NOT CARE LIKE THAT.

LIFE ON EASY MODE, RIGHT? YOU CAN JUST BURY ANY FLEETING LONELINESS WITH AN EASY VICTORY.

YOU'RE JUST ASSUMING STUFF ABOUT ME.

THERE'S LOTS OF STUFF I DON'T LIKE.

I HAVE PROBLEMS TOO, YOU KNOW.

ISN'T IT MORE LIKE THERE'S NO ONE YOU LIKE RIGHT NOW?

YOU REALLY BELIEVE THAT?

I THINK I'M GONNA HAVE A HARD TIME TRUSTING GUYS.

I MEAN, RIGHT NOW, BECAUSE OF MISAKI...

AT THE END OF THE DAY, YOU JUST INSIST ON HOW ENTITLED YOU ARE. YOU'RE GONNA BE A MEAN OLD LADY, SATO.

YOU DON'T ACTUALLY DO ANYTHING YOURSELF TO CHANGE THE SITUATION. A LOT OF TIMES YOU JUST SIT THERE PASSIVELY AND COMPLAIN.

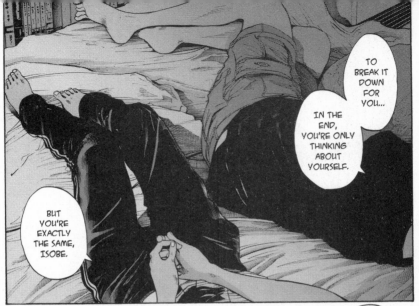

TO BREAK IT DOWN FOR YOU...

IN THE END, YOU'RE ONLY THINKING ABOUT YOURSELF.

BUT YOU'RE EXACTLY THE SAME, ISOBE.

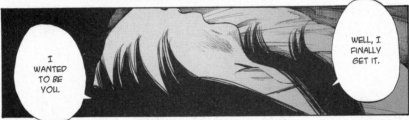

WELL, I FINALLY GET IT.

I WANTED TO BE YOU.

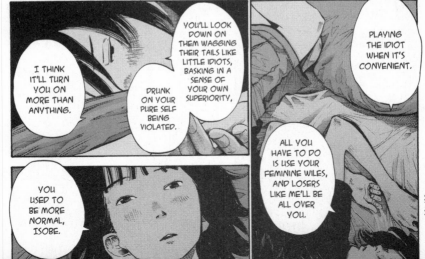

YOU'LL LOOK DOWN ON THEM WAGGING THEIR TAILS LIKE LITTLE IDIOTS, BASKING IN A SENSE OF YOUR OWN SUPERIORITY,

DRUNK ON YOUR PURE SELF BEING VIOLATED.

I THINK IT'LL TURN YOU ON MORE THAN ANYTHING.

PLAYING THE IDIOT WHEN IT'S CONVENIENT.

ALL YOU HAVE TO DO IS USE YOUR FEMININE WILES, AND LOSERS LIKE ME'LL BE ALL OVER YOU.

YOU USED TO BE MORE NORMAL, ISOBE.

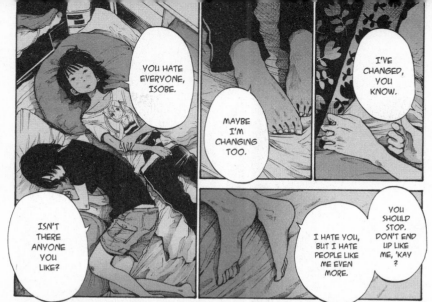

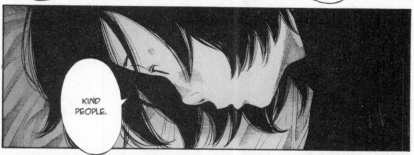

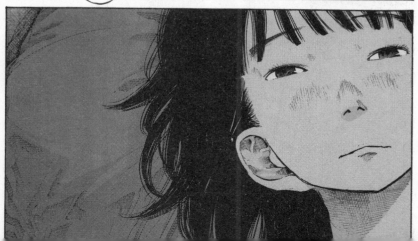

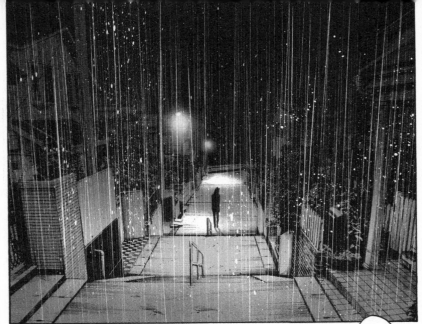

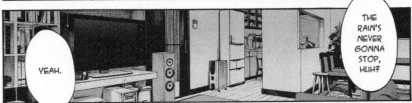

THE RAIN'S NEVER GONNA STOP, HUH?

YEAH.

IT'S LIKE I'M DROWNING. I CAN'T BREATHE.

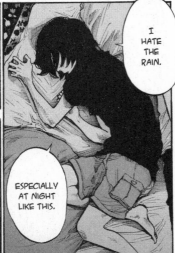

I HATE THE RAIN.

I KEEP BREATHING IN, BUT IT'S NEVER ENOUGH. I GET ALL SPACY.

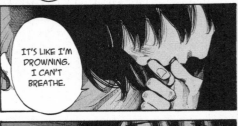

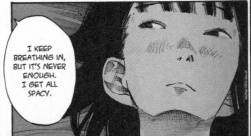

ESPECIALLY AT NIGHT LIKE THIS.

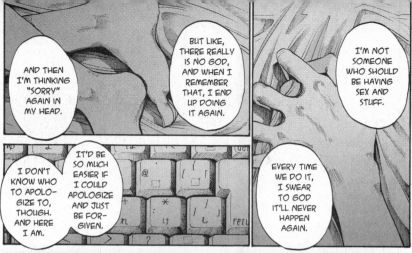

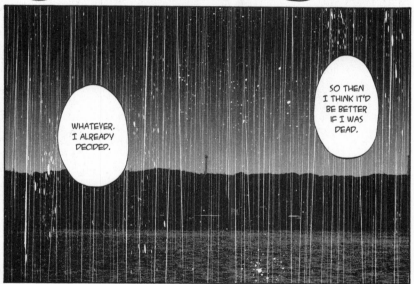

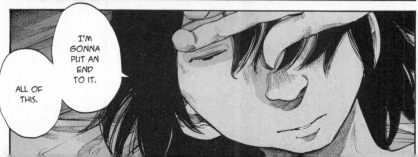

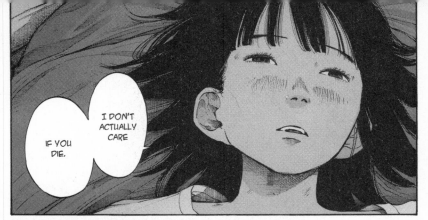

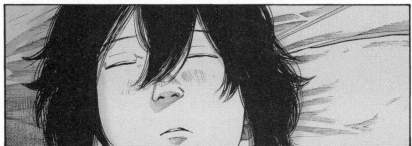

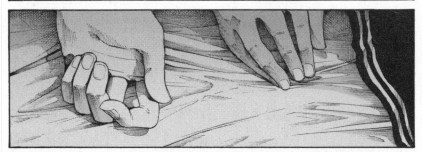

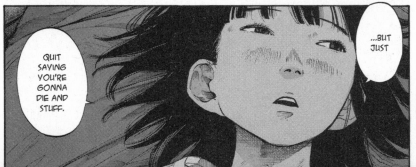

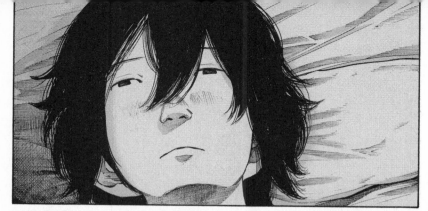

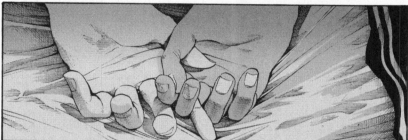

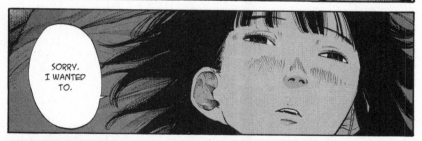

SORRY.
I WANTED
TO.

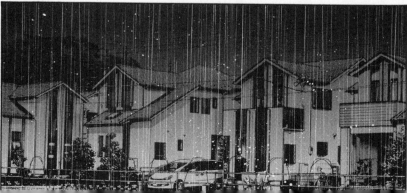

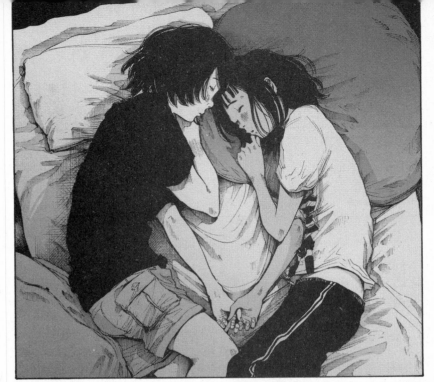

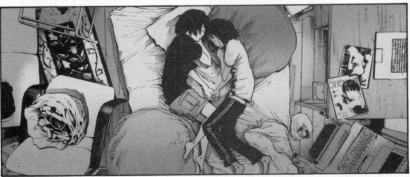

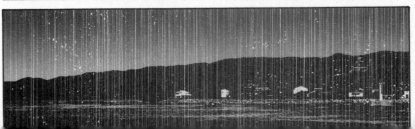

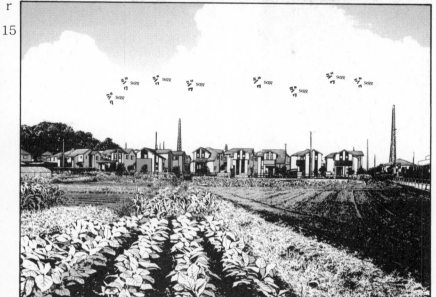

ジ
ジ
リ SKRR
ジ SKRR
リ SKRR
ジ
ジ SKRR
リ SKRR
ジ
リ SKRR

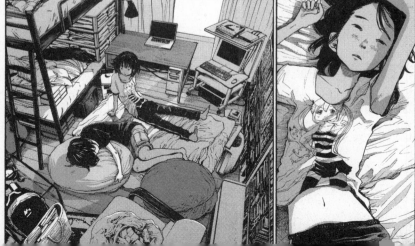

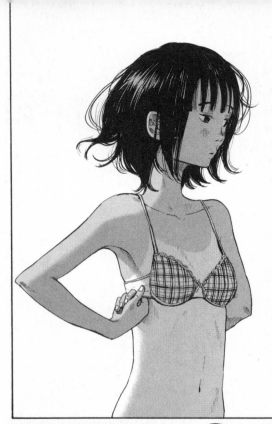

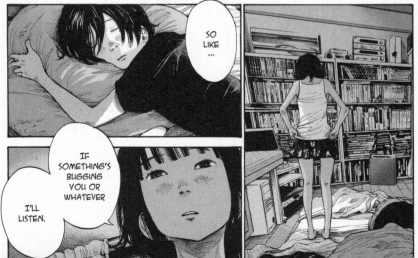

SO
LIKE
...

IF
SOMETHING'S
BUGGING
YOU OR
WHATEVER

I'LL
LISTEN.

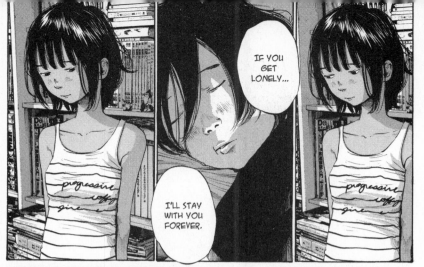

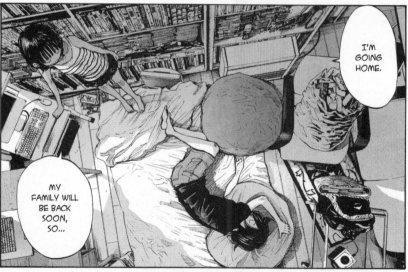

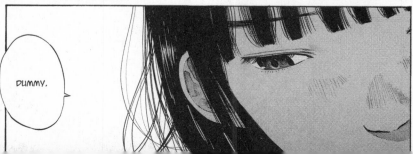

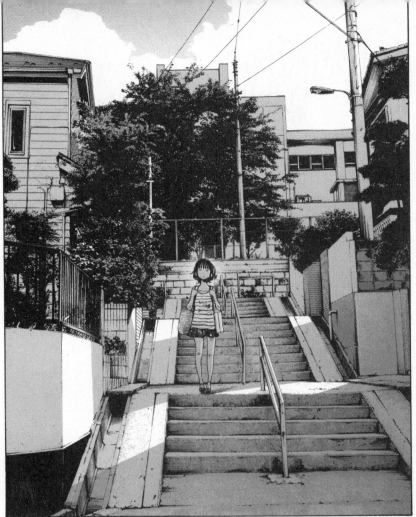

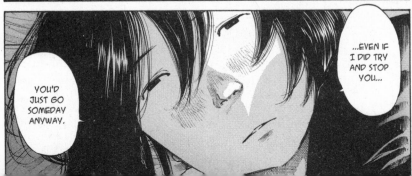

YOU'D JUST GO SOMEDAY ANYWAY.

...EVEN IF I DID TRY AND STOP YOU...

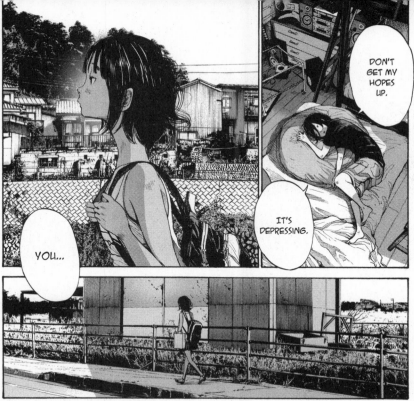

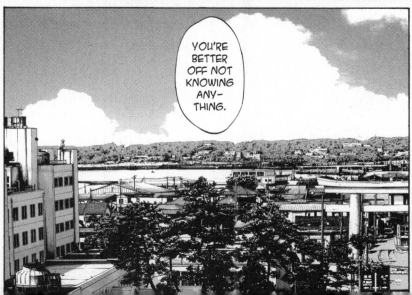

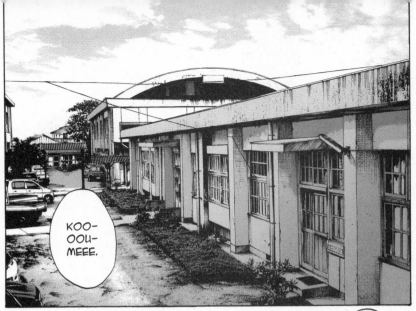

KOO-OOU-MEEE.

WHA-AAAT?

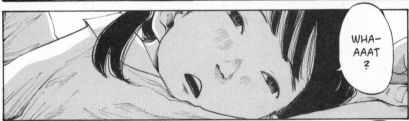

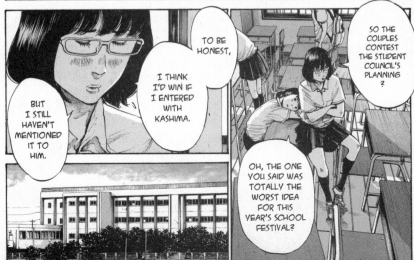

SO THE COUPLES CONTEST THE STUDENT COUNCIL'S PLANNING?

TO BE HONEST,

I THINK I'D WIN IF I ENTERED WITH KASHIMA.

BUT I STILL HAVEN'T MENTIONED IT TO HIM.

OH, THE ONE YOU SAID WAS TOTALLY THE WORST IDEA FOR THIS YEAR'S SCHOOL FESTIVAL?

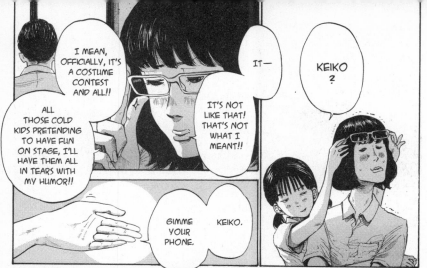

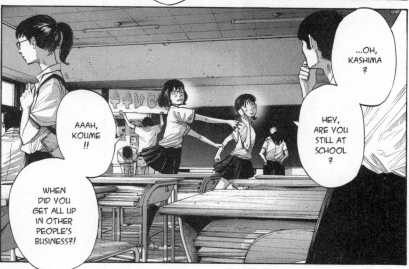

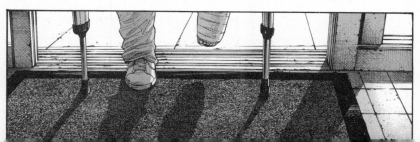

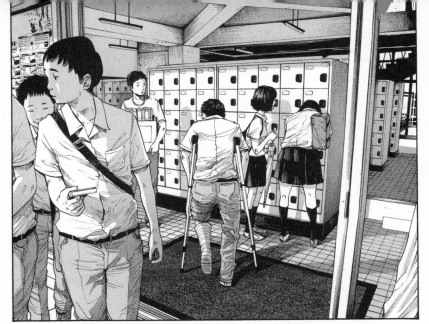

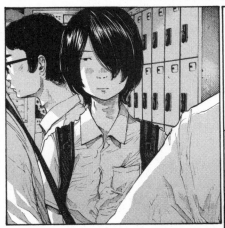

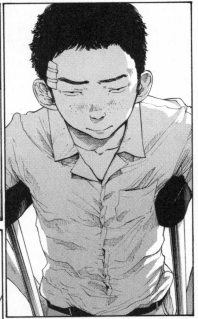

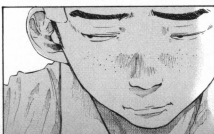

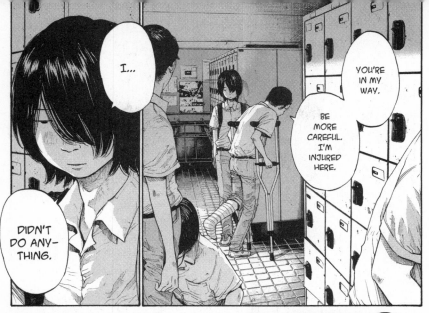

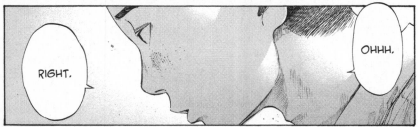

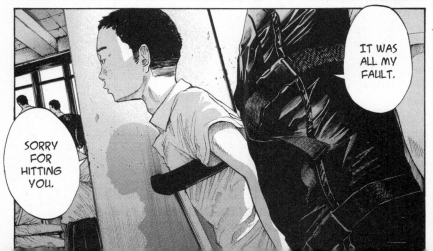

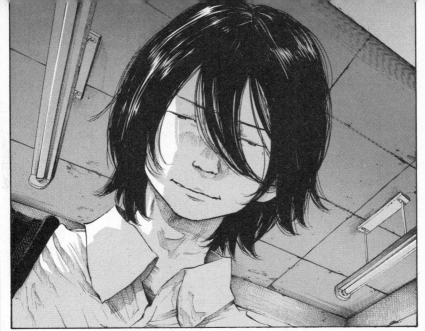

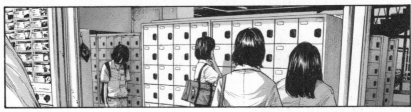

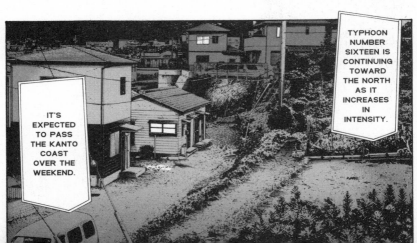

TYPHOON NUMBER SIXTEEN IS CONTINUING TOWARD THE NORTH AS IT INCREASES IN INTENSITY.

IT'S EXPECTED TO PASS THE KANTO COAST OVER THE WEEKEND.

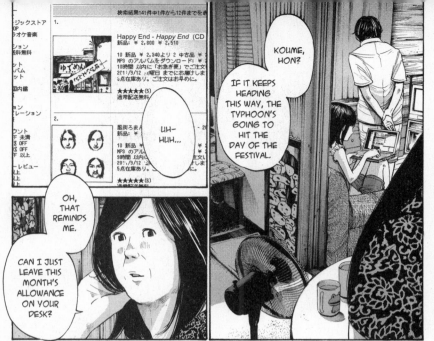
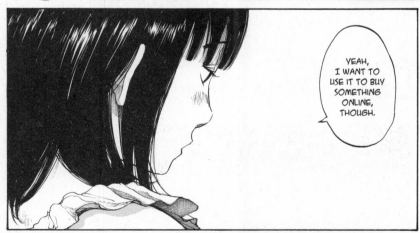
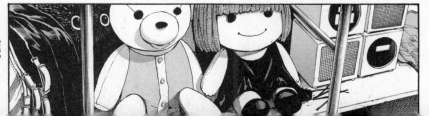

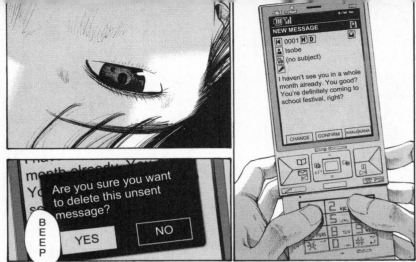

NEW MESSAGE

0001

Isobe

(no subject)

I haven't see you in a whole month already. You good? You're definitely coming to school festival, right?

CHANGE | CONFIRM | KANJI·KANA

Are you sure you want to delete this unsent message?

BEEP

YES | NO

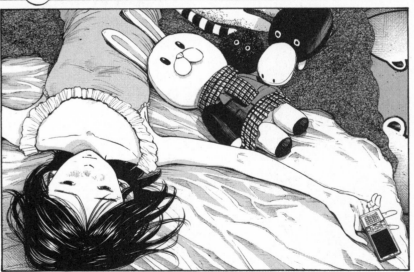

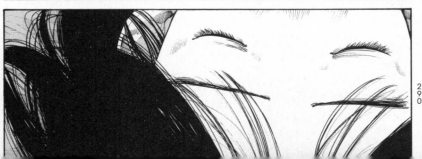

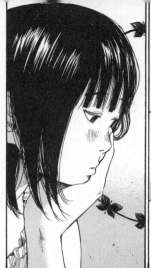
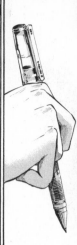
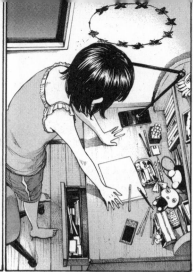
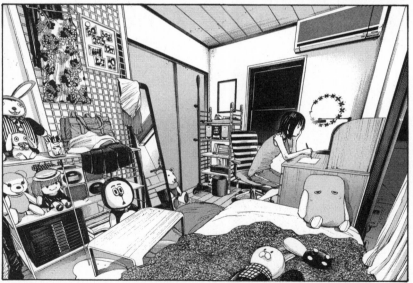
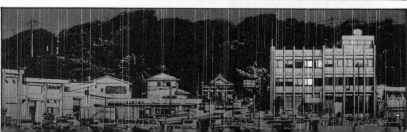

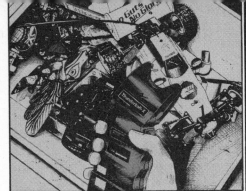

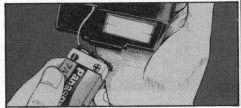

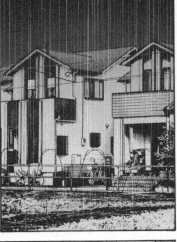

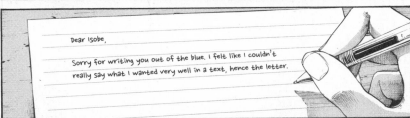

Dear Isobe,

Sorry for writing you out of the blue. I felt like I couldn't really say what I wanted very well in a text, hence the letter.

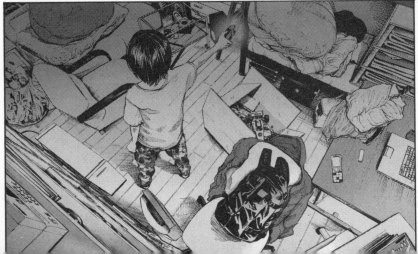

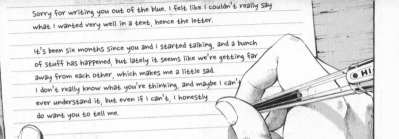

Sorry for writing you out of the blue. I felt like I couldn't really say what I wanted very well in a text, hence the letter.

It's been six months since you and I started talking, and a bunch of stuff has happened, but lately it seems like we're getting far away from each other, which makes me a little sad.
I don't really know what you're thinking, and maybe I can't ever understand it, but even if I can't, I honestly do want you to tell me.

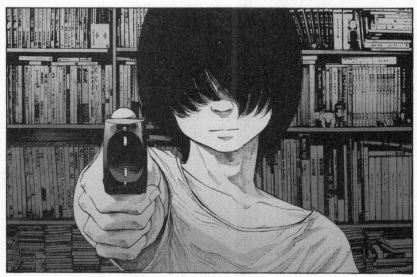

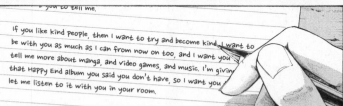

If you like kind people, then I want to try and become kind. I want to be with you as much as I can from now on too, and I want you to tell me more about manga, and video games, and music. I'm givin that Happy End album you said you don't have, so I want you let me listen to it with you in your room.

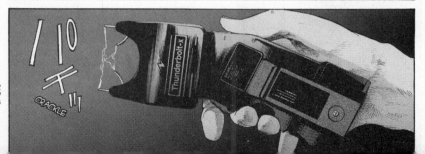

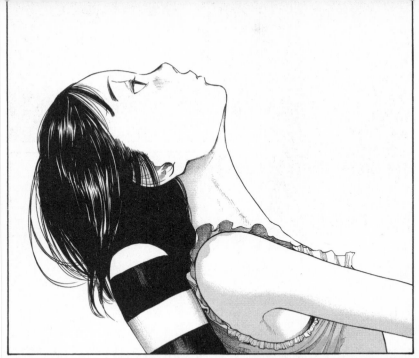

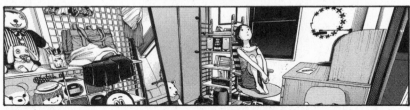

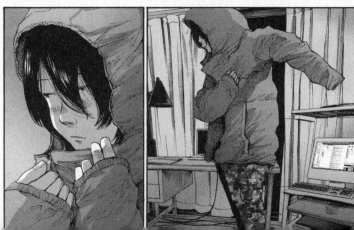

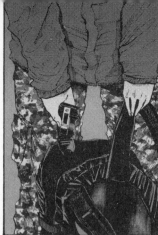

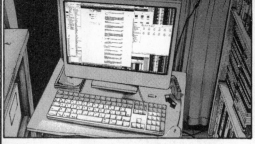

Mishamisha@shuhei maxxxxxxxx!!!
Daaaaamn! I won ten pool games for money in a row right now! (´ ▽ `))
All friends and neighbors who want to finance me, come on down! ＼(＾ｏ＾)／
23 minutes ago

Mishamisha@shuhei maxxxxxxxx!!!
@hageponchi-cho-cho Nice!
September 10

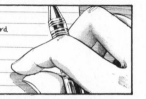

let me listen to it with you in your room.

Just writing this, my heart is seriously pounding. It's hard. I don't want to think that maybe there'll come a time when I'll never see you again.

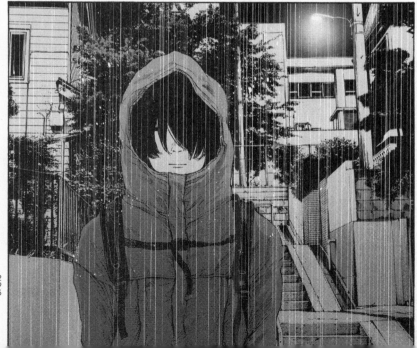

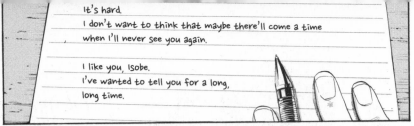

It's hard.
I don't want to think that maybe there'll come a time
when I'll never see you again.

I like you, Isobe.
I've wanted to tell you for a long,
long time.

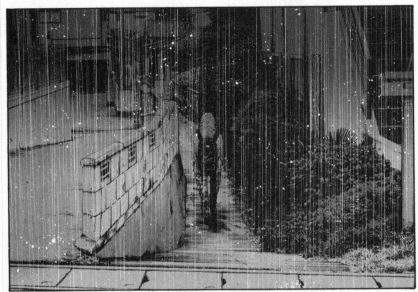

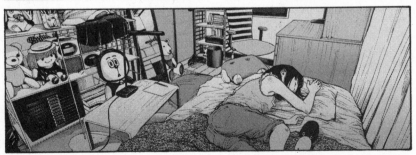

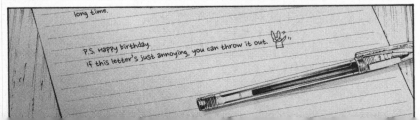

long time.

P.S. Happy birthday.
If this letter's just annoying, you can throw it out.

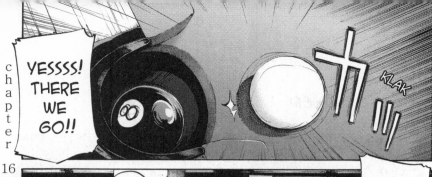
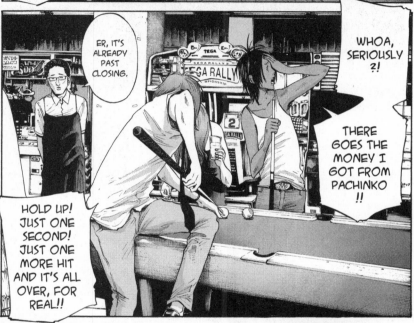

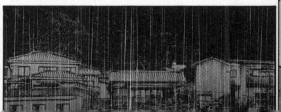
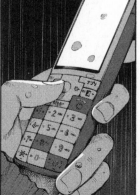

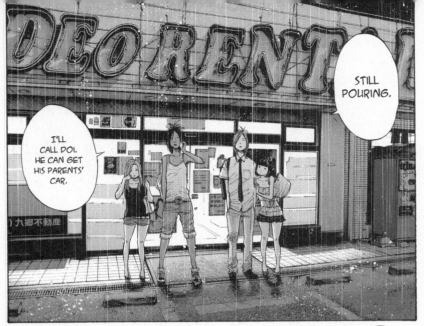

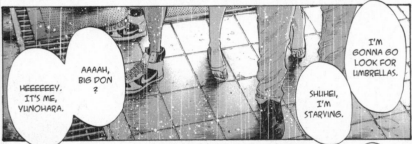

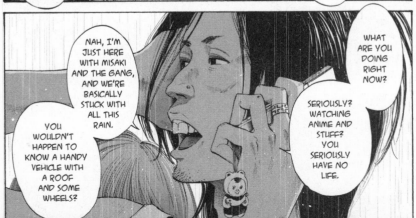

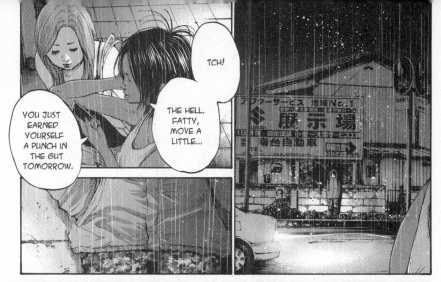

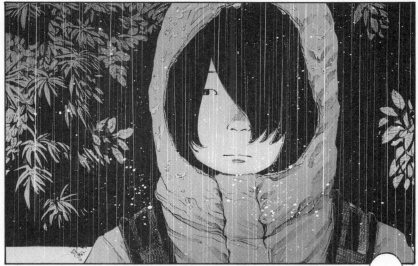

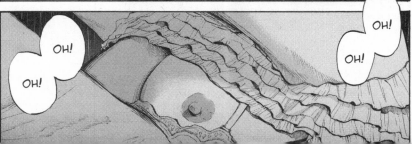

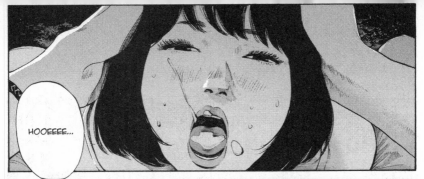

HOOEEEE...

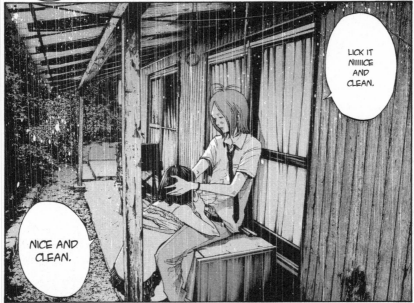

LICK IT NIIIIICE AND CLEAN.

NICE AND CLEAN.

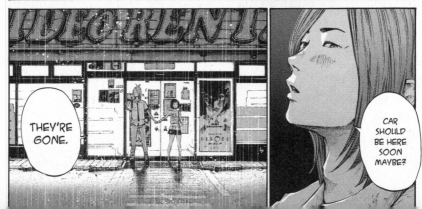

THEY'RE GONE.

CAR SHOULD BE HERE SOON MAYBE?

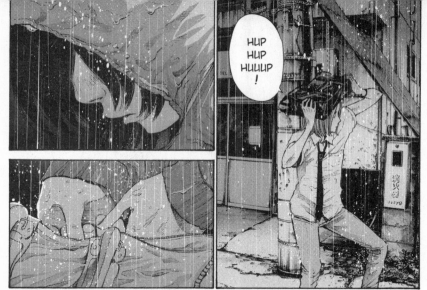

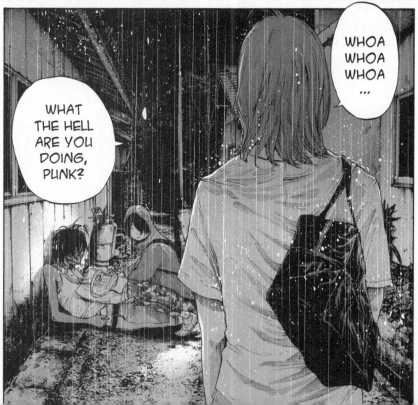

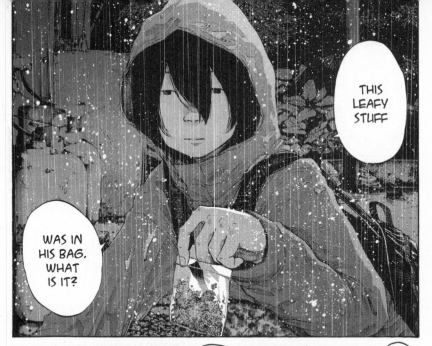

THIS LEAFY STUFF

WAS IN HIS BAG. WHAT IS IT?

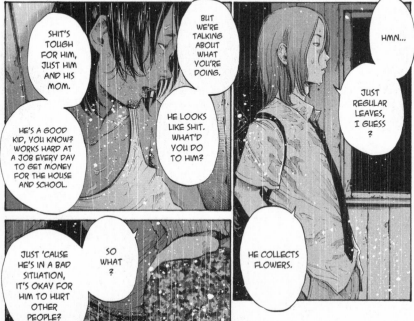

SHIT'S TOUGH FOR HIM, JUST HIM AND HIS MOM.

BUT WE'RE TALKING ABOUT WHAT YOU'RE DOING.

HMN...

JUST REGULAR LEAVES, I GUESS?

HE'S A GOOD KID, YOU KNOW? WORKS HARD AT A JOB EVERY DAY TO GET MONEY FOR THE HOUSE AND SCHOOL.

HE LOOKS LIKE SHIT. WHAT'D YOU DO TO HIM?

JUST 'CAUSE HE'S IN A BAD SITUATION, IT'S OKAY FOR HIM TO HURT OTHER PEOPLE?

SO WHAT?

HE COLLECTS FLOWERS.

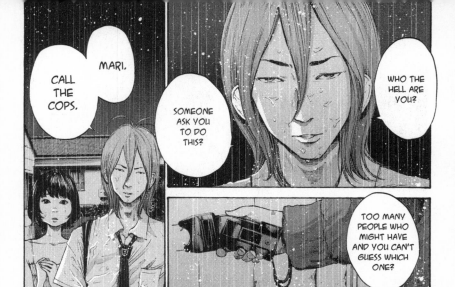

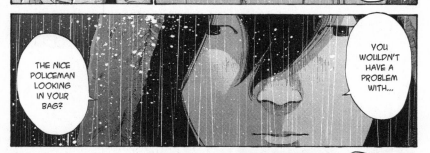

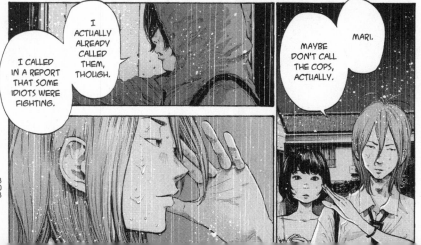

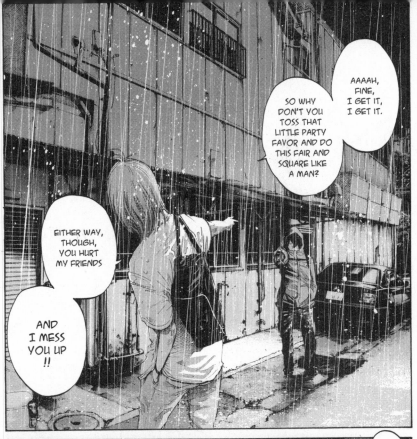

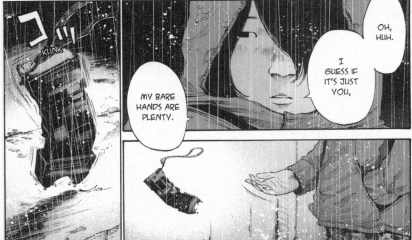

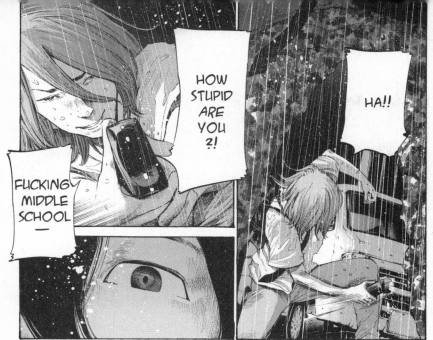

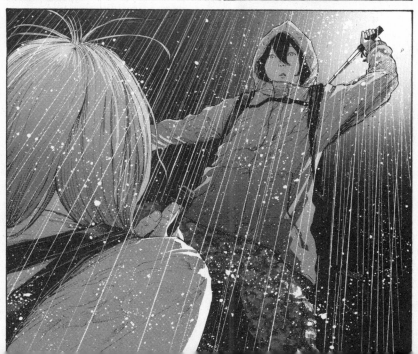

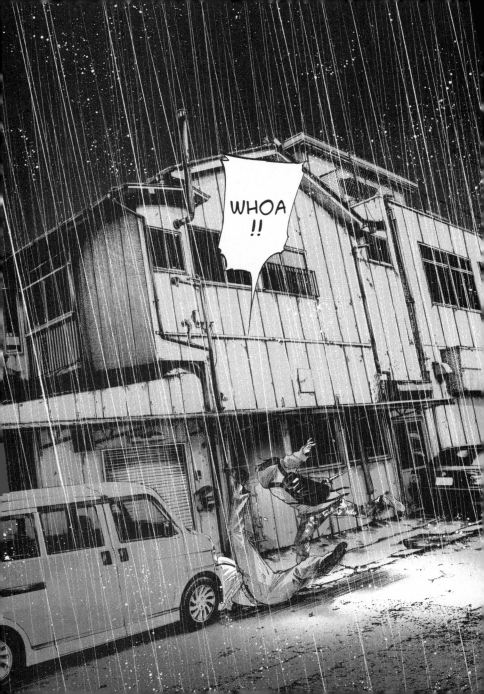

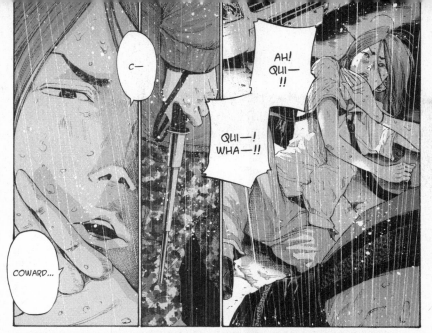

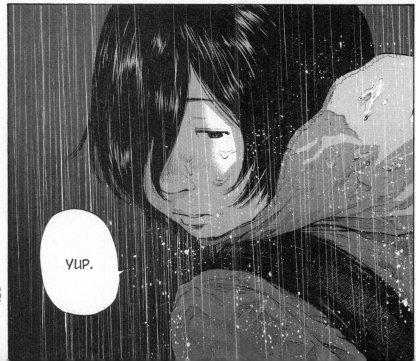

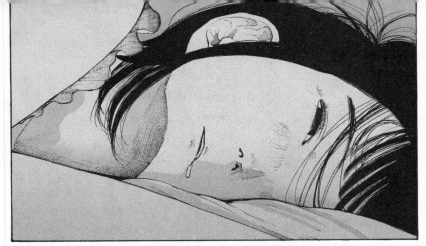

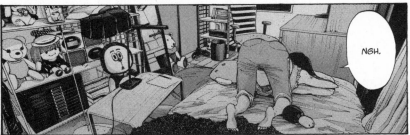

NGH.

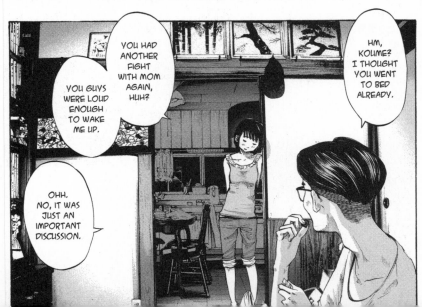

YOU HAD ANOTHER FIGHT WITH MOM AGAIN, HUH?

YOU GUYS WERE LOUD ENOUGH TO WAKE ME UP.

HM, KOUME? I THOUGHT YOU WENT TO BED ALREADY.

OHH. NO, IT WAS JUST AN IMPORTANT DISCUSSION.

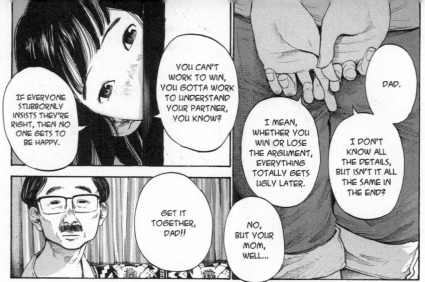

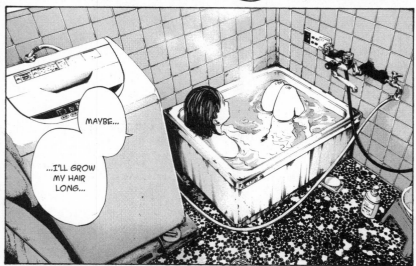

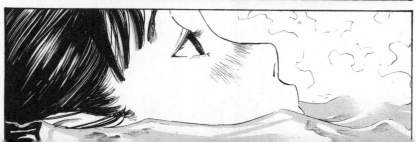

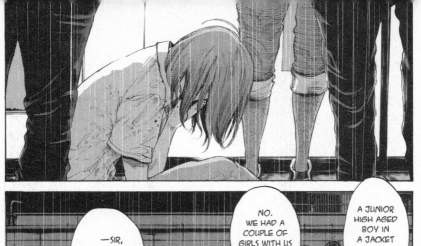

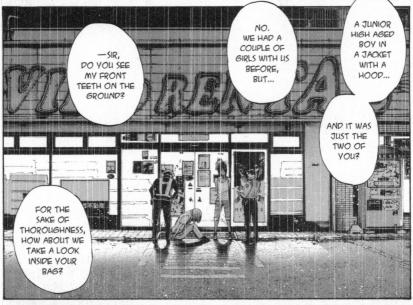

—SIR,
DO YOU SEE
MY FRONT
TEETH ON THE
GROUND?

NO.
WE HAD A
COUPLE OF
GIRLS WITH US
BEFORE,
BUT...

A JUNIOR
HIGH AGED
BOY IN
A JACKET
WITH A
HOOD...

AND IT WAS
JUST THE
TWO OF
YOU?

FOR THE
SAKE OF
THOROUGHNESS,
HOW ABOUT WE
TAKE A LOOK
INSIDE YOUR
BAG?

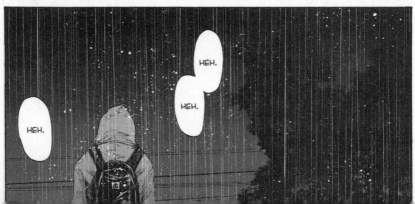

HEH.

HEH.

HEH.

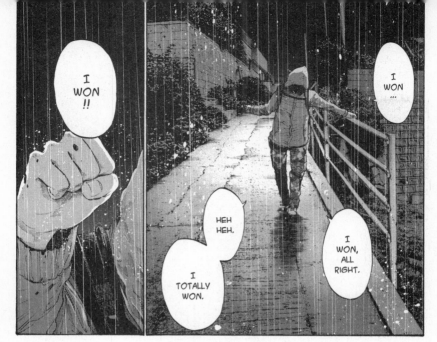

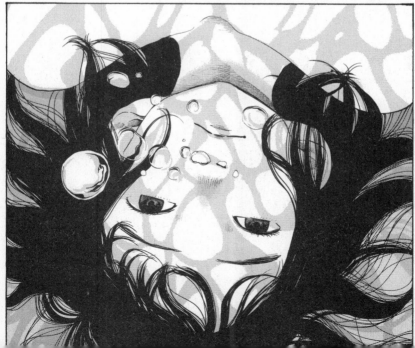

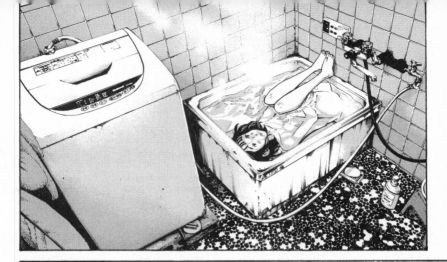

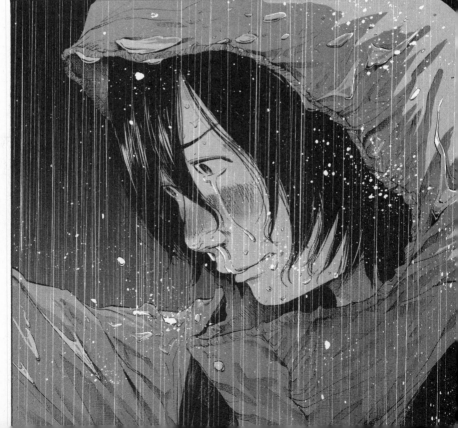

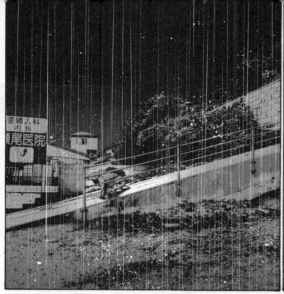
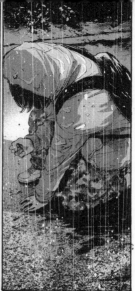
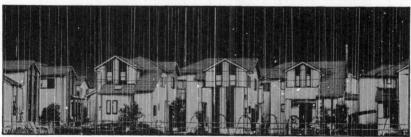
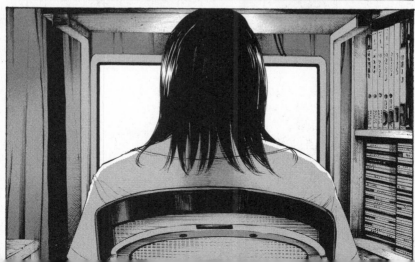

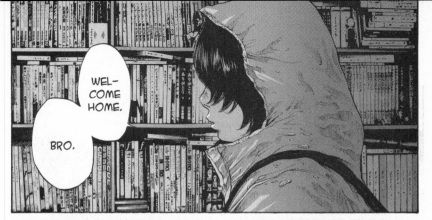

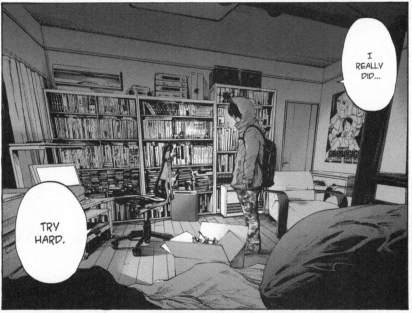

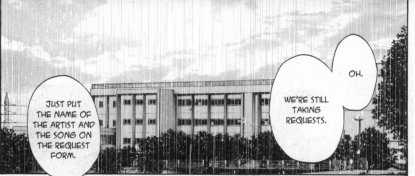

JUST PUT THE NAME OF THE ARTIST AND THE SONG ON THE REQUEST FORM.

WE'RE STILL TAKING REQUESTS.

OH.

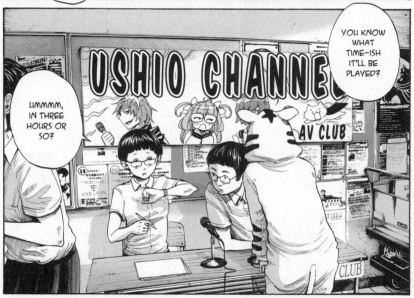

YOU KNOW WHAT TIME-ISH IT'LL BE PLAYED?

UMMMM, IN THREE HOURS OR SO?

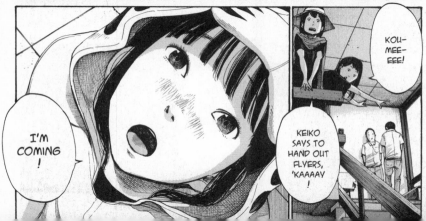

KOU-MEE-EEE!

KEIKO SAYS TO HAND OUT FLYERS, 'KAAAAY!

I'M COMING!

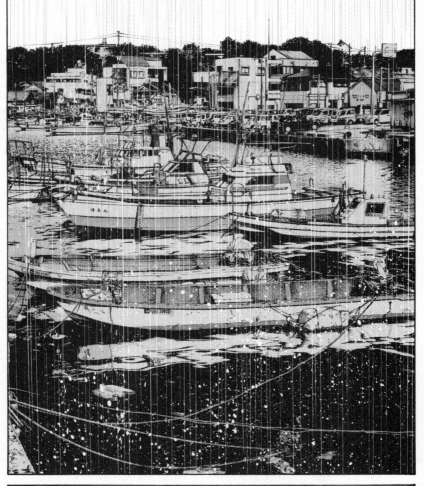

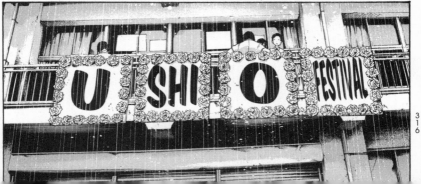

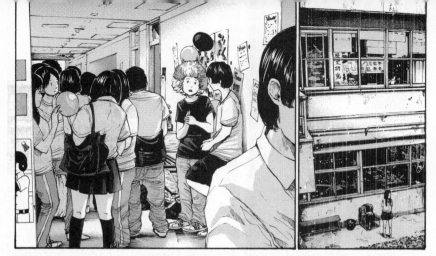

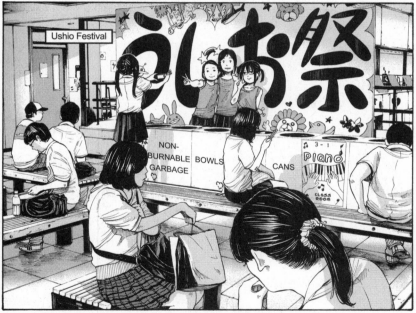

Ushio Festival

NON-BURNABLE GARBAGE

BOWLS

CANS

3-1
Piano
CLASS ROOM

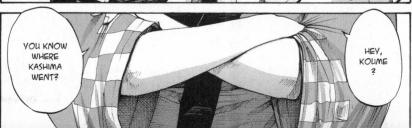

YOU KNOW WHERE KASHIMA WENT?

HEY, KOUME?

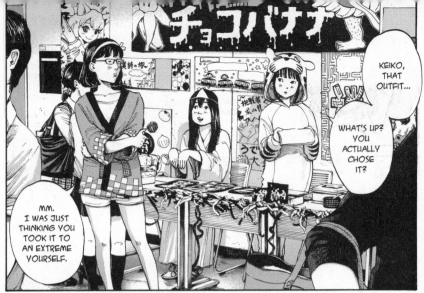

チョコバナナ

KEIKO, THAT OUTFIT...

WHAT'S UP? YOU ACTUALLY CHOSE IT?

MM. I WAS JUST THINKING YOU TOOK IT TO AN EXTREME YOURSELF.

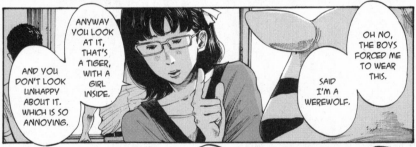

ANYWAY YOU LOOK AT IT, THAT'S A TIGER, WITH A GIRL INSIDE.

AND YOU DON'T LOOK UNHAPPY ABOUT IT. WHICH IS SO ANNOYING.

SAID I'M A WEREWOLF.

OH NO, THE BOYS FORCED ME TO WEAR THIS.

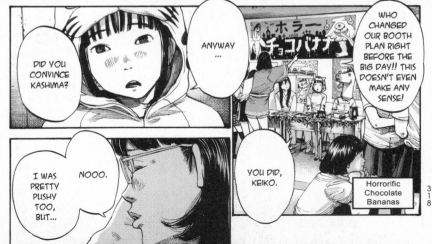

DID YOU CONVINCE KASHIMA?

ANYWAY...

ホラー チョコバナナ

WHO CHANGED OUR BOOTH PLAN RIGHT BEFORE THE BIG DAY!! THIS DOESN'T EVEN MAKE ANY SENSE!

I WAS PRETTY PUSHY TOO, BUT...

NOOO.

YOU DID, KEIKO.

Horrorific Chocolate Bananas

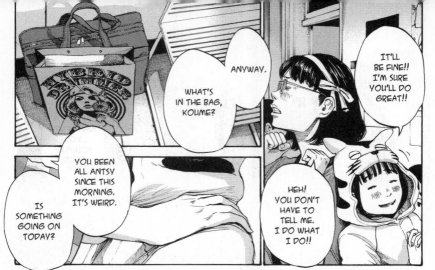

ANYWAY.

WHAT'S IN THE BAG, KOUME?

IT'LL BE FINE!! I'M SURE YOU'LL DO GREAT!!

YOU BEEN ALL ANTSY SINCE THIS MORNING. IT'S WEIRD.

IS SOMETHING GOING ON TODAY?

HEH! YOU DON'T HAVE TO TELL ME. I DO WHAT I DO!!

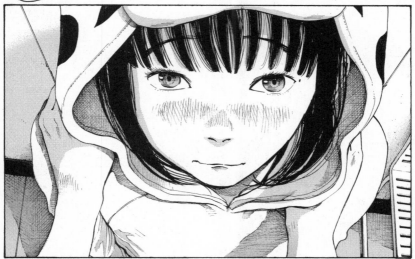

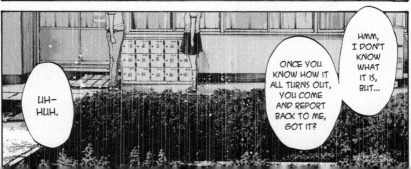

ONCE YOU KNOW HOW IT ALL TURNS OUT, YOU COME AND REPORT BACK TO ME, GOT IT?

HMM, I DON'T KNOW WHAT IT IS, BUT...

UH-HUH.

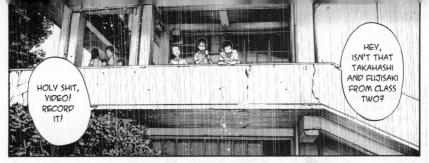

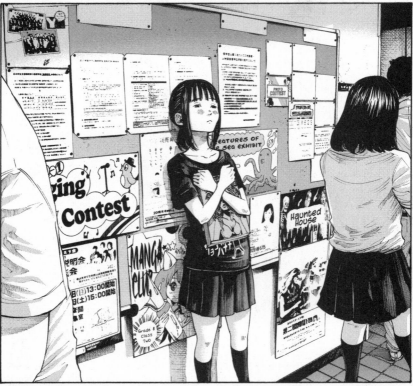

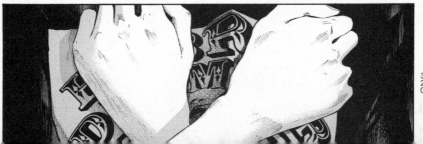

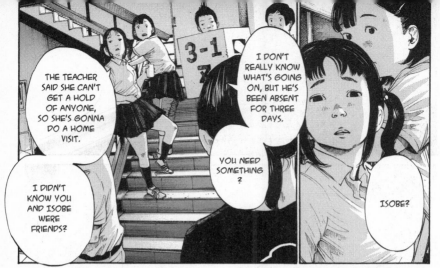

THE TEACHER SAID SHE CAN'T GET A HOLD OF ANYONE, SO SHE'S GONNA DO A HOME VISIT.

I DON'T REALLY KNOW WHAT'S GOING ON, BUT HE'S BEEN ABSENT FOR THREE DAYS.

YOU NEED SOMETHING?

ISOBE?

I DIDN'T KNOW YOU AND ISOBE WERE FRIENDS?

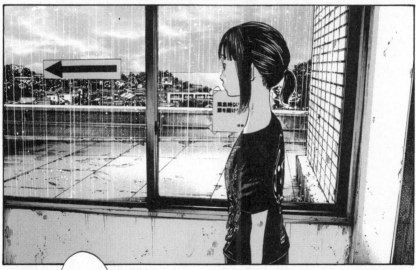

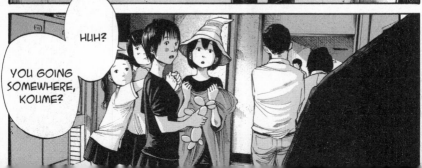

HUH?

YOU GOING SOMEWHERE, KOUME?

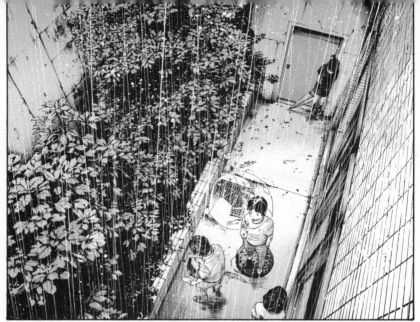

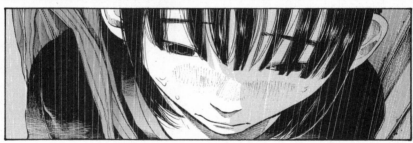

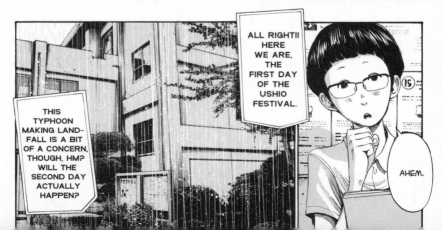

ALL RIGHT!! HERE WE ARE, THE FIRST DAY OF THE USHIO FESTIVAL.

THIS TYPHOON MAKING LANDFALL IS A BIT OF A CONCERN, THOUGH, HM? WILL THE SECOND DAY ACTUALLY HAPPEN?

AHEM.

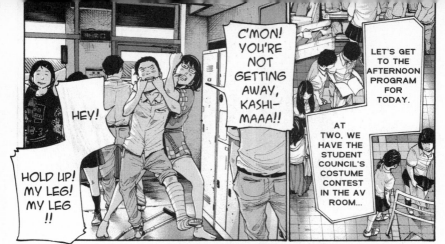

C'MON! YOU'RE NOT GETTING AWAY, KASHI-MAAA!!

HEY!

HOLD UP! MY LEG! MY LEG !!

LET'S GET TO THE AFTERNOON PROGRAM FOR TODAY.

AT TWO, WE HAVE THE STUDENT COUNCIL'S COSTUME CONTEST IN THE AV ROOM...

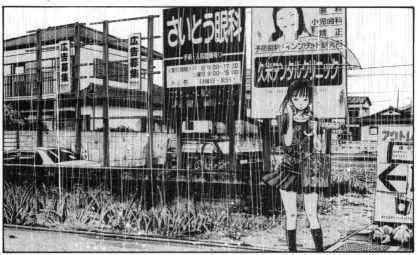

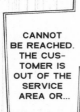

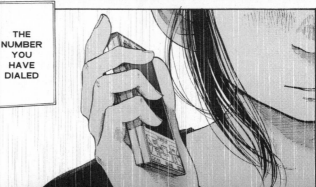

THE NUMBER YOU HAVE DIALED

CANNOT BE REACHED. THE CUS-TOMER IS OUT OF THE SERVICE AREA OR...

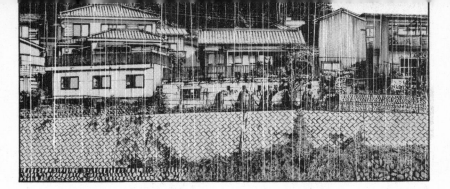

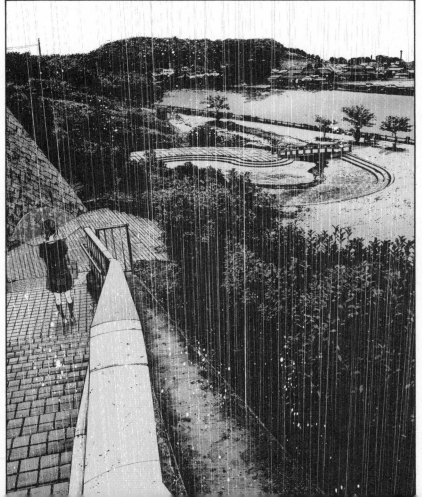

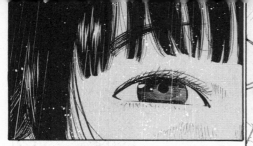

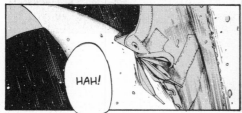

HAH!

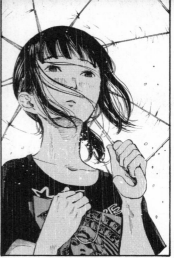

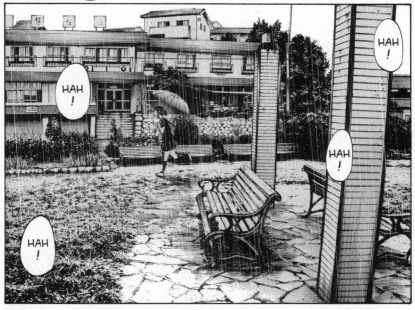

HAH
!

HAH
!

HAH
!

HAH
!

HAH
!

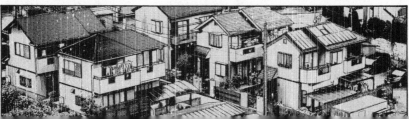

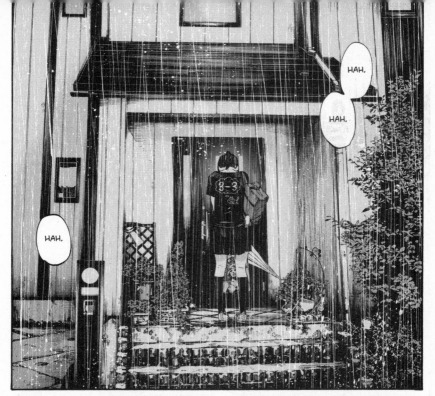

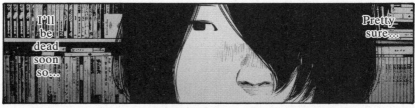

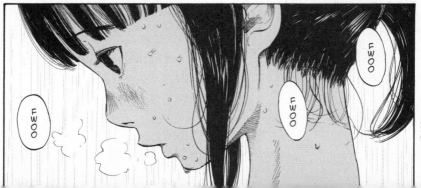

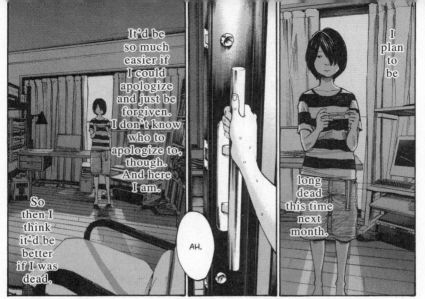

It'd be so much easier if I could apologize and just be forgiven. I don't know who to apologize to, though. And here I am.

So then I think it'd be better if I was dead.

AH.

I plan to be

long dead this time next month.

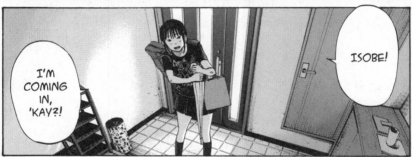

I'M COMING IN, 'KAY?!

ISOBE!

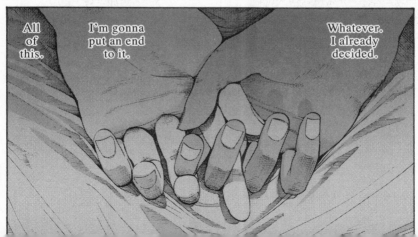

All of this.

I'm gonna put an end to it.

Whatever. I already decided.

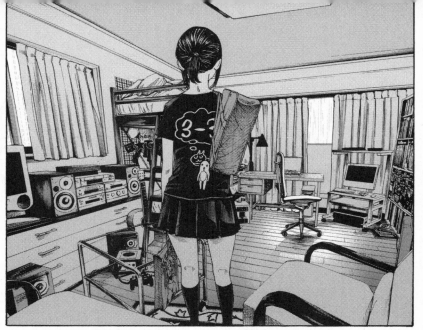

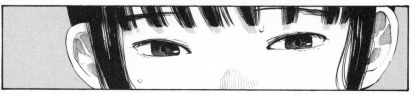

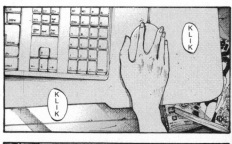

KLIK

KLIK

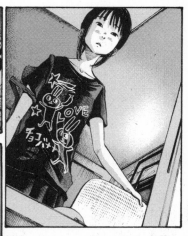

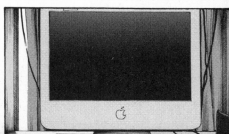

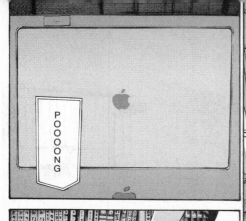
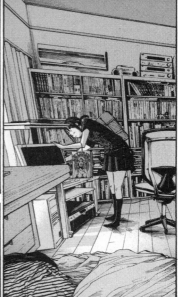
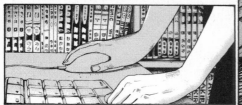
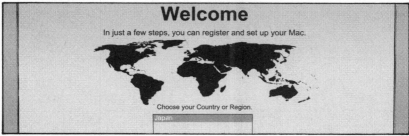
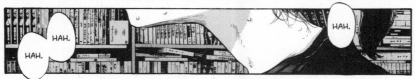
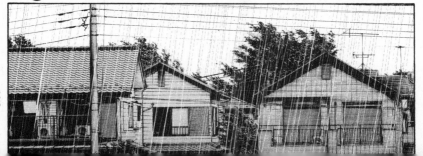

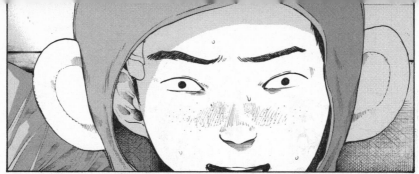

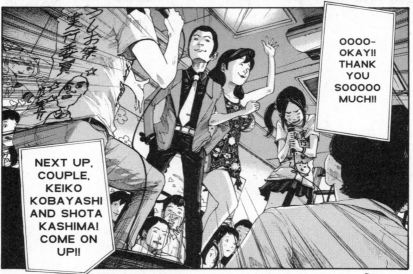

OOOO-OKAY!! THANK YOU SOOOOO MUCH!!

NEXT UP, COUPLE, KEIKO KOBAYASHI AND SHOTA KASHIMA! COME ON UP!!

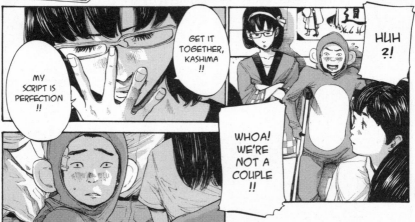

MY SCRIPT IS PERFECTION!!

GET IT TOGETHER, KASHIMA!!

HUH?!

WHOA! WE'RE NOT A COUPLE!!

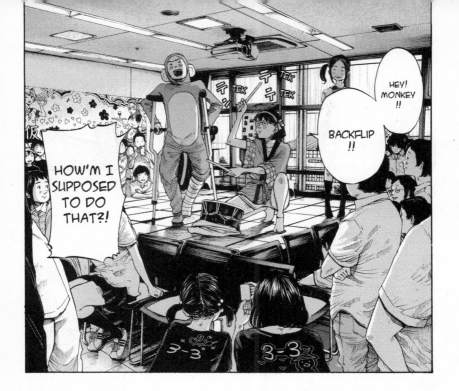

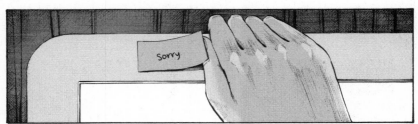

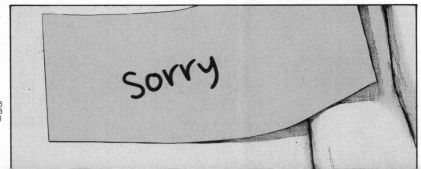

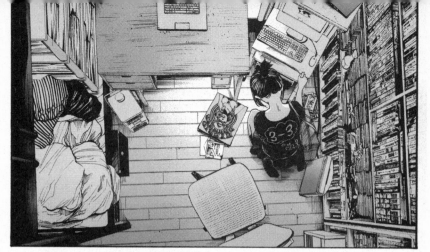

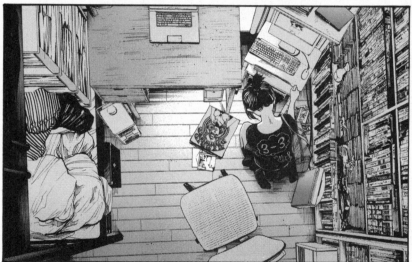

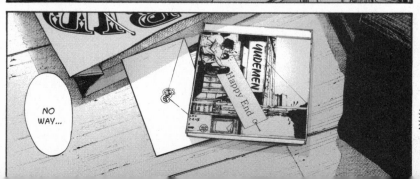

NO
WAY...

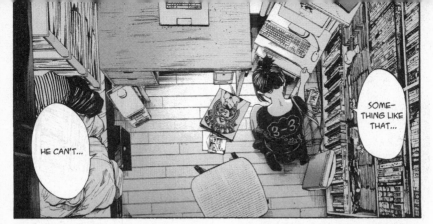

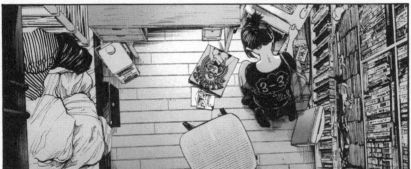

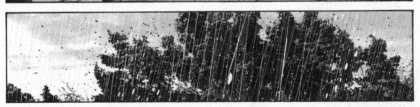

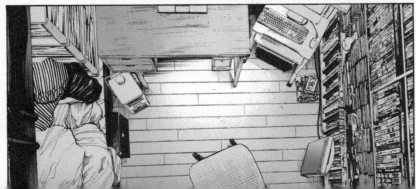

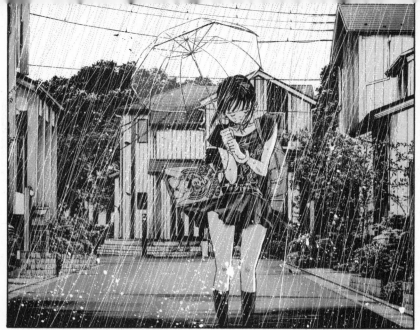

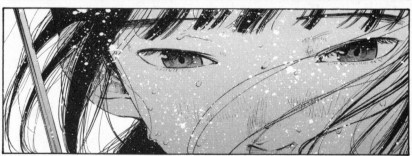

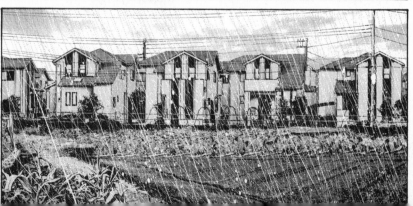

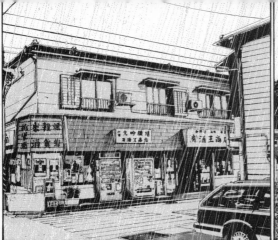

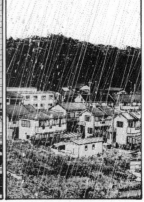

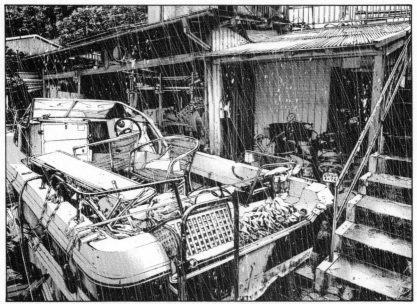

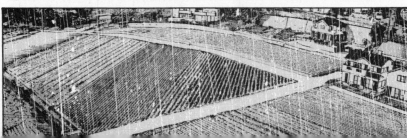

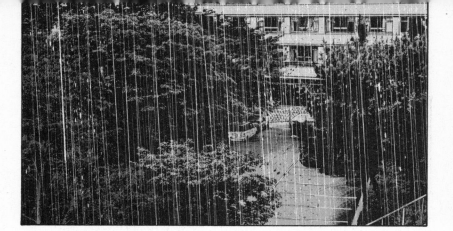

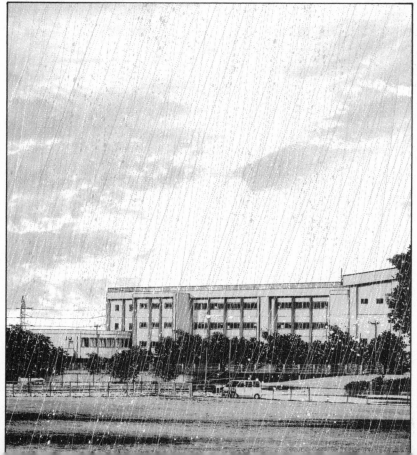

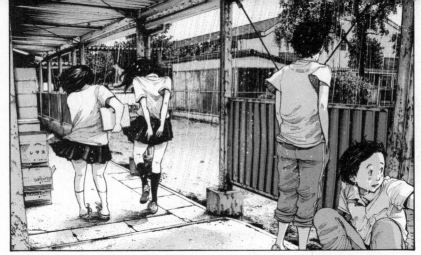

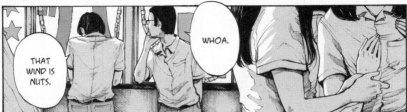

THAT WIND IS NUTS.

WHOA.

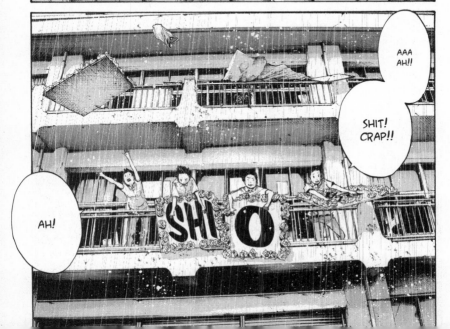

AAA AH!!

SHIT! CRAP!!

AH!

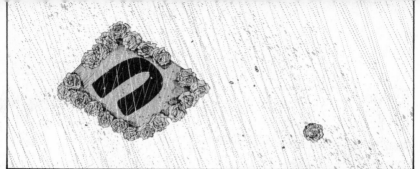

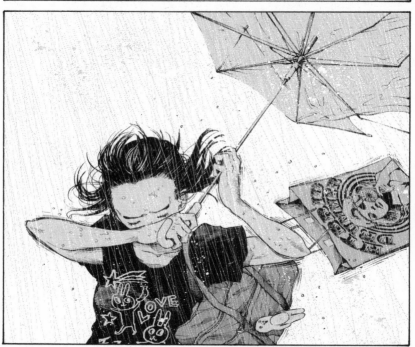

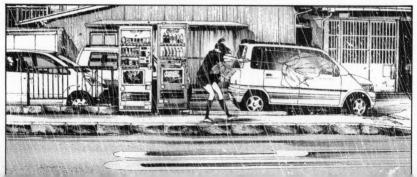

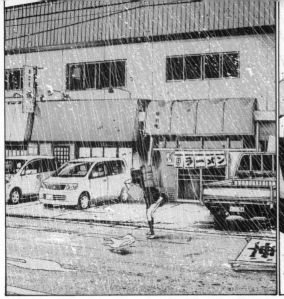

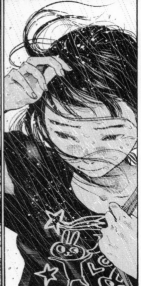

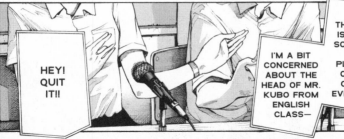

HEY! QUIT IT!!

I'M A BIT CONCERNED ABOUT THE HEAD OF MR. KUBO FROM ENGLISH CLASS—

WOW. THAT WIND IS REALLY SOMETHING, HUH? PLEASE BE CAREFUL OUTSIDE, EVERYBODY.

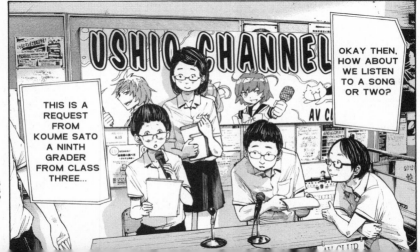

THIS IS A REQUEST FROM KOUME SATO A NINTH GRADER FROM CLASS THREE...

OKAY THEN, HOW ABOUT WE LISTEN TO A SONG OR TWO?

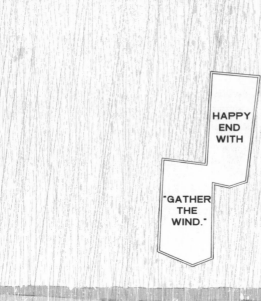

HAPPY
END
WITH

"GATHER
THE
WIND."

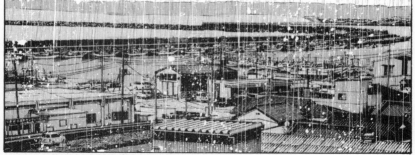

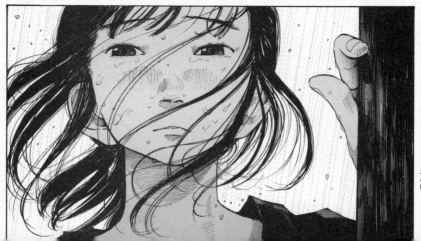

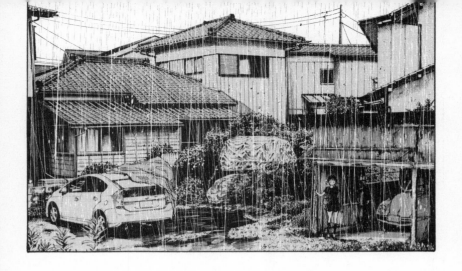

Walking down a road stretching out on the outskirts of town...

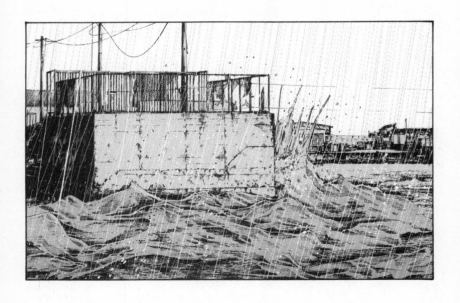

...beyond the stained early morning haze...

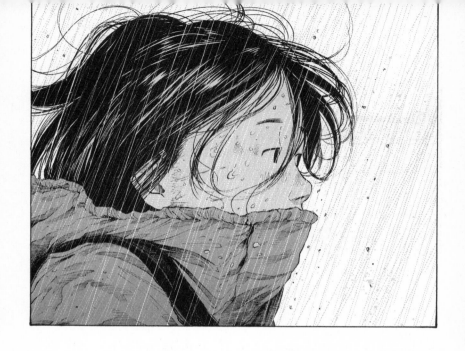

...I saw a streetcar rising from sleep to cross the ocean.

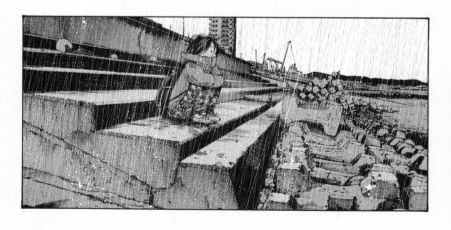

And I wanted to gather up the wind, gather up the wind...

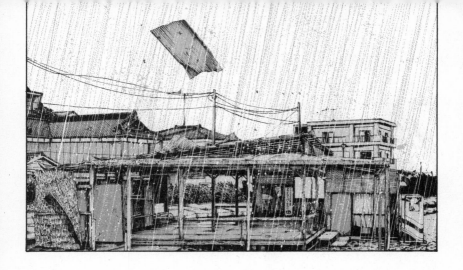

...and race through the blue sky, the clear, blue sky.

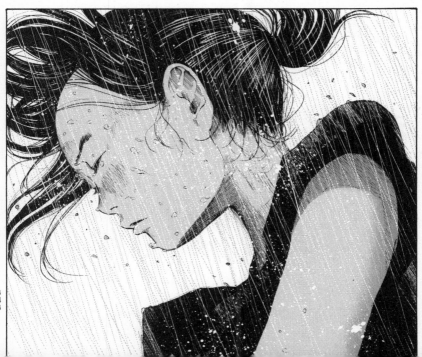

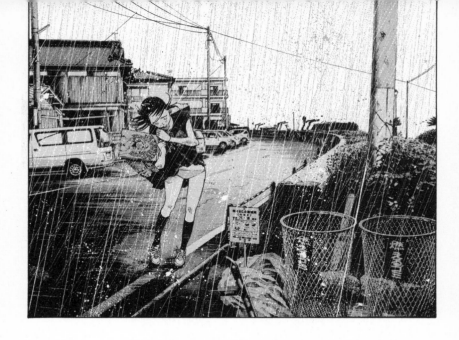

Passing through a spectacular sunrise...

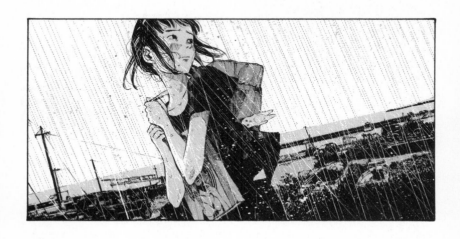

...beyond the deserted breakwater...

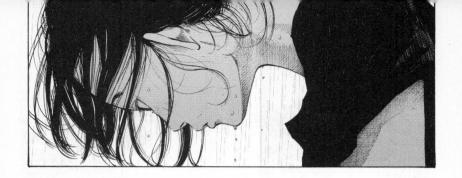

I saw a city crimson sails raised, anchored at port...

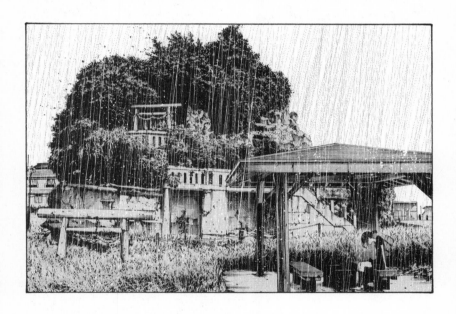

And I wanted to gather up the wind, gather up the wind...

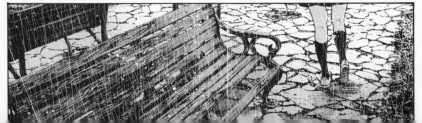

...and race through the blue sky, the clear, blue sky.

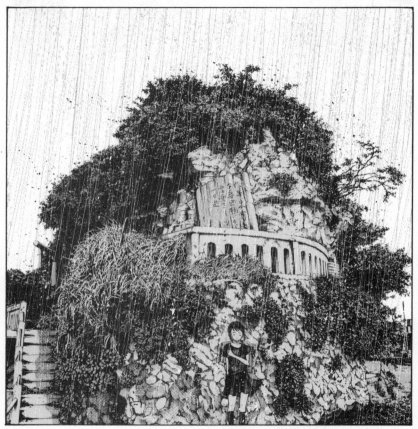

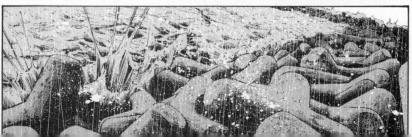

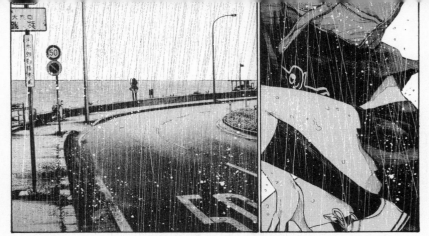

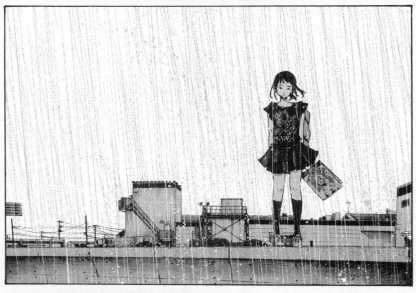

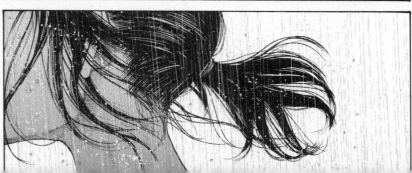

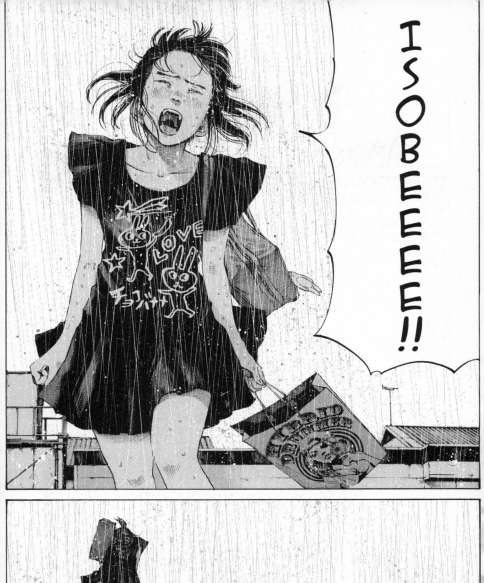

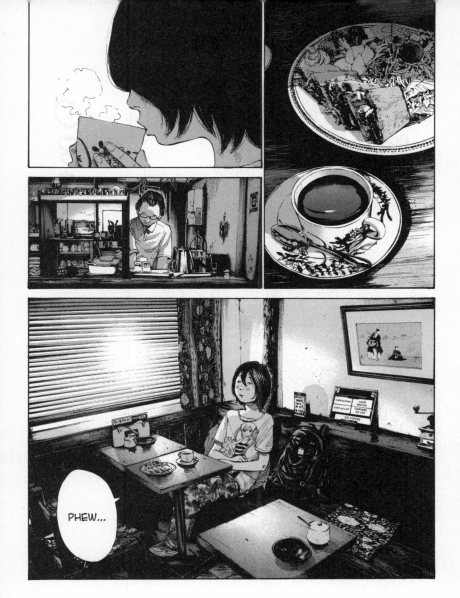

Killing time in a quiet coffee shop in the morning...

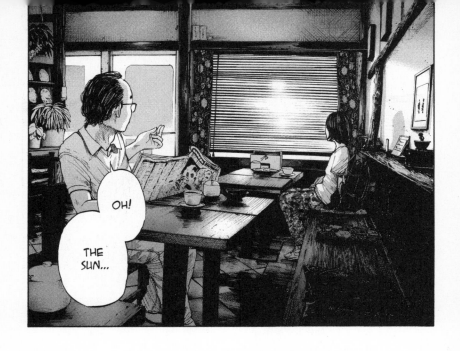

...beyond the cracked glass...

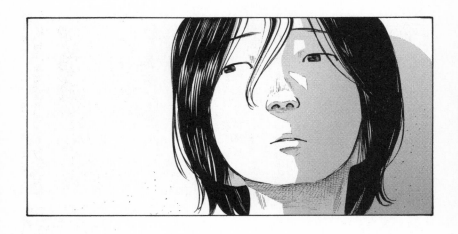

...I saw the rustling skyscrapers' silks dip onto the pavement.

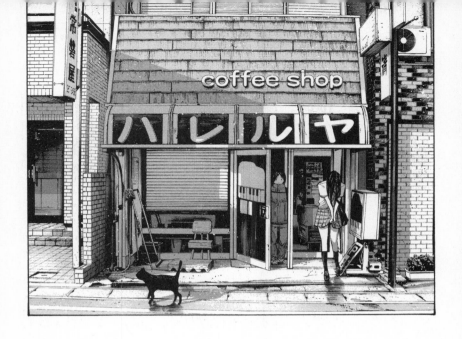

And I wanted to gather up the wind, gather up the wind...

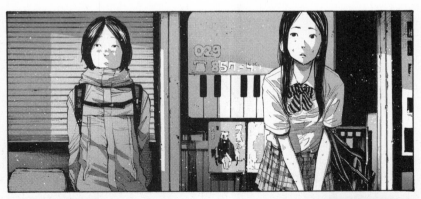

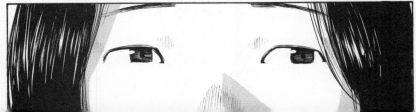

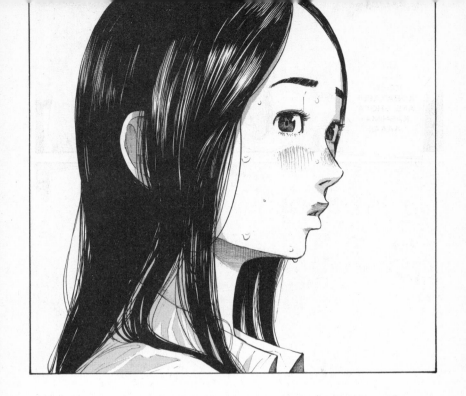

...and race through the blue sky, the clear, blue sky.

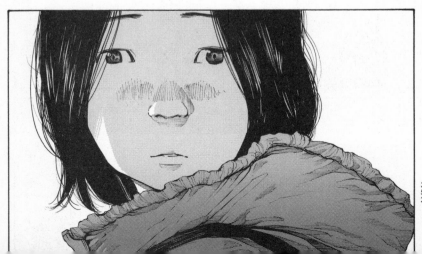

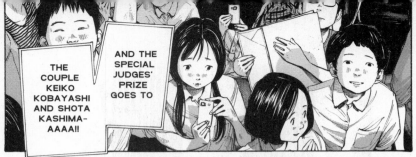

THE COUPLE KEIKO KOBAYASHI AND SHOTA KASHIMA-AAAA!!

AND THE SPECIAL JUDGES' PRIZE GOES TO

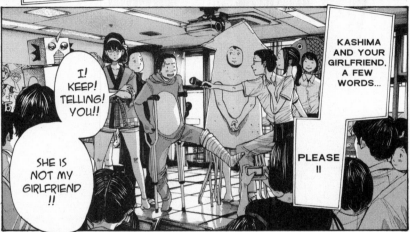

I! KEEP! TELLING! YOU!!

SHE IS NOT MY GIRLFRIEND!!

KASHIMA AND YOUR GIRLFRIEND, A FEW WORDS...

PLEASE!!

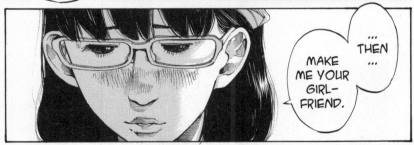

...THEN...

MAKE ME YOUR GIRL-FRIEND.

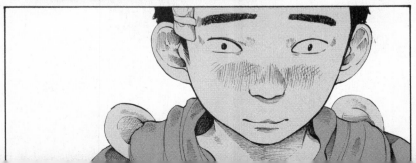

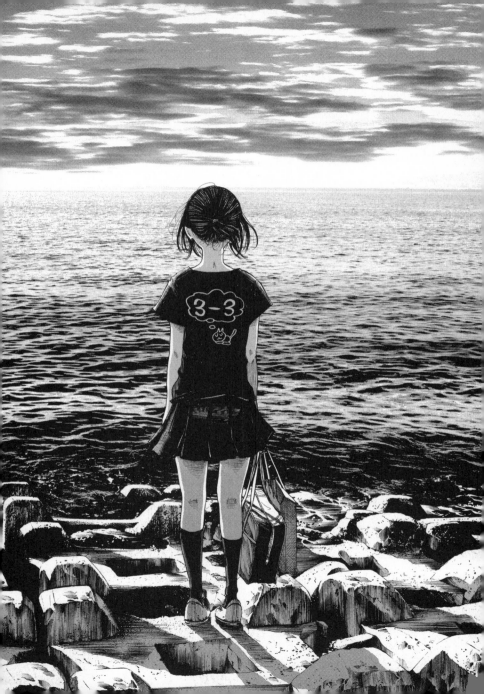

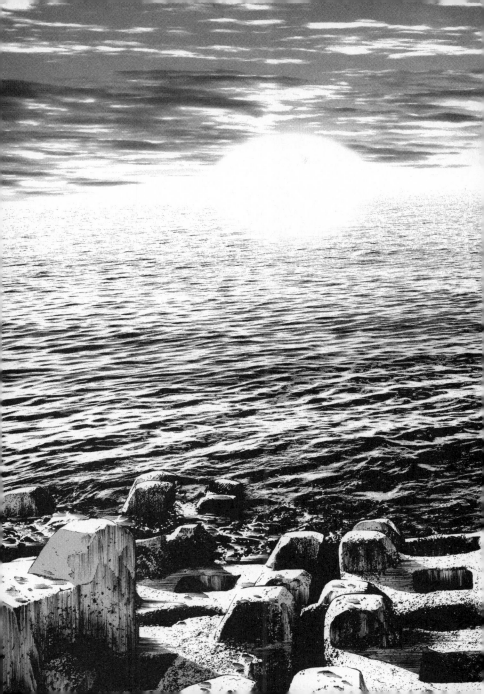

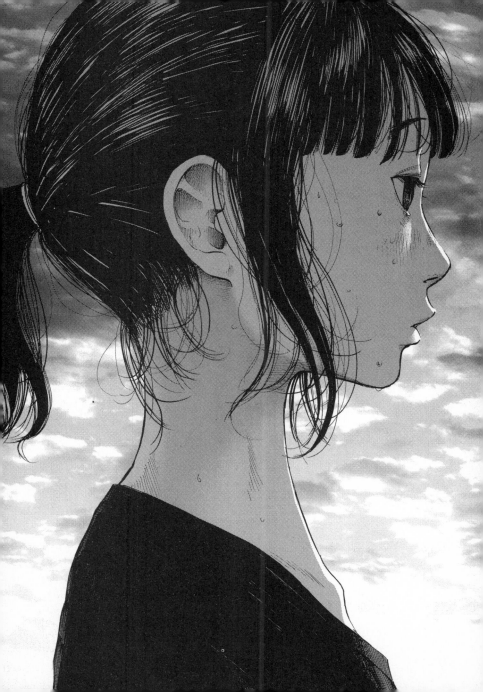

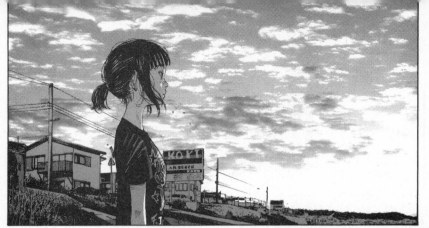

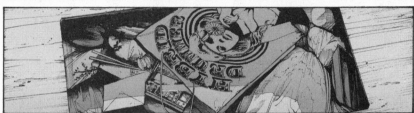

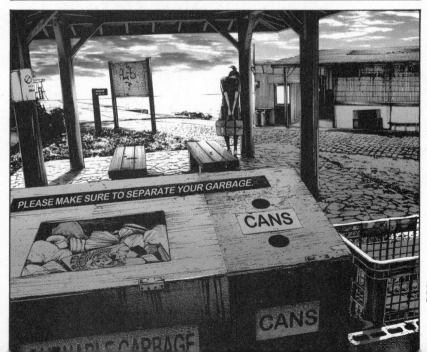

PLEASE MAKE SURE TO SEPARATE YOUR GARBAGE.

CANS

CANS

HEY GUYS! LISTEN TO THIS!!

YESTERDAY, KEIKO AND KASHIMA K—

RIIIIIIIGHT ?!

YOU BIG BLABBER MOUTH! YOU GOT IT ALL WRONG !!

C'MON, KEIKO. IT'S STILL ONLY BEEN A WEEK. THAT'S TOO FAST!

I KNOW IT'S THE FIRST DAY OF CRAM SCHOOL AND ALL, BUT YOU'RE A LITTLE TOO DOWN, KOUME?

C'MON !!

LET'S GO, KOUME !

I'M NOT ACTUALLY...

OH.

SURE.

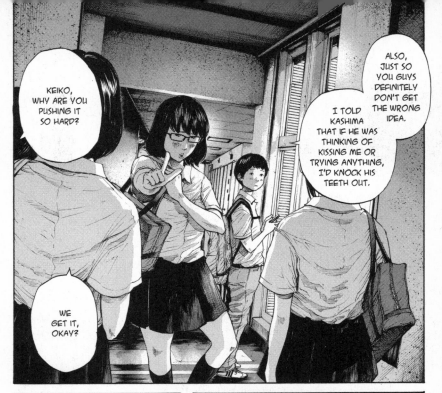

KEIKO, WHY ARE YOU PUSHING IT SO HARD?

I TOLD KASHIMA THAT IF HE WAS THINKING OF KISSING ME OR TRYING ANYTHING, I'D KNOCK HIS TEETH OUT.

ALSO, JUST SO YOU GUYS DEFINITELY DON'T GET THE WRONG IDEA.

WE GET IT, OKAY?

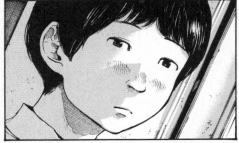

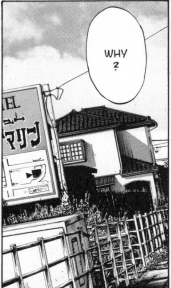

WHY?

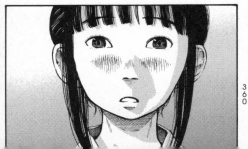

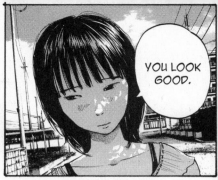

YOU LOOK GOOD.

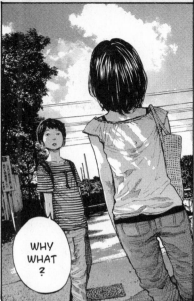

WHY WHAT?

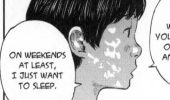

WHAT'D YOU CALL ME OUT FOR ANYWAY?

ON WEEKENDS AT LEAST, I JUST WANT TO SLEEP.

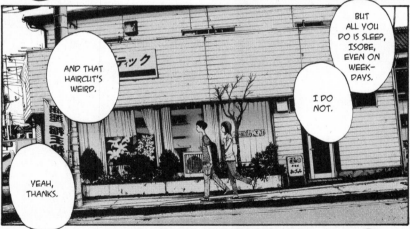

AND THAT HAIRCUT'S WEIRD.

BUT ALL YOU DO IS SLEEP, ISOBE, EVEN ON WEEKDAYS.

I DO NOT.

YEAH, THANKS.

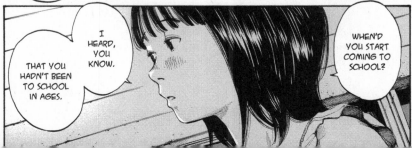

THAT YOU HADN'T BEEN TO SCHOOL IN AGES.

I HEARD, YOU KNOW.

WHEN'D YOU START COMING TO SCHOOL?

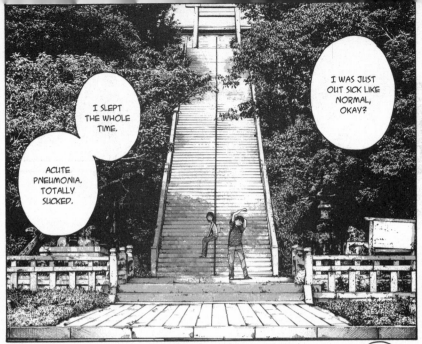

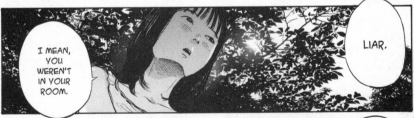

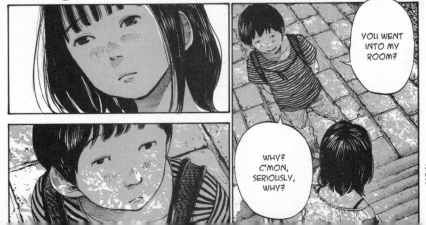

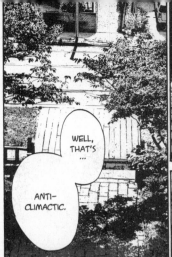
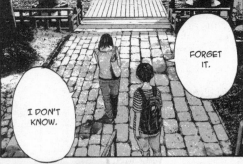
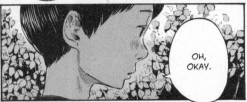
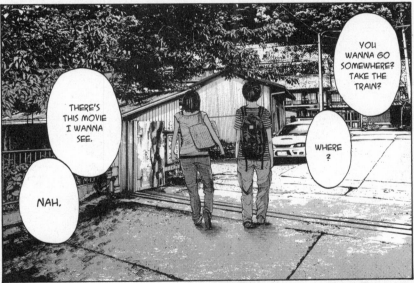
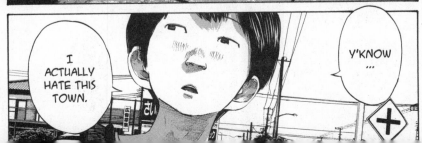

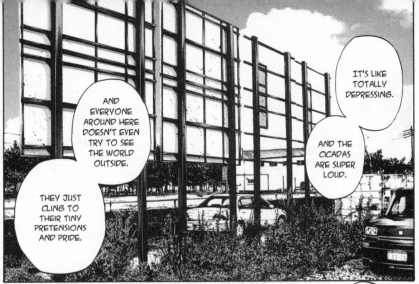

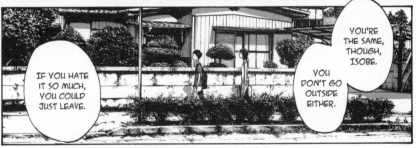

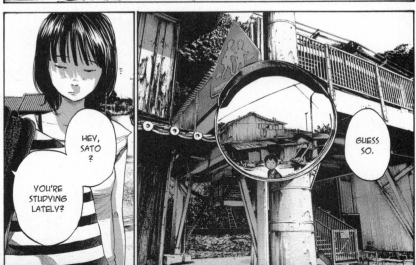

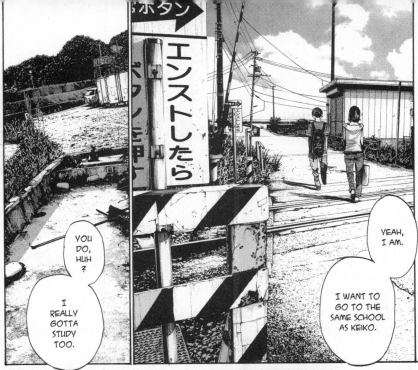

YOU DO, HUH?

I REALLY GOTTA STUDY TOO.

YEAH, I AM.

I WANT TO GO TO THE SAME SCHOOL AS KEIKO.

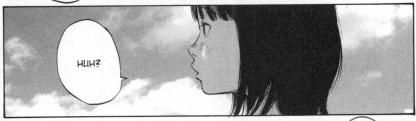

HUH?

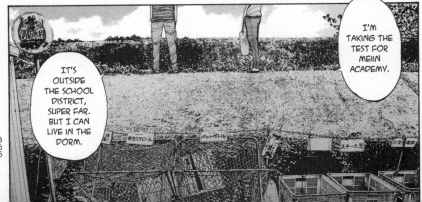

I'M TAKING THE TEST FOR MEIIN ACADEMY.

IT'S OUTSIDE THE SCHOOL DISTRICT, SUPER FAR, BUT I CAN LIVE IN THE DORM.

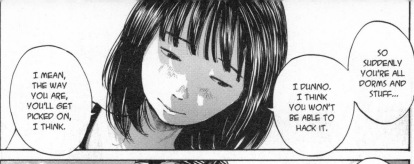

I MEAN, THE WAY YOU ARE, YOU'LL GET PICKED ON, I THINK.

I DUNNO. I THINK YOU WON'T BE ABLE TO HACK IT.

SO SUDDENLY YOU'RE ALL DORMS AND STUFF...

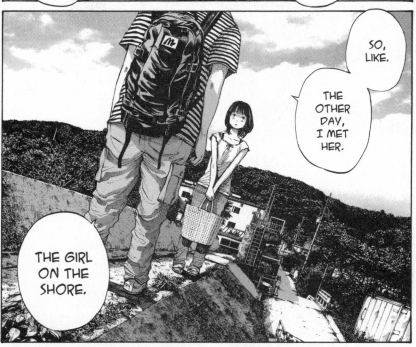

SO, LIKE.

THE OTHER DAY, I MET HER.

THE GIRL ON THE SHORE.

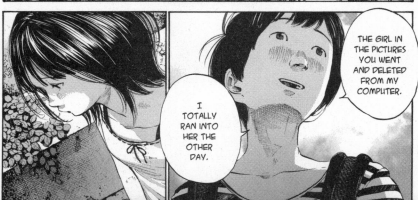

THE GIRL IN THE PICTURES YOU WENT AND DELETED FROM MY COMPUTER.

I TOTALLY RAN INTO HER THE OTHER DAY.

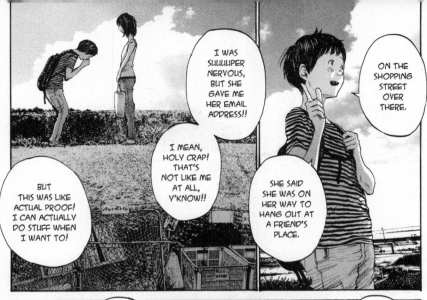

I WAS SUUUUPER NERVOUS, BUT SHE GAVE ME HER EMAIL ADDRESS!!

ON THE SHOPPING STREET OVER THERE.

I MEAN, HOLY CRAP! THAT'S NOT LIKE ME AT ALL, Y'KNOW!!

BUT THIS WAS LIKE ACTUAL PROOF! I CAN ACTUALLY DO STUFF WHEN I WANT TO!

SHE SAID SHE WAS ON HER WAY TO HANG OUT AT A FRIEND'S PLACE.

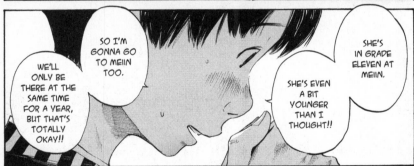

SO I'M GONNA GO TO MEIIN TOO.

WE'LL ONLY BE THERE AT THE SAME TIME FOR A YEAR, BUT THAT'S TOTALLY OKAY!!

SHE'S IN GRADE ELEVEN AT MEIIN,

SHE'S EVEN A BIT YOUNGER THAN I THOUGHT!!

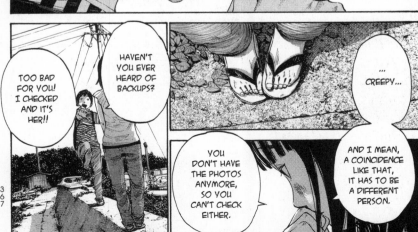

TOO BAD FOR YOU! I CHECKED AND IT'S HER!!

HAVEN'T YOU EVER HEARD OF BACKUPS?

...CREEPY...

YOU DON'T HAVE THE PHOTOS ANYMORE, SO YOU CAN'T CHECK EITHER.

AND I MEAN, A COINCIDENCE LIKE THAT, IT HAS TO BE A DIFFERENT PERSON.

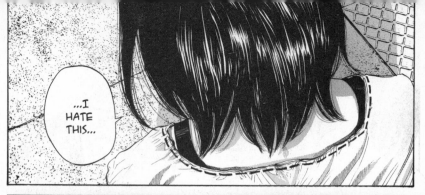

...I HATE THIS...

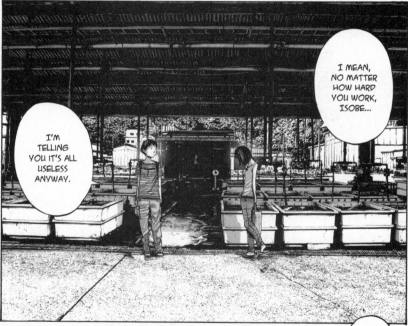

I MEAN, NO MATTER HOW HARD YOU WORK, ISOBE...

I'M TELLING YOU IT'S ALL USELESS ANYWAY.

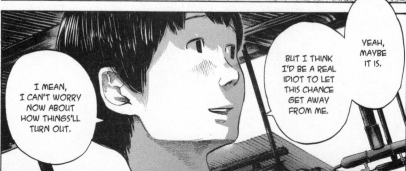

YEAH, MAYBE IT IS.

BUT I THINK I'D BE A REAL IDIOT TO LET THIS CHANCE GET AWAY FROM ME.

I MEAN, I CAN'T WORRY NOW ABOUT HOW THINGS'LL TURN OUT.

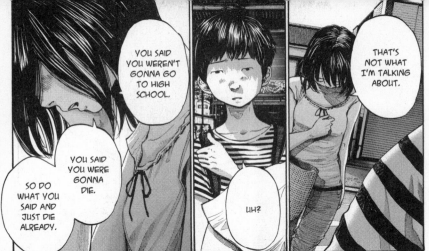

YOU SAID YOU WEREN'T GONNA GO TO HIGH SCHOOL.

THAT'S NOT WHAT I'M TALKING ABOUT.

YOU SAID YOU WERE GONNA DIE.

SO DO WHAT YOU SAID AND JUST DIE ALREADY.

UH?

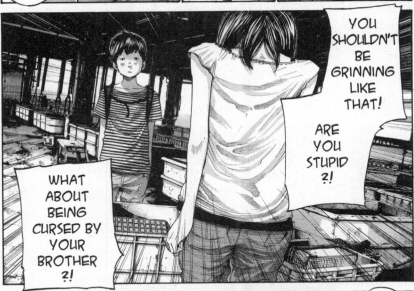

YOU SHOULDN'T BE GRINNING LIKE THAT!

ARE YOU STUPID ?!

WHAT ABOUT BEING CURSED BY YOUR BROTHER ?!

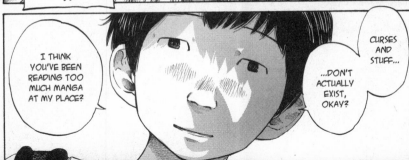

I THINK YOU'VE BEEN READING TOO MUCH MANGA AT MY PLACE?

CURSES AND STUFF...

...DON'T ACTUALLY EXIST, OKAY?

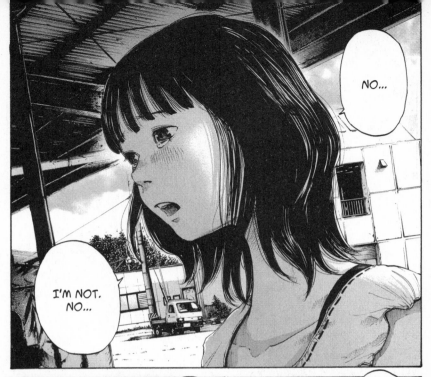

NO...

I'M NOT.
NO...

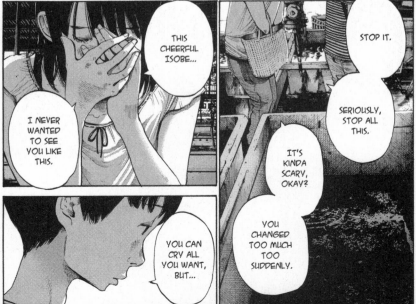

THIS
CHEERFUL
ISOBE...

I NEVER
WANTED
TO SEE
YOU LIKE
THIS.

YOU CAN
CRY ALL
YOU WANT,
BUT...

STOP IT.

SERIOUSLY,
STOP ALL
THIS.

IT'S
KINDA
SCARY,
OKAY?

YOU
CHANGED
TOO MUCH
TOO
SUDDENLY.

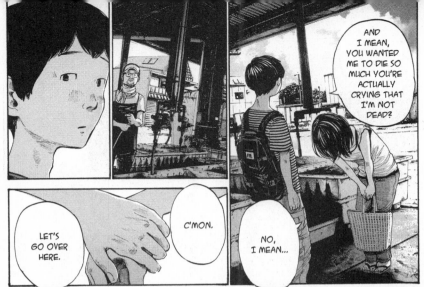

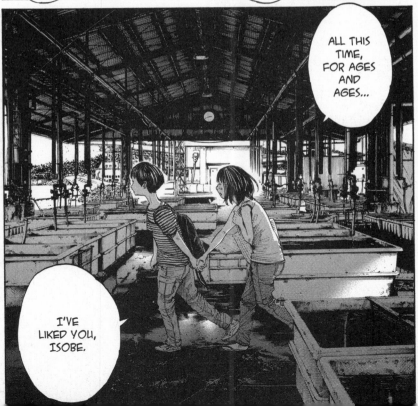

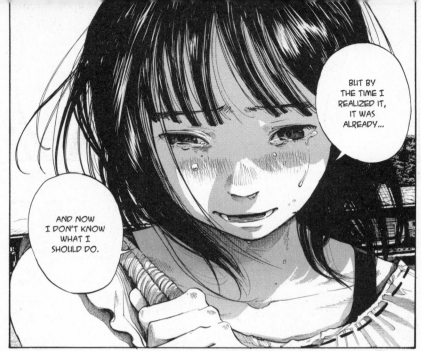

BUT BY THE TIME I REALIZED IT, IT WAS ALREADY...

AND NOW I DON'T KNOW WHAT I SHOULD DO.

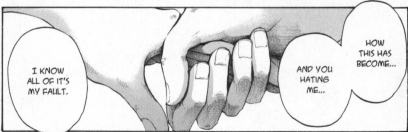

HOW THIS HAS BECOME...

AND YOU HATING ME...

I KNOW ALL OF IT'S MY FAULT.

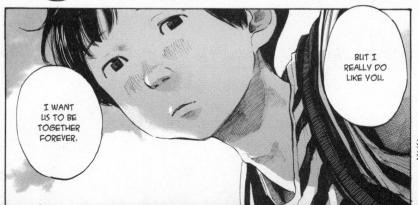

BUT I REALLY DO LIKE YOU.

I WANT US TO BE TOGETHER FOREVER.

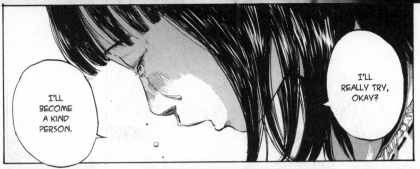

I'LL BECOME A KIND PERSON.

I'LL REALLY TRY, OKAY?

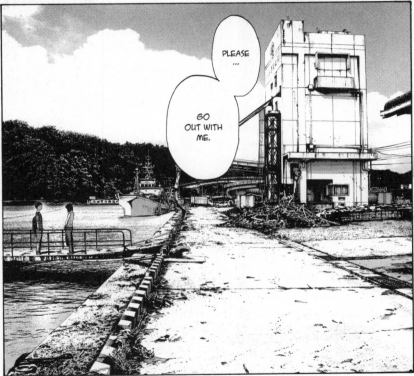

PLEASE ...

GO OUT WITH ME.

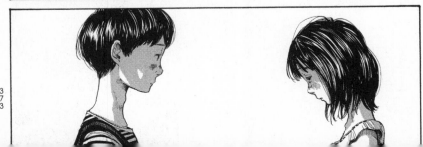

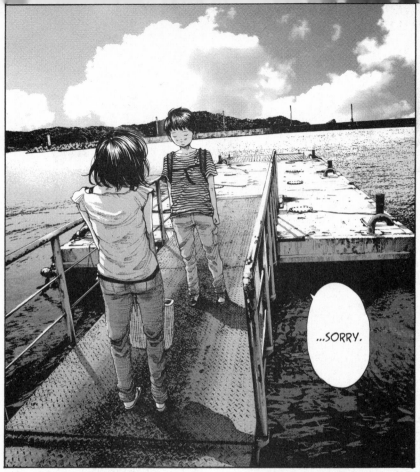

...SORRY.

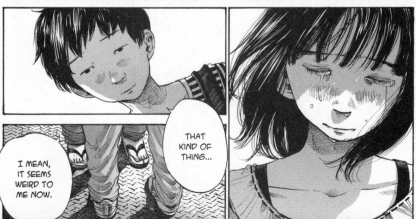

I MEAN, IT SEEMS WEIRD TO ME NOW.

THAT KIND OF THING...

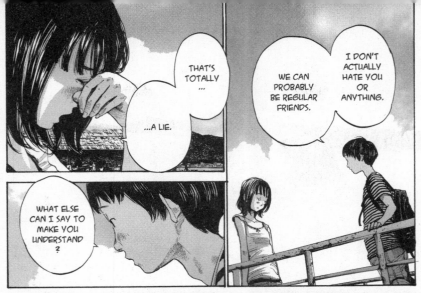

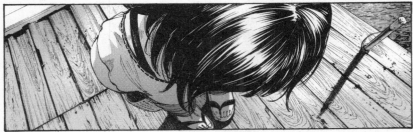

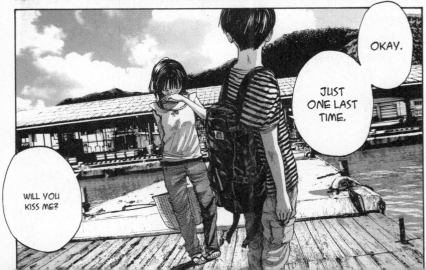

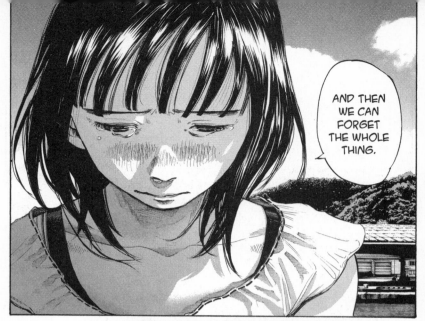

AND THEN WE CAN FORGET THE WHOLE THING.

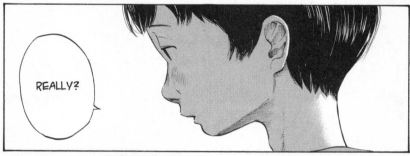

REALLY?

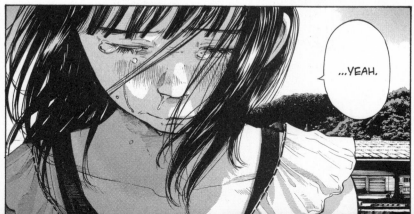

...YEAH.

376

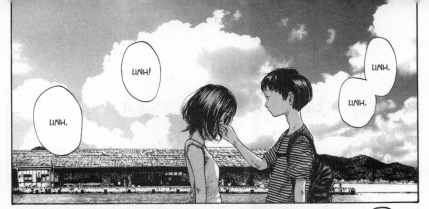

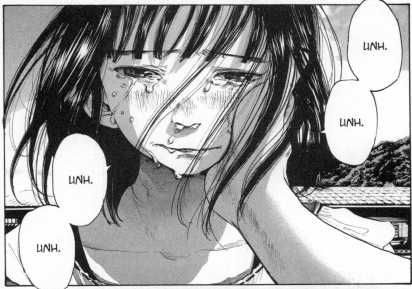

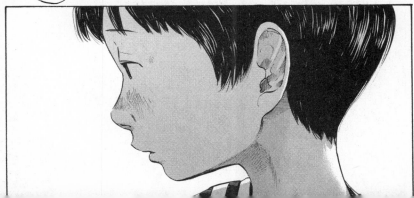

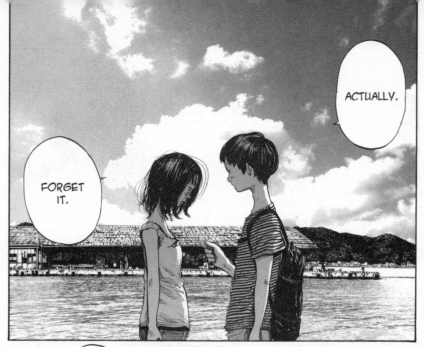

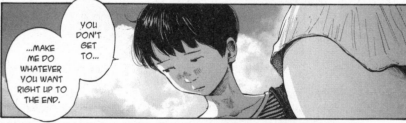

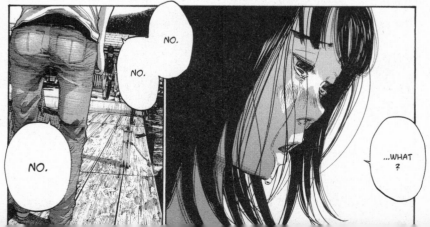

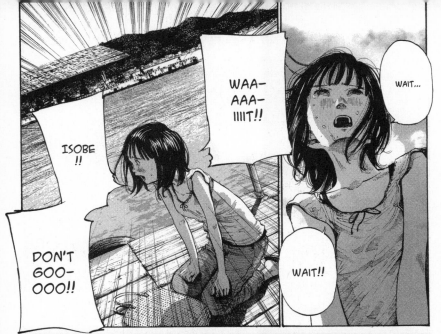

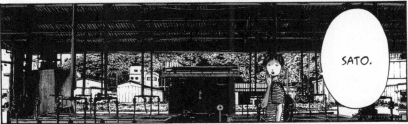

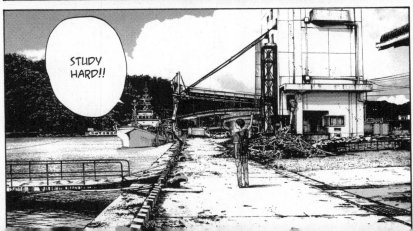

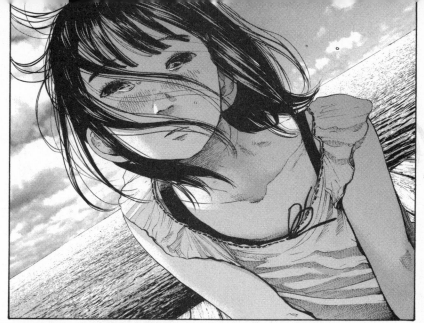

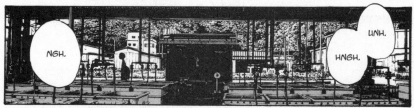

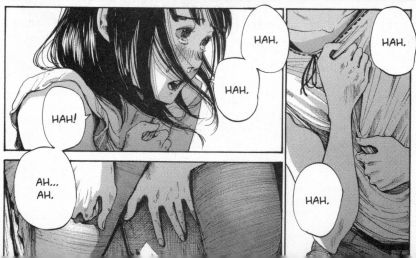

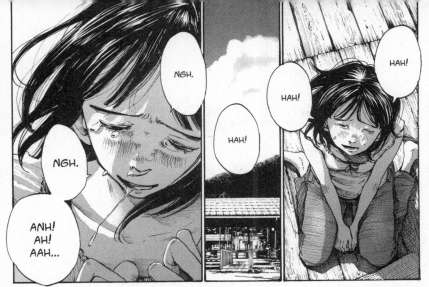

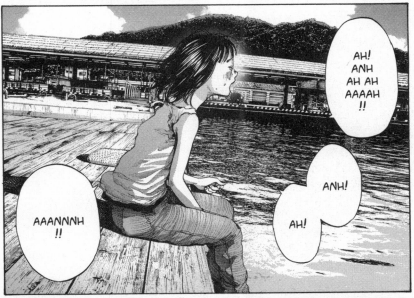

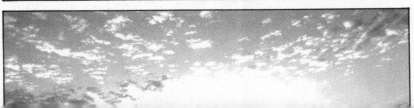

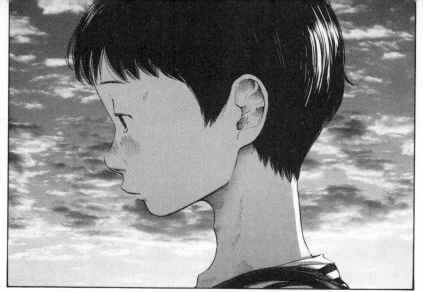
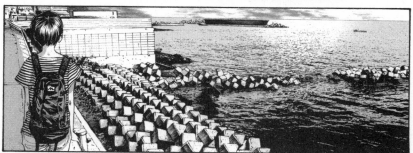
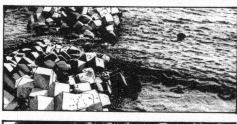
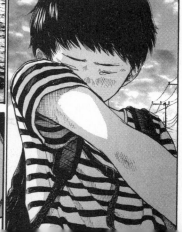
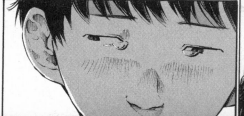

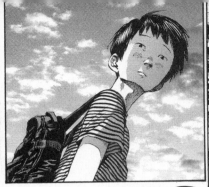

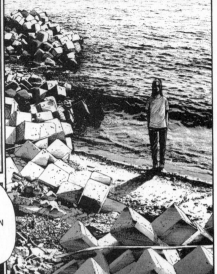

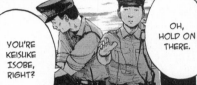

YOU'RE KEISUKE ISOBE, RIGHT?

OH, HOLD ON THERE.

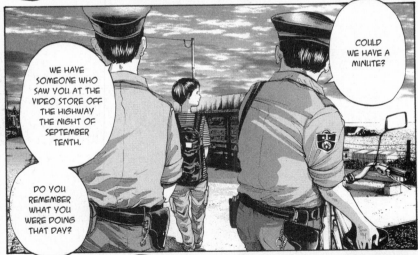

WE HAVE SOMEONE WHO SAW YOU AT THE VIDEO STORE OFF THE HIGHWAY THE NIGHT OF SEPTEMBER TENTH.

DO YOU REMEMBER WHAT YOU WERE DOING THAT DAY?

COULD WE HAVE A MINUTE?

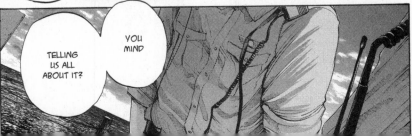

TELLING US ALL ABOUT IT?

YOU MIND

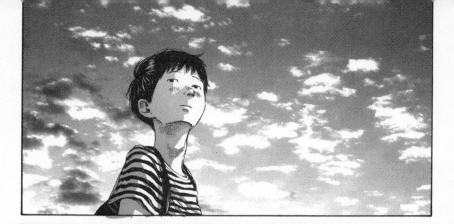

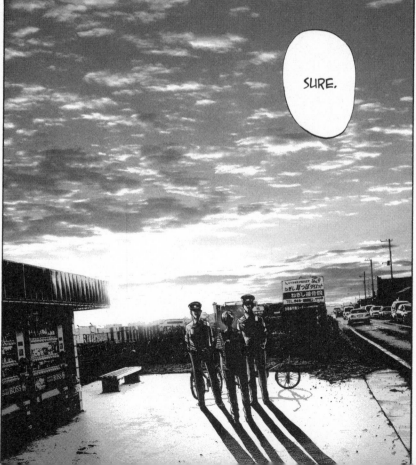

SURE.

A

Girl

on the

Shore

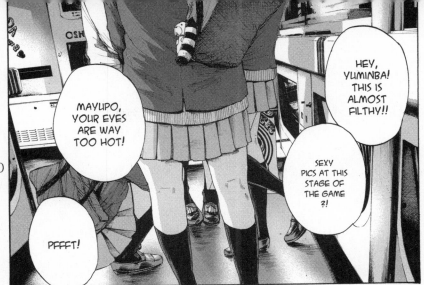

HEY, YUMINBA! THIS IS ALMOST FILTHY!!

MAYUPO, YOUR EYES ARE WAY TOO HOT!

SEXY PICS AT THIS STAGE OF THE GAME ?!

PFFFT!

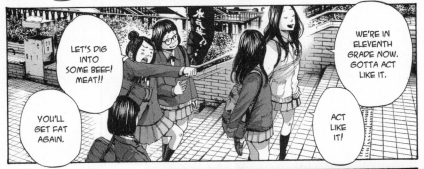

LET'S DIG INTO SOME BEEF! MEAT!!

WE'RE IN ELEVENTH GRADE NOW. GOTTA ACT LIKE IT.

YOU'LL GET FAT AGAIN.

ACT LIKE IT!

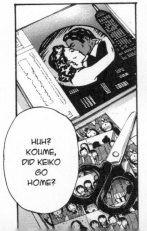

HUH? KOUME, DID KEIKO GO HOME?

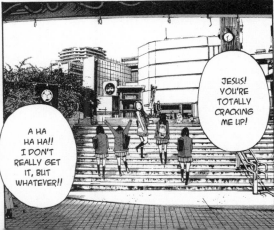

JESUS! YOU'RE TOTALLY CRACKING ME UP!

A HA HA HA!! I DON'T REALLY GET IT, BUT WHATEVER!!

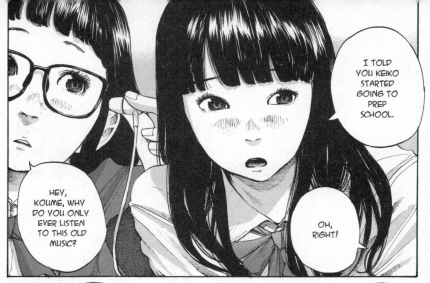

HEY, KOUME, WHY DO YOU ONLY EVER LISTEN TO THIS OLD MUSIC?

I TOLD YOU KEIKO STARTED GOING TO PREP SCHOOL.

OH, RIGHT!

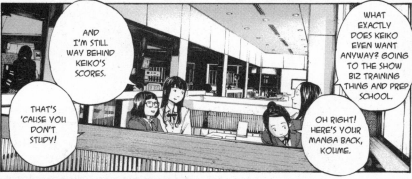

AND I'M STILL WAY BEHIND KEIKO'S SCORES.

THAT'S 'CAUSE YOU DON'T STUDY!

WHAT EXACTLY DOES KEIKO EVEN WANT ANYWAY? GOING TO THE SHOW BIZ TRAINING THING AND PREP SCHOOL.

OH RIGHT! HERE'S YOUR MANGA BACK, KOUME.

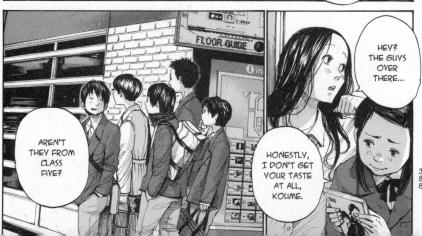

AREN'T THEY FROM CLASS FIVE?

HEY? THE GUYS OVER THERE...

HONESTLY, I DON'T GET YOUR TASTE AT ALL, KOUME.

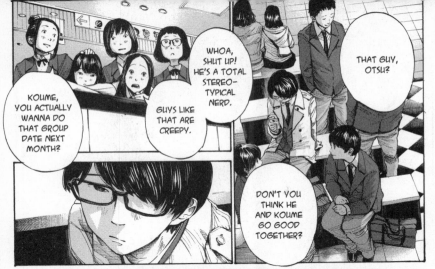

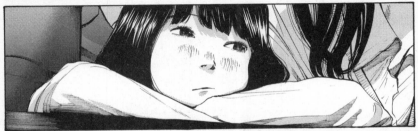

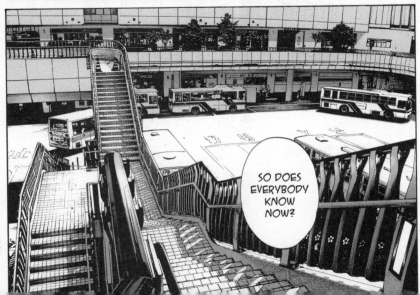

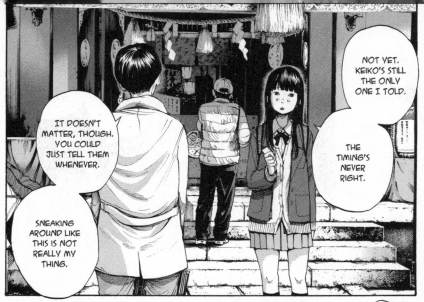

IT DOESN'T MATTER, THOUGH. YOU COULD JUST TELL THEM WHENEVER.

SNEAKING AROUND LIKE THIS IS NOT REALLY MY THING.

NOT YET. KEIKO'S STILL THE ONLY ONE I TOLD.

THE TIMING'S NEVER RIGHT.

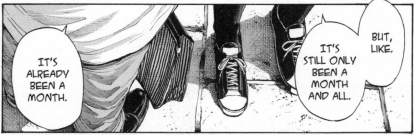

IT'S ALREADY BEEN A MONTH.

IT'S STILL ONLY BEEN A MONTH AND ALL.

BUT, LIKE,

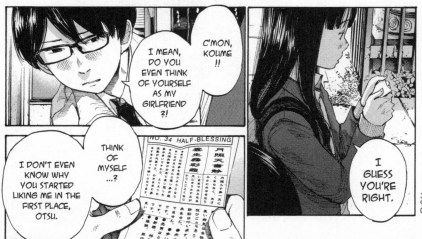

I MEAN, DO YOU EVEN THINK OF YOURSELF AS MY GIRLFRIEND?!

C'MON, KOUME!!

I DON'T EVEN KNOW WHY YOU STARTED LIKING ME IN THE FIRST PLACE, OTSU.

THINK OF MYSELF...?

NO. 34 HALF-BLESSING

I GUESS YOU'RE RIGHT.

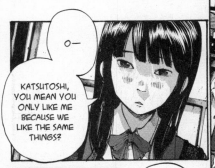

HAVING THINGS WE CAN TALK ABOUT LIKE THAT'S IMPORTANT, Y'KNOW?

YOU LIKE BANDS FROM THE SIXTIES AND SEVENTIES, YOU KNOW A LOT ABOUT MANGA.

O—

KATSUTOSHI, YOU MEAN YOU ONLY LIKE ME BECAUSE WE LIKE THE SAME THINGS?

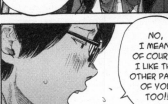

NO, I MEAN, OF COURSE, I LIKE THE OTHER PARTS OF YOU TOO!!

AND STOP CALLING ME OTSU.

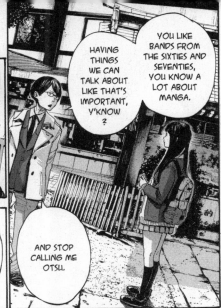

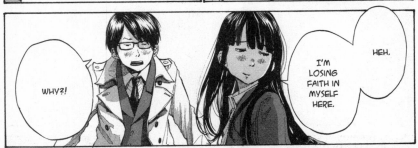

WHY?!

I'M LOSING FAITH IN MYSELF HERE.

HEH.

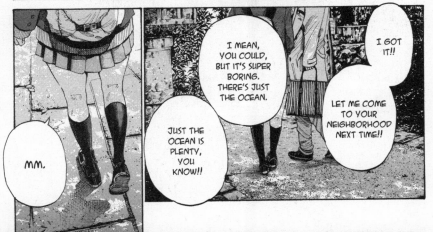

I MEAN, YOU COULD, BUT IT'S SUPER BORING. THERE'S JUST THE OCEAN.

I GOT IT!!

LET ME COME TO YOUR NEIGHBORHOOD NEXT TIME!!

JUST THE OCEAN IS PLENTY, YOU KNOW!!

MM.

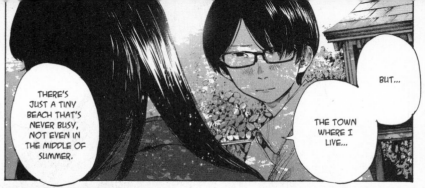
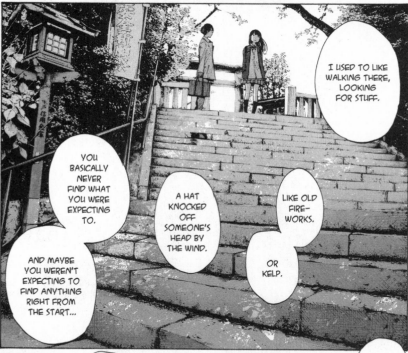
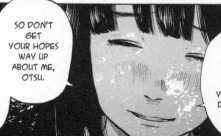

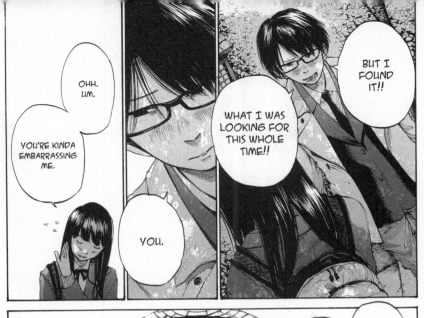

OHH, UM.

YOU'RE KINDA EMBARRASSING ME.

WHAT I WAS LOOKING FOR THIS WHOLE TIME!!

BUT I FOUND IT!!

YOU.

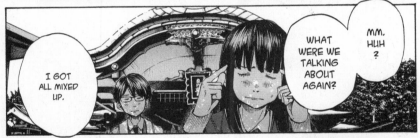

I GOT ALL MIXED UP.

WHAT WERE WE TALKING ABOUT AGAIN?

MM, HUH?

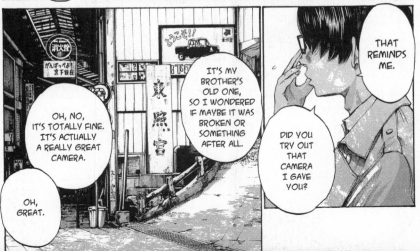

OH, NO, IT'S TOTALLY FINE. IT'S ACTUALLY A REALLY GREAT CAMERA.

IT'S MY BROTHER'S OLD ONE, SO I WONDERED IF MAYBE IT WAS BROKEN OR SOMETHING AFTER ALL.

DID YOU TRY OUT THAT CAMERA I GAVE YOU?

THAT REMINDS ME.

OH, GREAT.

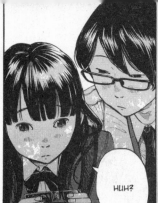
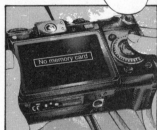
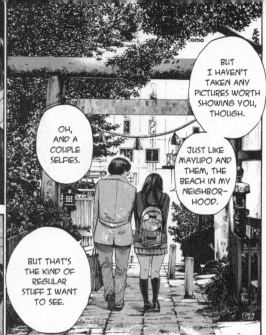
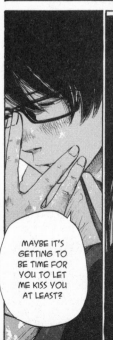
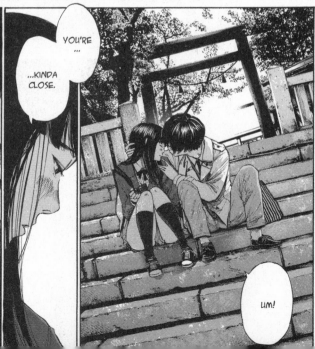

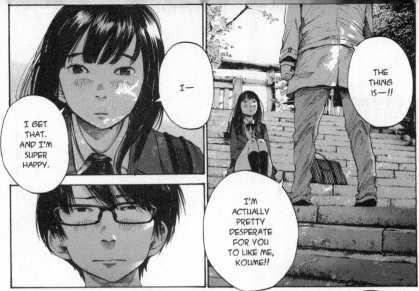

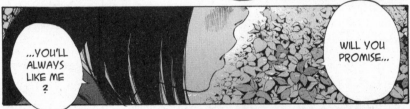

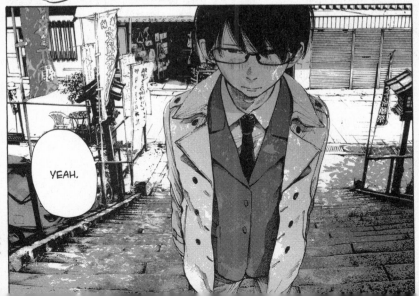

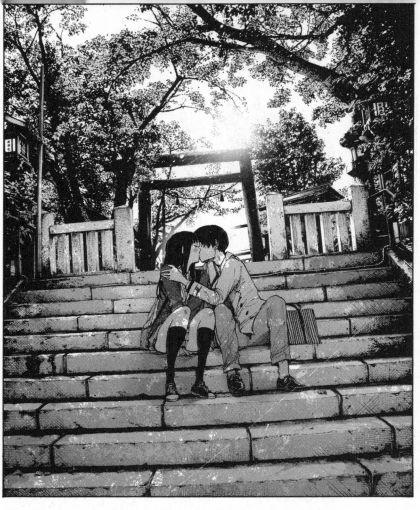

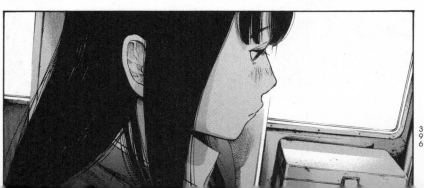

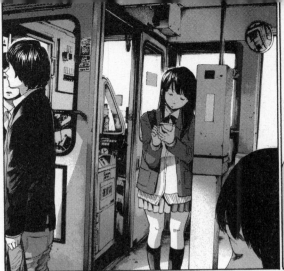

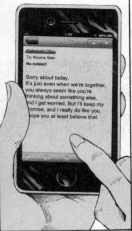

Kabukura Chisa
To: Koume Sato
No subject

Sorry about today.
It's just even when we're together,
you always seem like you're
thinking about something else,
and I get worried. But I'll keep my
promise, and I really do like you.
I hope you at least believe that.

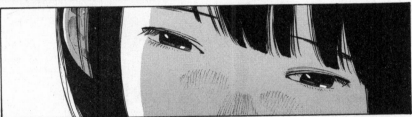

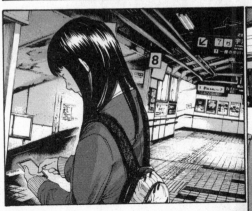

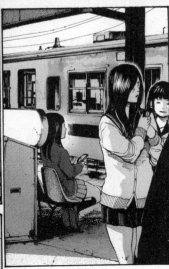

Subject: Re:

I super like you too, you know. (´−'*)

Sent from my iPhone

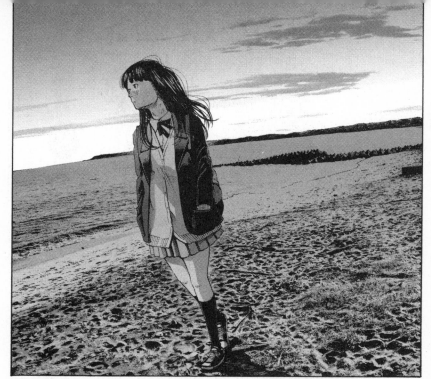

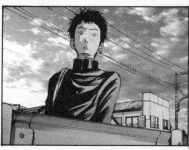

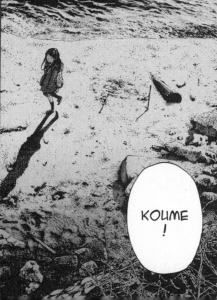

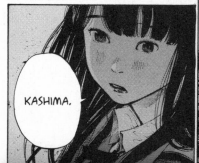

KASHIMA.

KOUME
!

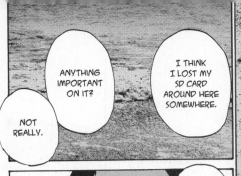

ANYTHING IMPORTANT ON IT?

I THINK I LOST MY SD CARD AROUND HERE SOMEWHERE.

NOT REALLY.

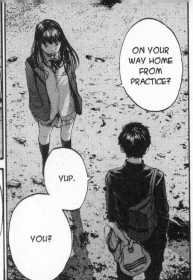

ON YOUR WAY HOME FROM PRACTICE?

YUP.

YOU?

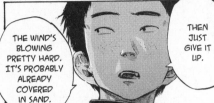

THE WIND'S BLOWING PRETTY HARD. IT'S PROBABLY ALREADY COVERED IN SAND.

THEN JUST GIVE IT UP.

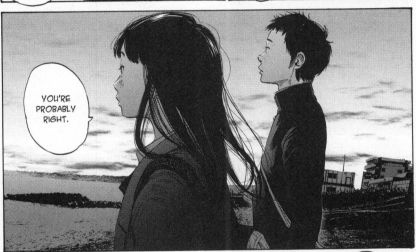

YOU'RE PROBABLY RIGHT.

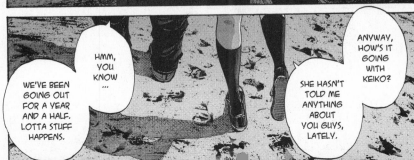

WE'VE BEEN GOING OUT FOR A YEAR AND A HALF. LOTTA STUFF HAPPENS.

HMM, YOU KNOW ...

SHE HASN'T TOLD ME ANYTHING ABOUT YOU GUYS, LATELY.

ANYWAY, HOW'S IT GOING WITH KEIKO?

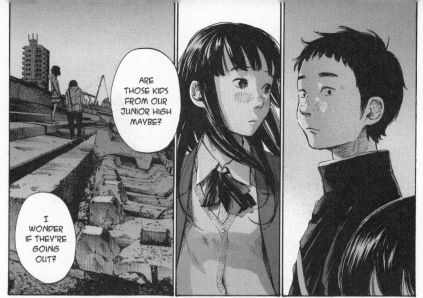

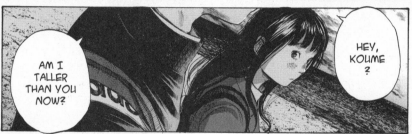

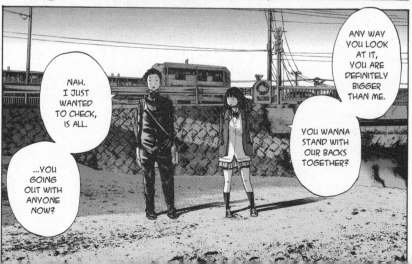

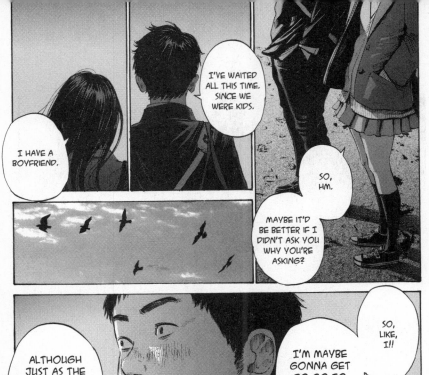

I'VE WAITED ALL THIS TIME. SINCE WE WERE KIDS.

I HAVE A BOYFRIEND.

SO, HM.

MAYBE IT'D BE BETTER IF I DIDN'T ASK YOU WHY YOU'RE ASKING?

SO, LIKE, I!!

I'M MAYBE GONNA GET TO GO TO NATIONALS AT KOSHIEN !!

ALTHOUGH JUST AS THE MANAGER!! PRETTY AMAZING, HUH?!

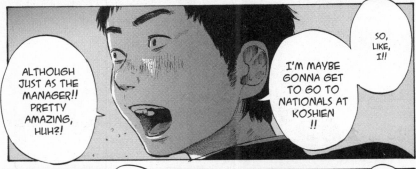

I WAS PRETTY GLOOMY ABOUT THE WHOLE MANAGER THING AT FIRST.

NO WAY!

THAT IS TOTALLY AMAZING!!

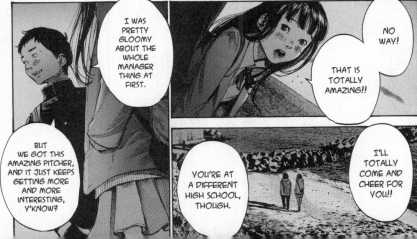

BUT WE GOT THIS AMAZING PITCHER, AND IT JUST KEEPS GETTING MORE AND MORE INTERESTING, Y'KNOW?

YOU'RE AT A DIFFERENT HIGH SCHOOL, THOUGH.

I'LL TOTALLY COME AND CHEER FOR YOU!!

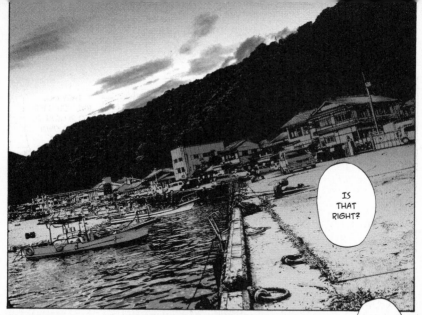

IS THAT RIGHT?

I THINK MAYBE IT'S MORE LIKE I'M JUST ACTING LIKE IT'S FUN.

BUT WHEN I THINK ABOUT WHETHER IT'S FUN EVERY DAY,

THAT'S GREAT. YOU'RE LUCKY.

I MEAN, I DON'T HATE SCHOOL OR ANYTHING.

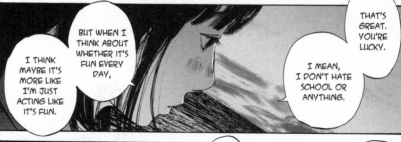

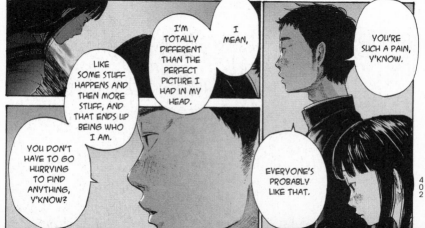

I MEAN,

I'M TOTALLY DIFFERENT THAN THE PERFECT PICTURE I HAD IN MY HEAD.

YOU'RE SUCH A PAIN, Y'KNOW.

LIKE SOME STUFF HAPPENS AND THEN MORE STUFF, AND THAT ENDS UP BEING WHO I AM.

YOU DON'T HAVE TO GO HURRYING TO FIND ANYTHING, Y'KNOW?

EVERYONE'S PROBABLY LIKE THAT.

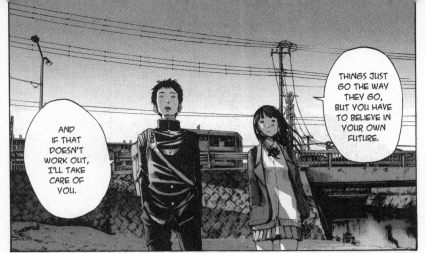

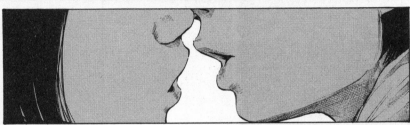

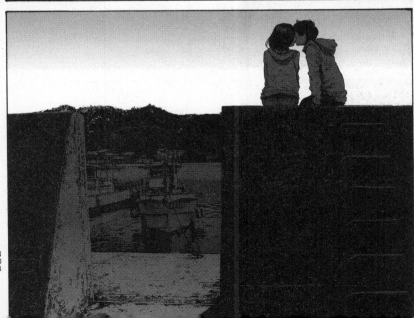

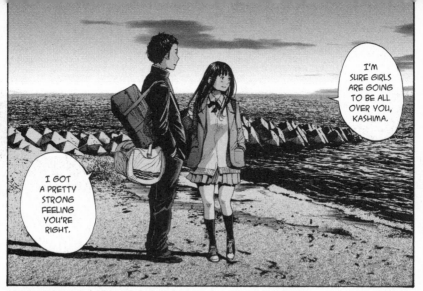

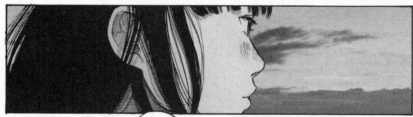

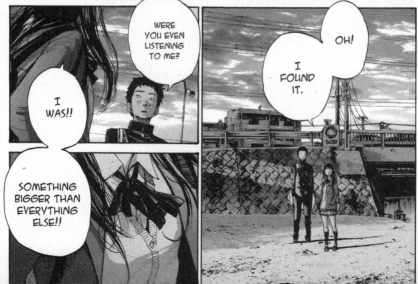

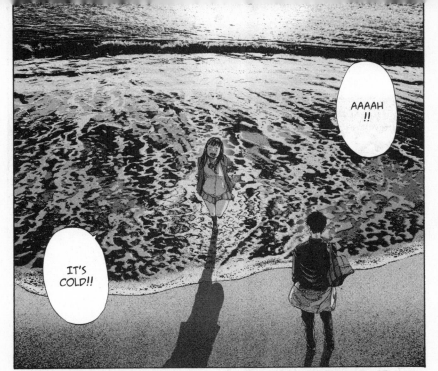

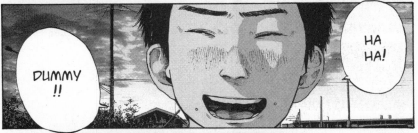

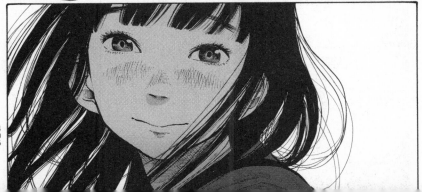

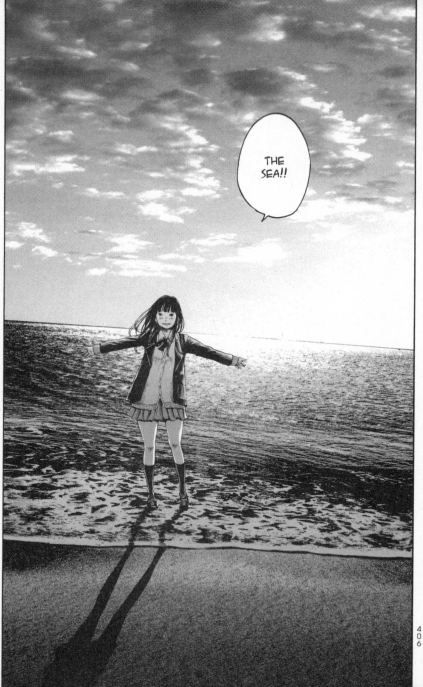

E N D

A Girl on the Shore
A Vertical Comics Edition

Translation: Jocelyne Allen
Production: Risa Cho
          Nicole Dochych

UMIBE NO ONNANOKO
© Inio Asano 2011
All rights reserved
First published in Japan in 2011, 2013 by Ohta Publishing Co., Tokyo.
English translation rights arranged with Ohta Publishing Co.
through Tuttle—Mori Agency, Inc., Tokyo.

Translation provided by Vertical Comics, 2016
Published by Vertical Comics, an imprint of Vertical, Inc., New York

Originally published in Japanese as *Umibe no Onnanoko 1, 2*
by Ohta Publishing Co., 2011, 2013
Umibe no Onnanoko first serialized in *Manga Erotics f,*
Ohta Publishing Co., 2009—11, 2011—13

This is a work of fiction.

ISBN: 978—1—941220—85—6

Manufactured in Canada

First Edition

Fourth Printing

Vertical, Inc.
451 Park Avenue South
7th Floor
New York, NY 10016
www.vertical—comics.com

Vertical books are distributed through Penguin—Random House Publisher Services.